ECONOMIC ESSAYS BY DAVID RICARDO

ECONOMIC ESSAYS

BY

DAVID RICARDO

Edited with Introductory Essay and Notes by

E. C. K. GONNER

FRANK CASS & CO. LTD.

1966

Published by Frank Cass & Co. Ltd.,
10 Woburn Walk, London W.C.1
by arrangement with G. Bell & Sons, Ltd.

First Edition 1923
New Impression 1966

Printed in Great Britain by
Thomas Nelson (Printers) Ltd., London and Edinburgh.

PREFACE

The present volume is designed as a companion to *The Principles of Political Economy and Taxation*, edited and published in 1891. It contains the five important pamphlets published by Ricardo, the only economic writings omitted being the two entitled respectively *Plan for a National Bank* and *Essay on the Funding System*, both of which are ephemeral in their interest and neither of which seems to call for reproduction. The Table of Accounts given in Appendix V. to the *Proposals for an Economical and Secure Currency* is also omitted.

The five pamphlets now republished are writings of the greatest importance, because both of the subjects with which they deal and of the principles laid down in their treatment of those subjects.

Writing on Ricardo after the lapse of nearly thirty years, I feel that the trend of economic thought and the new importance attached to economic inquiry make more valuable than ever the study of a writer whose attitude was so disinterested and who, despite his short-comings, sought in all he wrote, on the one hand to elucidate facts by reference to principles and on the other hand to build up out of the data at his command a system of coherent thought.

E. C. K. GONNER.

THE UNIVERSITY,
LIVERPOOL.

TABLE OF CONTENTS

HIGH PRICE OF BULLION.

PAGE

§ 1. Mode of distribution of the precious metals among the various countries explained 3
§ 2. Effect of the discovery in a country of a mine. Corresponding effect of the establishment of a bank of issue 4
§ 3. Specie is only exported from a country when its exportation is advantageous 6
§ 4. Owing to the facilities of intercourse between countries there cannot for a long space of time be much difference between the value of the currency, proportionate quantities of the precious metals assumed, in the different countries 6
§ 5. So long as notes were payable in specie increased issue would mean nothing more than exportation of gold, despite the law against exportation of money . . 7
§ 6. Such exportation constituting, as it is termed, an unfavourable balance, takes place only owing to a currency comparatively redundant 9
§ 7. Thus specie is only sent abroad when it is the cheapest exportable commodity 12
§ 8. In further considering the subject, it becomes necessary to consider which metal is the standard in England 14
§ 9. Mode in which par of exchange can be ascertained, as, for instance, between England and Holland . . 17
§ 10. Expenses of transport, &c., the limits of an unfavourable exchange 19
§ 11. Present condition of the issue of notes by the bank . 21
§ 12. These must be examined with reference to the rate of exchange and the price of bullion. Former policy of the bank with regard to its paper . . . 21
§ 13. It may be concluded that depreciation of the paper money is due to its over-issue 24
§ 14. The best mode of preparing for the repeal of the Restriction Act 26
§ 15. That bank notes are depreciated is shown by, firstly, the unfavourable rate of exchange . . . 28
§ 16. Secondly, the continued high price of bullion . . 28

PAGE

§ 17. It is not, moreover, correct that these notes are representative of silver and not of gold. Even if they were, the price of bullion would not be so high as it now is 29
§ 18. Nor is it true that they are representative of the debased silver coin 30
§ 19. The assertion that the amount of bank notes has not increased disproportionably is both unproved and inconclusive 30
§ 20. The issues of bank paper regulate the issues of country paper 32
§ 21. The further assertion that the rate of interest is the criterion by which we can judge of the abundance of paper money is thoroughly unsound . . 32
§ 22. Though it cannot be denied that at each time of issue the rate of interest might be affected . . . 35
§ 23. The remedy for the present bad condition of the currency lies in the gradually withdrawal of notes . 37
§ 24. The extraordinary powers of the bank directors . 39
§ 25. On the evils of debased money and depreciated paper currency 39

REPLY TO MR. BOSANQUET'S PRACTICAL OBSERVATIONS ON THE REPORT OF THE BULLION COMMITTEE.

CHAPTER I.

PRELIMINARY OBSERVATIONS—MR. BOSANQUET'S OBJECTIONS TO THE CONCLUSIONS OF THE BULLION COMMITTEE BRIEFLY STATED.

§ 1. Preliminary observations and Mr. Bosanquet's attack 63
§ 2. The principal positions which he attacks stated in six propositions 65

CHAPTER II.

MR. BOSANQUET'S ALLEGED FACTS, DRAWN FROM THE HISTORY OF THE STATE OF EXCHANGE, CONSIDERED.

SECTION I.

Exchange with Hamburgh.

§ 3. The first proposition attacked, stated and illustrated 66
§ 4. Alleged facts cited in opposition 67
§ 5. Errors in the table relied upon by Mr. Bosanquet. The table corrected 68
§ 6. Very different conclusion to be drawn from the amended table with regard to exchange with Hamburgh 71

PAGE

§ 7. The meaning of the original proposition . . . 72
§ 8. Reasons why balance between England and Hamburgh favourable to former country during 1797 and 1798 73
§ 9. Further errors made in Mr. Bosanquet's calculations . 75

SECTION II.

Exchange with Paris.

§ 10. Par between London and Paris ascertained . . 77
§ 11. High seignorage in France 80
§ 12. Mr. Bosanquet's calculations erroneous as based on faulty data 81

SECTION III.

Supposed fact of a Premium on English Currency in America. Favourable Exchange with Sweden.

§ 13. Apparent error in the assertion that a premium on English currency exists in America . . . 83
§ 14. From such facts as appear it would seem that both in Sweden and England there is a depreciated paper currency 84

SECTION IV.

A Statement concerning the Par of Exchange, by the Bullion Committee examined.

§ 15. This statement considered 85

CHAPTER III.

MR. BOSANQUET'S ALLEGED FACTS, IN SUPPOSED REFUTATION OF THE CONCLUSION THAT A RISE IN THE MARKET PRICE OF BULLION ABOVE THE MINT PRICE PROVES A DEPRECIATION OF THE CURRENCY, CONSIDERED.

SECTION I.

That the Negation of the above Conclusion implies the Impossibility of Melting or Exporting English Coin—an Impossibility contended for by nobody.

§ 16. The correct statement of the proposition is established 88
§ 17. The one thing that would effectively disprove its correctness would be the efficacy of the law against melting and exportation 89
§ 18. Facts cited by the committee in support of their proposition 90
§ 19. The question of the efficacy of the law . . . 92

SECTION II.

Consequences which would follow on the Supposition that the Currencies of other Countries (exclusive of England) were diminished or increased one half.

§ 20. Suppositions made as above 93
§ 21. Analogous case of issue of paper 94

PAGE

SECTION III.

The Trifling Rise in the Price of Gold on the Continent owing solely to a Variation in the Relation of Silver to Gold.

§ 22. Gold at Hamburgh, for instance, has not risen more than 3 per cent. 95
§ 23. The relative prices show that it is paper that has fallen in England, not gold that has risen 96
§ 24. Further errors of Mr. Bosanquet with regard to this point 97

SECTION IV.

Failure ascribed to Mr. Locke's Theory relative to the Recoinage in 1696.

§ 25. A similarity of Locke's theory to that upheld . . 101
§ 26. It did not fail, if for no other reason, because it was not followed 101
§ 27. Lord Liverpool's account of the recoinage and Mr. Bosanquet's error 102

CHAPTER IV.

MR. BOSANQUET'S OBJECTION TO THE STATEMENT THAT THE BALANCE OF PAYMENTS HAS BEEN IN FAVOUR OF GREAT BRITAIN, EXAMINED.

§ 28. The controversy between Mr. Bosanquet and the committee as to the facts relating to imports and exports unimportant so far as the principles are concerned. 104
§ 29. The meaning of the fact that the balance of payments has been against England 105
§ 30. The exportation of gold a matter of choice and not of necessity 106
§ 31. In opposition to certain writers it is contended that a depreciation in the currency owing to an increase of paper does not lead to a rise in price of bullion so long as gold continues a part of that currency . 107

CHAPTER V.

MR. BOSANQUET'S ARGUMENT TO PROVE THAT THE BANK OF ENGLAND HAS NOT THE POWER OF FORCING THE CIRCULATION OF BANK NOTES, CONSIDERED.

§ 32. What is meant by the power of the bank to force the circulation of bank notes 113
§ 33. Mr. Bosanquet's attempt to distinguish between production of gold coin from a mine and issue of paper by the bank 114
§ 34. The analogy upheld 115

PAGE

§ 35. The refusal to discount any but *bonâ fide* bills would not produce the limitation of the circulation imagined 118

CHAPTER VI.

OBSERVATION ON THE PRINCIPLES OF SEIGNORAGE.

§ 36. Principles and consequences of seignorage . . 120
§ 37. The bullion value retained by a country for its circulation remains unchanged, its commerce remaining the same 121
§ 38. Nor can there be depreciation of currency save from excess 122

CHAPTER VII.

MR. BOSANQUET'S OBJECTIONS TO THE PROPOSITION THAT THE CIRCULATION OF THE BANK OF ENGLAND REGULATES THAT OF THE COUNTRY BANKS, CONSIDERED.

§ 39. This proposition, like the others laid down by the committee, has the support of practical men. . 124
§ 40. Mr. Bosanquet's misinterpretation of the term excess of currency 125
§ 41. The way in which the issues of the country banks depend on that of the Bank of England, exhibited . 127

CHAPTER VIII.

MR. BOSANQUET'S OPINION, THAT YEARS OF SCARCITY AND TAXES HAVE BEEN THE SOLE CAUSE OF THE RISE OF PRICES, EXCESSIVE CIRCULATION NO CAUSE, CONSIDERED.

§ 42. Mr. Bosanquet urges that depreciation of paper has not occurred because the increase of taxes has been greater than the additions to the paper currency . 132
§ 43. He alleges that the cause of rise in prices is due, first, scarcity of corn in 1800 and 1801, and secondly, to increase of taxes since 1793. That the first must have some effect is true 135
§ 44. The mode in which taxes, and what taxes, affect the prices of commodities, canvassed 136
§ 45. It does not follow that more money is needed to circulate commodities generally 138

CHAPTER IX.

MR. BOSANQUET'S OPINION, THAT EVIL WOULD RESULT FROM THE RESUMPTION OF CASH PAYMENTS, CONSIDERED.

§ 46. The opinions held by Mr. Bosanquet generally considered 140

PROPOSALS FOR AN ECONOMICAL AND SECURE CURRENCY, WITH OBSERVATIONS ON THE PROFITS OF THE BANK OF ENGLAND AS THEY REGARD THE PUBLIC AND THE PROPRIETORS OF BANK STOCK.

PAGE

SECTION I.

In the Medium of Circulation, Cause of Uniformity is Cause of Goodness.

§ 1. On uniformity is the value of money . . . 157
§ 2. On the causes determining the quantity of metal used as money 158
§ 3. The first of which is value of money. 158
§ 4. The second, the number of transactions 159
§ 5. The third, the substitutes for money in use . . 160

SECTION II.

Use of a Standard Commodity—Objections to it Considered.

§ 6. A money to be perfect should not vary in value. . 161
§ 7. That it is impossible in practice to judge of the value of money by a reference to its relation to the mass of commodities 162

SECTION III.

The Standard, its Imperfections. Variations below without Allowance of the Countervailing Variations above the Standard, their Effects. Correspondence with the Standard the Rule for Paper Money.

§ 8. Imperfections in gold and silver as standard . . 164
§ 9. The inconvenience of a double standard and the relative advantages of gold and of silver . . 165
§ 10. Despite its imperfections, the standard when established should be adhered to 165

SECTION IV.

An Expedient to bring the English Currency as near as Possible to Perfection.

§ 11. Advantages of a well-regulated system of paper currency too great to be readily surrendered. . 167
§ 12. Means of retaining these and of securing conformity of paper money with standard 168
§ 13. Advantages of system thus proposed as compared with present inconveniences 169
§ 14. What these latter were in case of country banks . 171
§ 15. The reason for state control over issues of money . 172
§ 16. That this should be extended to issue of notes by country banks 173

PAGE

SECTION V.

A Practice which creates a great Mass of Mercantile Inconvenience. Remedy proposed.

§ 17. Inconvenience caused by withdrawal of money for payment of quarterly dividends 175
§ 18. How this may be remedied 176

SECTION VI.

The Public Services of the Bank excessively overpaid. Remedy proposed.

§ 19. Large profits made by the bank from the public deposits 177
§ 20. Erroneous contention with regard to these by the bank directors 178
§ 21. Report of committee of 1807 on this point . . 179
§ 22. Profits and expenditure of the bank 181
§ 23. Resolutions to be proposed in Parliament with reference to the gains made by the bank . . 185
§ 24. Circumstances attending the renewal of the charter in 1800. 187

SECTION VII.

Bank Profits and Savings. Misapplication. Proposed Remedy.

§ 25. Profits of the bank and the right of proprietors of bank stock to share in them by increased dividends. 193
§ 26. Attempt to estimate these profits and savings . . 194
§ 27. The surplus capital thus accumulated should by law be divided among the proprietors by increased dividends 200
§ 28. Whether such accumulation is expedient. . . 203
§ 29. Irregularities in the conduct of the bank . . . 206

INFLUENCE OF A LOW PRICE OF CORN ON THE PROFITS OF STOCK.

§ 1. Relation between rent, wages and profits discussed and defined, with particular reference to effects ensuing from the nature of rent 225
§ 2. Effect on profits of the circumstances which lead to rent and its development 227
§ 3. As these come into importance the rate of profits diminishes, that is if other things remain the same. 231
§ 4. Price of corn rises as a nation increases in wealth and its population grows 233

PAGE

§ 5. This to the advantage of the landowner . . . 235

§ 6. Principles governing profits recapitulated and considered 236

§ 7. The view criticised, that extension of trade by itself tends to a rise in the rate of profits . . . 237

§ 8. In answer to this it is asserted that rate of profits initially depends on circumstances allowing a low price of food 239

§ 9. Such being the case, the restriction on importation requires strong arguments 240

§ 10. These considered, with reference to the contentions that importation involves a danger in time of war and enables foreign countries to withhold supplies. 240

§ 11. Any such action would be disastrous to the exporting country and is most unlikely to be successful even if attempted 241

§ 12. Great advantage to England of obtaining food supplies from a variety of countries, subject to different conditions 244

§ 13. The present investment of agricultural capital a reason, however, for gradual withdrawal of corn laws, but not for their permanent retention . . 244

§ 14. The view that a low money price of corn disadvantageous to poorer classes combated . . . 247

§ 15. It is pointed out that though restriction on importation of food may not and probably would not diminish foreign trade, it would diminish the profits arising from it. 248

§ 16. Other points considered. General effect of rise in prices considered 248

§ 17. Effect on production of employment of capital respectively in agriculture and in manufacture . . 249

§ 18. Effect of low price of corn on the holders of national stock 251

ON PROTECTION TO AGRICULTURE.

Section I.

On Remunerating Price.

§ 1. Remunerative price defined. It is shown that the remunerative price in the case of corn rises as recourse takes place to inferior soils . . . 259

§ 2. Such price therefore rises as progress takes place and population increases. This does not justify a restriction on importation designed to maintain high prices 261

PAGE

SECTION II.

On the Influence of a Rise in Wages on the Price of Corn.

§ 3. But while this admitted by many, so long as such rise is due to natural causes, it has been argued that that where due to taxation, a justification exists 262
§ 4. This, however, when taxation is general, an argument for restriction on everything and not on corn alone. 262
§ 5. The imposition of protective duties on all commodities is futile 262
§ 6. Argument that a rise in price of corn involves a rise in all prices criticised 264

SECTION III.

On the Effects of Taxes imposed on a Particular Commodity.

§ 7. It is admitted that some protection accompanied by a drawback may be given in respect of taxes peculiarly affecting growers of corn . . . 265

SECTION IV.

On the Effect of Abundant Crops on the Price of Corn.

§ 8. The price of corn peculiarly sensitive to alterations in the quantity produced 267

SECTION V.

On the Effect produced on the Price of Corn by Mr. Peel's Bill for restoring the Ancient Standard.

§ 9. The argument that present alterations in price due to Peel's Bill considered. The effect of this very limited 270
§ 10. Ricardo's own proposals recapitulated with a view to showing that its adoption would have further modified this 272
§ 11. The attibution of agricultural distress wholly to alterations in currency further considered. These limited in themselves. Further, the landowners, if now injured, were formerly benefited by the Restriction Bill 276
§ 12. But if the effect of currency changes were so great, similar distress would have been produced in other quarters. This not the case 278
§ 13. Observations on the refusal of the bank to lend at 4 per cent. 279

SECTION VI.

On the Effects of a Low Price of Corn on the Rate of Profits.

§ 14. Furthermore, in the interests of progress a low price of corn desirable, because it allows of a high rate of profits 281

PAGE

§ 15. An enhancement of the price of corn discourages industry and may banish capital from the country . 283
§ 16. Landlords, moreover, injured by want of steadiness in prices 284

SECTION VII.

Under a System of Protecting Duties, established with a view to give the Monopoly of the Home Market to the Home Grower of Corn, Prices cannot be otherwise than Fluctuating.

§ 17. Protective duties tend towards fluctuation. This so in case of fixed duties 286
§ 18. Particularly so in case of present system of duties . 287
§ 19. Ricardo's own proposals. To meet the special burdens previously considered (Section III.); a limited countervailing duty, accompanied by a drawback suggested 288
§ 20. Report of the Committee on Agricultural Distress in 1821 and that on Agriculture, 1822, considered . 290
§ 21. The argument that protection to agriculture necessary because of existing protection to manufacture, considered 295

SECTION VIII.

On the Project of Advancing Money on Loan, to Speculators in Corn, at a Low Interest.

§ 22. The recommendation that the Government should make advances at a low rate of interest, criticised . 297

SECTION IX.

Can the Present State of Agricultural Distress be attributed to Taxation?

§ 23. The view that the existing agricultural distress was due to taxation, disputed 299
§ 24. Fall of raw produce since 1819 due to a limited extent to alteration in the value of the currency, but mainly to abundance 303

CONCLUSION.

§ 25. General summary attempted 305
§ 26. Part played by corn laws in aggravating the difficulties 306
§ 27. Policy of gradual withdrawal advocated . . . 306

INTRODUCTORY ESSAY

THE minor economic writings of Ricardo, now included in this volume, fall under two headings, those relating to monetary and financial subjects, and those concerned with the agricultural conditions of the country and the remedies proposed for the existing difficulties. These groups of writings are alike in certain particulars. They treat of concrete difficulties and are in the main an attempt to deal with actual phenomena. The principles enunciated are brought into close relation to fact. Thus in both instances inductive reasoning plays a very considerable part. This, however, is less obviously truc in the two essays relating to agricultural matters, since in these the abstract argument which underlies Ricardo's theory of Distribution occupies a prominent position. In the financial writings, on the other hand, the contact with fact is much closer. Nor is this surprising, since in such matters Ricardo had an amount of expert knowledge which is always appearing, and serves as an immediate and direct basis for theory and generalization. Both the width of this knowledge and the reliancc of the writer upon facts is best seen in the reply made to Mr Bosanquet's attack on the Report of the Bullion Committee and incidentally upon the principles contained in Ricardo's own pamphlet. Facts are treated throughout as the essential basis of theory, as the phenomena, that is, out of which theory is evolved.

Thus, quite apart from their value in themselves these

writings are of considerable importance as explaining the attitude of Ricardo as a thinker. He is in reality far less abstract and far more inductive than many of his critics have allowed. This must not be taken as a denial of his use of hypothesis. Of his assumptions many are overstrained and many are incorrect. But they are introduced in lieu of and in the absence of attainable facts, and his theories are in the main an attempt to connect and interpret such facts as there were.

This explains another feature which careful criticism has brought to light. In certain cases, at least, Ricardo's conclusions, which seem incorrect at the present time, are in consonance with fact as it then existed. As is pointed out below, and as has been pointed out by other writers, some theories which seem least true in general are so because they correspond most to the concrete facts of a particular and somewhat exceptional period.

I.

The financial and monetary pamphlets occupy the larger part of the present volume and deserve prior consideration not only for this reason but for other reasons given above. He writes with an authority and with a familiarity with his subject-matter, which is less apparent in other instances. Of these the two most important are *The High Price of Bullion* and *The Reply to Mr Bosanquet's Practical Observations.* In the first of these there is more system and completeness, but in the latter contradiction and opposition gave the author the opportunity of showing the luminous sureness of his touch. So Mr Bosanquet served a cause which he did not favour, by eliciting from his opponent still more proofs of the depreciation of the bank paper in addition to those given in the earlier publication. In some ways the later tract is even more convincing by reason of the greater vivacity and point with which it is written.

Turning to the consideration of the subjects dealt with in the financial pamphlets, we may select three as at once the most important and requiring most explanation:

1. The High Price of Bullion and Depreciation of Paper Money.
2. Monetary Theory.
3. The Position of the Bank of England.

These matters, indeed, are treated in very close connection. They are linked together by the action of the Bank of England. Both in the issue of paper money under the Restriction Act and in the ensuing discussions that body took up a position which in Ricardo's eyes could not but be highly detrimental to the general well-being. In so doing it enunciated, or its defenders enunciated on its behalf, a theory of currency totally at variance with that laid down so lucidly and so emphatically by Ricardo himself; it also raised the question whether its existence and continuance was compatible with the best interest of the state. On all these questions Ricardo had much to say. The immediate occasion for the financial and currency pamphlets was afforded by practical difficulties, and in the first instance, first both in importance and in time, by the consequences arising out of the operations of the bank under the Bank Restriction Act.

1. *The High Price of Bullion and Depreciation of Paper Money.*—In the two treatises already singled out for notice Ricardo devotes himself to discussing, first, the means at his disposal for testing the value of the paper money, and, secondly, the action of the bank with regard to its issue. But before the former could be employed with any security he had to determine what constituted the standard in England and of what money the bank notes were representative. The standard he proves clearly to

be gold owing both to usage and to the restrictions placed on the employment of silver, while, with regard to the representative character of the paper, he establishes the position that these notes are representative of gold. In answer to objections, he urges that the legal limitation placed on the use of silver precludes the notes from being representative of that metal, and, with a sharp turn to the real point at issue, he remarks that even were the objection granted, the difference between the value of bullion and notes would be wholly different from what it was. Nor can these, he continues, be representative of the debased silver coin then in circulation, for the very simple reason that for all payments above 25*l.* silver was a legal tender only by weight.

From this preliminary discussion he turns to the leading principles which he wishes to establish.

First with regard to the possible means of detecting depreciation. There are two tests, both simple and, as he considers, certain. In the first place, a continued unfavourable exchange which has fallen below the point at which it begins to be profitable to export gold is, he says, an evidence of such. The exchanges, as he knew and expressly states, are often against a country and heavily against a country, but he urges that the extent to which they can continue thus unfavourable is rigidly limited by the expenses attending the exportation of the precious metals from the country, against which they thus run, for as soon as they exceed this a bullion export trade becomes profitable and will continue to be profitable till they are brought within the limits previously indicated. In order, then, to form an accurate judgment of the estimation in which the money of England is held it is only necessary to compare the exchanges as they run with the true par of exchange, to be discovered by a comparison of the standard of England with the standard of the other country as, for instance, Hamburgh. This important contention rests very largely on two subsidiary positions established by Ricardo. Bullion, like all other commodities, is transferred when it is the most advantageous commodity to make payments in, a condition most frequently brought about by a redundancy of the currency in the particular country. Again, so long as the money of the country consists of the precious metals, an adverse exchange below the expenses of transport will only lead to increased exportations of the precious metals, for in no branch of trade are small profits more speedily and surely taken advantage of. Is it not evident, then, that a continued unfavourable exchange implies depreciation ?

The rise of the market price of bullion above the Mint price, if continued, is a proof almost as convincing as the foregoing of the depreciation which has taken place in the money of the country. The one thing wanted, according to Ricardo, to make this proposition self-evident is the admission or the proof " that the law which forbids the conversion of gold coin into gold bullion cannot be successfully executed." The principle laid down here is, to quote once more, " not that gold as a commodity may not rise above its value as coin, but that it cannot continue so, because the convertibility of coin into bullion would soon equalize their value."

Against these two tests a host of criticisms were levelled, those to which Ricardo replied being chiefly such as embodied facts alleged to be irreconcilable with the argument that the divergences thus laid stress on are necessarily evidence of an over-issue of paper. The facts brought forward by Mr Bosanquet did not bear a searching examination. They were inaccurate and incomplete, and when amended sometimes served to illustrate the principles which they were intended to overthrow.

But another important question remained. Could the bank force an undue amount of paper on the country ?

To this the partisans of that institution responded, firstly, that it could not if the circulation was already adequate; secondly, that its issues could have no such effect so long as the bills it discounted were those for *bonâ fide* transactions; and thirdly, that the bank was only one of several issuers, the country bank issues being important. To the first of these objections, Ricardo developed very elaborately the opinion he had already expressed. He has already explained that to speak of a currency as redundant is to employ a term of comparison, as there is no amount which on depreciation cannot be absorbed in the circulation of the country, the one effectual check, as far as a single country is concerned, being exportation, a check inapplicable of course in the case of over-issued paper. Here he concluded with the remark, "Of this I am fully convinced, that if the principle advanced by the bank directors be correct, not a bank note could ever have been permanently kept in circulation nor would the discovery of the mines of America have added one guinea to the circulation of England." The additional gold would, according to this system, have found a circulation already adequate, and in which no more could be admitted. With regard to the second objection, he says, "The refusal to discount any bills but those for *bonâ fide* transactions would be as little effectual in limiting the circulation; because, though the directors should have the means of distinguishing such bills, which can by no means be allowed, a greater portion of paper currency might be called into circulation, not than the wants of commerce could employ but greater than what could remain in the channel of currency without depreciation. It is well known that the same 1000*l.* may settle twenty *bonâ fide* transactions in one day. It may pay for a ship; the seller of a ship may pay with it his ropemaker; he, again, may pay the Russian merchants for hemp, &c., &c. Now, as each of these was a *bonâ fide* transaction, a bill might have been drawn by each, and the bank, by their rule, might discount them all; so that 20,000*l.* might be called into circulation to perform those payments for which 1000*l.* was equal." The connection between the issues of the country banks is explained, while in addition Ricardo points out that several country bankers admitted, in their evidence before the Bullion Committee, that they were, as a matter of course, influenced in their issues by the action of the Bank of England.

Despite the evils which Ricardo attributed to the action of the Restriction Act and the unrebutting vigour with which he pursued its supporters, the practical measures which he advocated were anything but hasty or revolutionary. They were judiciously adapted to bring about the change desired without undue interruption. "The remedy," says he, "which I propose for all the evils in our currency, is that the bank should gradually decrease the amount of their notes in circulation, &c." This was to precede the repeal of the act which, taken suddenly and alone, could not but produce many and grave evils.

2. *Monetary Theory.*—The more systematic considerations of the conditions and theories of money are to be found in *Principles of Political Economy*, Chapter XXVII., *High Price of Bullion*, earlier paragraphs, and the *Proposals for an Economical and Secure Currency*, §§ 1—18. In addition to these, many valuable suggestions are made in other portions of the minor writings. Without writing a formal treatise on the subject, Ricardo has, I think, contributed more to our correct understanding of the theory of money than any other writer. He has the immense advantage of not overlooking fundamental principles when engaged in discussing some matter of detail. He has no illusions about money. Thus gold and silver never cease to be commodities to him. Like other commodities, they lose their value with an increase in

quantity, they gain in value with a diminution. A bank note "may be considered as a piece of money on which the seignorage is enormous, amounting to all its value."

The main conceptions which obtain prominence in these writings are:—

(*a*) The quantitative theory of money which he applies to the issue of paper money, the nature of which is discussed at length.

(*b*) The mode of the distribution of the precious metals throughout Europe, and the conditions under which modifications of the existing distribution take place.

(*c*) The nature of a standard of value and the use of the precious metals as such.

In all these instances he made valuable additions to the knowledge of the time while even now his considerations, though sometimes a little obscured by a loose use of terms, merit the attention of students of the theory of money. Thus, in treating of the first, he explains the connection existing between the quantity and the value of money as such by saying "The quantity of metal, employed as money, in effecting the payments of any particular country, using metallic money, or the quantity of metal for which paper money is the substitute, if paper money be partly or wholly used, must depend on three things: first, on its value; secondly, on the amount or value of the payments to be made; and, thirdly, on the degree of economy practised in effecting those payments." After this follows an explanation of the three points taken consecutively. In the particular case of an over-issue of inconvertible paper Ricardo avoids the error so frequently made at the time that the consequent depreciation proceeded from general discredit of the financial position of the bank and the country.

With the explanation of the gradual and certain dispersal of the precious metals among the various countries of Europe he completed the discomfiture of the mercantile theorists who, though by no means committed to the mistakes of their predecessors, still continued to attribute particular qualities to the precious commodity which served as money. It still remains the classical exposition of the subject. What Ricardo suggested then is now recognized as true: save in face of some unusual event or as a consequence of the export of gold from the country in which the mines are situated, the transfers of bullion are comparatively small.

With regard to the nature of the standard of value and the position which the precious metals hold with regard to it, Ricardo made certain incidental observations which affect two of the most interesting monetary questions of the present day. In the *Proposals for an Economical and Secure Currency* (Section II., §§ 7, 8) he examines the difficulties which lie in the way of what are called *index numbers.* It must, indeed, be conceded at once that the idea of a currency without what is here termed "a specific standard" is impracticable, but I do not think that Ricardo's argument at all destroys the position taken by those who, while adopting a metallic standard, consider that the variations in it may be gauged and its irregularities corrected by a comparison with the mass of commodities. True, these may vary, but it is equally true that the variations taking place among a large number of commodities in general use are likely to correct each other and so to exclude the almost inevitable evil which must ensue on an unyielding reliance on one commodity. Again, with regard to Bi-metallism, Ricardo, no doubt, shows himself fully cognizant of the nature and of the difficulties attending the establishment of such an alternating standard. He says rightly that the standard will change from one metal to the other according to their fluctuations from the ratio. He further points out that in consequence the variations in the standard will be more frequent. This is no doubt true, but it is more important to remember that they will in all probability be less extreme than would be the case with a single standard. This would seem to have been overlooked by Ricardo, for he decides in favour of a single standard on account of the foregoing reason as well as because of the inconvenience which, he says, resulted from the use of the two metals. He does not, however, deem either of these by any means a perfect standard. "Experience has indeed taught us that though the variations in the value of gold and silver may be considerable on a comparison of distant periods, yet for short spaces of time their value is tolerably fixed." More recent changes cannot be said to substantiate this view, which, however, is important as showing the nature of the evidence which led Ricardo to the opinion which he repeatedly expressed on the subject of the standard.

But he himself had a proposal of his own to make. While desirous of establishing beyond question and recall a sound metallic basis, he was equally anxious to introduce into practice all possible economies in the use of money. The greatest of these consisted, as he thought, in substituting the use of paper for gold or silver, an almost valueless for a most valuable medium. To achieve this, it was necessary to place some restraint on the preference which he considers the community would display for gold in place of paper without at the same time rendering the latter inconvertible or partly so. Such was the problem; but this he deemed might be met as follows: "by subjecting the bank to the delivery of uncoined gold or silver at the Mint standard and price, in exchange for their notes, instead of the delivery of guineas; by which means paper would never fall below the value of bullion without being followed by a reduction of its quantity. To prevent the rise of paper above the value of bullion, the bank should be also obliged to give their paper in exchange for standard gold at the price of 3*l.* 17s. per ounce. Not to give too much trouble to the bank, the quantity of gold to be demanded in exchange for paper at the Mint price of 3*l.* 17s. 10½d., or the quantity to be sold to the bank at 3*l.* 17s., should never be less than twenty ounces.

3. *The Position of the Bank of England.*—The conflict into which Ricardo had come with the policy of the bank led him first into criticism and thence into a definite attack on its position. In his *Reply to the Practical Observations of Mr Bosanquet* he takes the directors to task very sharply for their action with regard to the public interest; in the latter sections (VI., VII.) of *Proposals for an Economical and Secure Currency* he urges on them the necessity of making liberal concessions to the Government of its extra and unusual profits; while he also suggested its supersession so far as its powers of issue are concerned by a body of National Commissioners. What were the grounds of this accusation? Owing to the great increase in public deposits and to other circumstances, the profits accruing to the bank had been much greater than had been estimated in previous years, and more particularly at the time when the charter was renewed in 1800. This, indeed, was virtually admitted. It was on this ground that Percival, when Chancellor of the Exchequer, claimed and secured certain unusually favourable loans. In the letter which he wrote with regard to these, he informs the directors that further increase may be met by further demands on behalf of the public. It was the contention of Mr Grenfell in Parliament and of Ricardo in his *Proposals for an Economical and Secure Currency* that the time for such demands had now arrived. It is needless to say that the bank directors did not agree with them. At first they met the contention by what amounted to a virtual denial of the right of the public to participate in these advantages, but when openly charged

with entertaining such views they receded. In the next place, they denied that they had received any advantage from the increase in the public deposits. This remarkable assertion was examined by Ricardo in the light of fact and with a stern logic that had an irony of its own. From this charge, by far the most prominent in his treatises, Ricardo passes to another. The directors had, he says, been guilty of grave irregularity in refusing the publication of their accounts and in accumulating a large and *quasi* secret reserve out of these increased profits, which, according to their charter, should have gone in increased dividends to the proprietors. But he does more than complain. He analyses the cost to the country of the Bank of England, and concludes by urging that the public services which it performs, as apart from its action as an ordinary bank, might well be rendered in a cheaper if not a better way.

II.

The two essays relating to agriculture and agricultural circumstances, namely, *The Influence of a Low Price of Corn on the Profits of Stock* and *On Protection to Agriculture,* are of particular importance in three respects. They deal with the question of Protection, both in general and in connection with the proposals and discussions of the time. The existing distress is considered, and the various causes alleged for it subjected to a somewhat keen criticism. Lastly, they throw considerable light on Ricardo's theory of Distribution, illustrating both its merits and its defects. While these must be dealt with in turn, a word or two on the essays in general will not be out of place. In structure they are compact, and the line of reasoning, as will be seen from the analytical table, is consecutive and little interrupted by digression. But perhaps the most noteworthy feature is their close relation to fact. There are many general passages, it is true, but the attempt throughout is to explain the facts of that particular time, and digressions, when they occur, arise in most cases from the necessity of considering explanations which had been advanced by recent writers. This leads at times to references, often not explicitly stated, to general principles. When these are under discussion a good deal is assumed and readers are credited with an acquaintance with general doctrines and in particular with Ricardo's doctrines, which few then possessed. At the present time many of the points are likely to be misunderstood, and so misinterpreted, unless read in connection with a knowledge of the times.

With regard to Protection, Ricardo deals both with the particular contentions with relation to agriculture and also, though more incidentally, with the question in general. The pleas for the corn duties are examined, in the main, with reference to their effect on profits, the leading contention being that such duties involved an increase in rent at the expense of profits. Of course here a good deal is assumed with regard to a standard of wages, and Ricardo, though he admitted, did not give adequate prominence to the effects produced by the want of relation between the variations in prices and the variations in wages. On the other hand, the remarks on the importance of a high rate of profits deserve a great deal of attention in view of the circumstances of the time. The need of capital in the development of the industries of the time was great, and Ricardo's contentions were, firstly, that savings were made out of the income received as profits, and, secondly, that an unduly low rate of profits might lessen the desire to accumulate. The first matter is not dealt with at any length; but it seems probable that at that time the particular capital required would be provided out of this part of the national income. The second matter, as has been pointed out with regard to

Ricardo's general treatment in the *Principles*, is largely qualified by other passages. It is at any rate not worked out. Another aspect presented itself in the plea that dependence on foreign supplies was a national danger. On this point, what Ricardo wrote then (*Influence of Low Price of Corn on the Profits of Stock*, §§ 10—13) has gained in reality from recent occurrences. He contends, in effect, that wide and varied sources of supply are most advantageous, and that an exporting trade in corn, when once built up, cannot be stopped without a great deal of damage to the *exporting* country and much consequent resentment. Writing at a time when the English control of the seas had been established, no attention is given to the relation of naval power and food supplies.

But while Ricardo attacked the corn laws, both in their general aspect and also in their particular form, it must be remembered that he did not advocate their instant or indeed their entire repeal. A gradual reduction was the policy he recommended, till only a small *fixed* duty was left sufficient to compensate for the particular taxes affecting the cultivation of the land.

In the references to a general protection, theoretical principles, rather than concrete facts, hold the ground. Few writers have depicted so concisely the real futility of wholesale protection and the close interdependence of exports and imports.

On the subject of the distress of the time and in particular of the distress in agriculture, some very useful information and criticism are supplied. It is pointed out that the extent to which such was attributable to changes in the value of money, owing to the Act of 1819, was very restricted. So far as the years 1819 and 1820 were concerned, the influence of Peel's Act restoring the money to a gold basis had to be measured not against the depreciation in paper when at its height, but against the measure of that depreciation just before the Act. This he estimated as at most a 10 per cent. alteration. The immediate relevance of this lay in the protective plea which attributed the ills of the time to the action of the Government and therefore demanded something by way of compensation from the state. But the alterations in the value of money owing to the issues of paper are equally important if applied to the earlier years of the century. Ricardo, of course, did not so apply them because he was treating of definite years and a definite contention. Next, with regard to the burden of taxation, which was again alleged with the same motive in view, it is shown that the effects of taxation would be experienced in industry as well as agriculture, and that great progress was taking place in industry. In other words, agriculture had no special grievances, and therefore no special claims could be advanced on its behalf. As against these efforts to seek the cause of distress in some action of the state, involving as these did an implied claim for redress by some such measure as Protection, Ricardo turned to discuss the connection of the trouble with underlying economic causes. He attributes the distress of 1820 and thereabouts largely, though not exclusively, to the good harvests and the great abundance of agricultural products. The action of such variations in supply was, he considered, accentuated by the particular effects of sliding scales, which tended, as he showed, to accentuate fluctuations in prices.

Though it cannot be contended that Ricardo's treatment is by any means exhaustive, he undoubtedly supplies evidence as to the action of certain factors which were overlooked at the time and which have been given an inadequate place in some late attempts to explain the difficulties of the period.

When we come to the theoretical argument which runs through and underlies his contention, it is necessary to turn from these essays to the position laid down in the *Principles*. As these have been fully dealt with in the *Introduction* to that volume, the task here is to trace their application to concrete phenomena.

The main argument is concerned with the problem of distribution, that is, with the division of the national income into rent, profits and wages. Ricardo throughout contends that the effect of Protection and the result of a high price of corn is a diminution in the rate of profits owing to a transfer to rent of what otherwise might have accrued in profits, and that such a change in the destination of a part of the total income is to the disadvantage of the community, inasmuch as a high rate of profits is essential to economic progress. These two propositions are separate. So far as the latter is concerned some remarks have been made above. The analysis of the relation between profits and accumulation is inadequate, indeed it is doubtful if the brief discussion should be dignified by the term analysis. Again, it may be contended that a large part of the accumulation is effected out of direct earnings or out of rental incomes. But here, again, we are brought to a standstill by a want of certainty in the use of the term profits of stock. It is probable that Ricardo considered the whole income of employers as separate in its determination from the income denoted as wages. But apart from technical defects of this kind there is, I think, a substantial meaning in the broad contention. He argues that the artificial increase in the amount allocated as rent implies the maintenance in a country of a class passive in economic progress at the expense of a class which is active. Of course his argument is limited to differential rent and must not be applied to returns directly derived from the application of capital in improved methods of cultivation.

It is, however, in connection with the first proposition that the more theoretical positions are developed. The keynote of the argument lies in § 7, *Influence of a Low Price of Corn on the Profits of Stock,* where a comparison is made of the ways in which a country may be benefited by trade. This is important as showing that Ricardo did not consider a high rate of profits as an ultimate aim in economic development. On the contrary, he expressly says that abundance of commodities owing to general improvements are to the advantage of mankind. Indeed he states that it is in this way only that nations benefit by industrial improvements and the extension of trade. Such abundance, however, he adds, does not in itself imply a "high rate of profits," and therefore, while indicative of general comfort at the time, does not lead to further advance. He admits, however, two exceptions, both very considerable. General abundance *may* lead to a *lower rate* of wages not, it must be remembered, to lower real wages, but to the same or even increased real wages being earned at the cost of a smaller proportion of the *effort* of the country. In this case a higher rate of profit may ensue and progress may be attained. With regard to this a good many things might be said. It might be said, for instance, that this means a continual sacrifice on the part of the working class for a future which will only see a like sacrifice enacted. The truth is that here Ricardo was hindered by the absence of any coherent theory of interest and by his habit of viewing the profit income as accruing to a class which would save and assist in progress and the wages income as going to a class which would not. In the second place, an extension of trade might lead to a readjustment of production whereby corn and other food might be procured without having to resort to the less favourable conditions which prevailed previously. This is undoubtedly true. But allowing for the correction made in the former of these exceptions, it is obvious that an increase in abundance, even on Ricardo's grounds, would very frequently lead to a rise in the "rate of profits," without any loss in the advantages accruing to mankind in general at the time. To him this did not appear to be the case. He regarded the exceptions, not perhaps as improbable, but certainly as of limited application. Thus the first of the two ways, indicated in the paragraph in question (§ 7), becomes more important.

The "rate of profit" depends, he says, essentially on the low price of corn, because agricultural profits in their rate determine the general rate. Now, of course, it is perfectly clear that it is to the general advantage if the food supply can be obtained without recourse to land inferior in fertility or less suitable in situation. But Ricardo goes a good deal further than this. He argues, in effect, that in the absence of two exceptional cases, invention and extension of trade offering though they do new opportunities for the employment of labour and capital, will not lead to a rise in the rate of profits "because they do not augment the produce compared with the cost of production on the land, and it is impossible that all other profits should rise whilst the profits on land are either stationary or retrograde." It is, of course, assumed that the demand for food is not diminished, and this may be granted. But what, it must be asked, would happen under the circumstances set out above, namely, an increase in industrial and commercial opportunities leaving unaffected agricultural processes. For the present the effect of a general improvement in production may be put on one side. Now Ricardo, to substantiate his general position, lays down a somewhat strange proposition. In effect, he contends that improvements and new opportunities in certain directions which might otherwise bring about a rise in profits, are precluded from exercising their influence in this direction because in agriculture no such change occurs. The normal result would be a rise in the price of agricultural produce, but this apparently he considers ineffective or impossible in view of the hypothesis that the demand for such produce remains unchanged. But this hypothesis to have any meaning implies a want of elasticity in demand and therefore the maintenance of the old demand at a higher price. This alteration in relative values means an equalisation in the return given for the use of capital. The disregard of this solution of the seeming paradox laid down was due, I think, to the confusion of this somewhat limited argument with one which is much wider and runs through his general teaching, namely, as to the effect of an increase in abundance on the *rate of profits*. This, which finds expression most clearly in the *Principles* (*v. inter alia, Value and Riches*) is dealt with in the *Introductory Essay* to that volume. Granted, however, the utility of the abstract relation thus established between the *rate of profits* and the *rate of wages*, its relevance in the present discussion must be considered. The point at issue is the maintenance or the acceleration of progress by the increase of capital. Surely an improvement in the return to effort will, other things remaining the same, increase both the revenue or ability of the class by which it is assumed saving is made, and also the amount saved as capital. If so, the end is attained.

The truth seems to be that whilst Ricardo's main contention is true, he went far beyond what was necessary to sustain it, on the one hand venturing on certain assumptions, including among these that as to the infrequency of the exceptions which he mentions, and on the other hand asserting that nothing else than the one cause which he had in view would secure the increase of capital. So far as the controversial end which was before him, his contention is undisturbed, the artificial efforts which occasioned a resort in agriculture to less favourable conditions were in themselves disadvantageous; and probably it is also true that part of these disadvantages lay in an encroachment on profits. So far as theory is concerned, the case is more doubtful. Certain possible tendencies and relations are indicated, but they depend on many assumptions and are subject to certain exceptions which are difficult to estimate.

THE HIGH PRICE

OF

BULLION

A PROOF OF THE

DEPRECIATION OF BANK NOTES

THE FOURTH EDITION

WITH AN APPENDIX

1811

HIGH PRICE OF BULLION

§ 1. The precious metals employed for circulating the commodities of the world, previously to the establishment of banks, have been supposed by the most approved writers on political economy to have been divided into certain proportions among the different civilized nations of the earth, according to the state of their commerce and wealth, and therefore according to the number and frequency of the payments which they had to perform. While so divided they preserved every where the same value, and as each country had an equal necessity for the quantity actually in use, there could be no temptation offered to either for their importation or exportation.

Gold and silver, like other commodities, have an intrinsic value, which is not arbitrary, but is dependent on their scarcity, the quantity of labour bestowed in procuring them, and the value of the capital employed in the mines which produce them.

"The quality of utility, beauty, and scarcity," says Dr Smith, "are the original foundation of the high price of those metals, or of the great quantity of other goods, for which they can every where be exchanged. This value was antecedent to, and independent of, their being employed as coin, and was the quality which fitted them for that employment."

If the quantity of gold and silver in the world employed as money were exceedingly small, or abundantly great, it would not in the least affect the proportions in which they would be divided among the different nations—the variation in their quantity would have produced no other effect than to make the commodities for which they were exchanged comparatively dear or cheap.

The smaller quantity of money would perform the functions of a circulating medium, as well as the larger. Ten millions would be as effectual for that purpose as 100 millions. Dr Smith observes, "that the most abundant mines of the precious metals would add little to the wealth of the world. A produce of which the value is principally derived from its scarcity is necessarily degraded by its abundance."

If in the progress towards wealth, one nation advanced more rapidly than the others, that nation would require and obtain a greater proportion of the money of the world. Its commerce, its commodities, and its payments, would increase, and the general currency of the world would be divided according to the new proportions. All countries, therefore, would contribute their share to this effectual demand.

In the same manner, if any nation wasted part of its wealth, or lost part of its trade, it could not retain the same quantity of circulating medium which it before possessed. A part would be exported, and divided among the other nations till the usual proportions were re-established.

While the relative situation of countries continued unaltered, they might have abundant commerce with each other, but their exports and imports would on the whole be equal. England might possibly import more goods from, than she would export to, France, but she would in consequence export more to some other country, and France would import more from that country; so that the exports and imports of all countries would balance each other; bills of exchange would make the necessary payments, but no money would pass because it would have the same value in all countries.

§ 2. If a mine of gold were discovered in either of these countries, the currency of that country would be lowered in value in consequence of the increased quantity of the precious metals brought into circulation, and would therefore no longer be of the same value as that of other countries. Gold and silver, whether in coin or in bullion, obeying the law which regulates all other commodities, would immediately become articles of exportation ; they would leave the country where they were cheap, for those countries where they were dear, and would continue to do so, as long as the mine should prove productive, and till the proportion existing between capital and money in each country before the discovery of the mine, were again established, and gold and silver restored every where to one value. In return for the gold exported, commodities would be imported ; and though what is usually termed the balance of trade would be against the country exporting money or bullion, it would be evident that she was carrying on a most advantageous trade, exporting that which was no way useful to her, for commodities which might be employed in the extension of her manufactures, and the increase of her wealth.

If instead of a mine being discovered in any country, a bank were established, such as the Bank of England, with the power of issuing its notes for a circulating medium ; after a large amount had been issued, either by way of loan to merchants, or by advances to Government, thereby adding considerably to the sum of the currency, the same effect would follow as in the case of the mine. The circulating medium would be lowered in value, and goods would experience a proportionate rise. The equilibrium between that and other nations would only be restored by the exportation of part of the coin.

The establishment of the bank, and the consequent issue of its notes, therefore, as well as the discovery of the mine, operate as an inducement to the exportation either of bullion, or of coin, and are beneficial only in as far as that object may be accomplished. The bank substitutes a currency of no value for one most costly, and enables us to turn the precious metals (which, though a very necessary part of our capital, yield no revenue), into a capital which will yield one. Dr A. Smith compares the advantages attending the establishment of a bank to those which would be obtained by converting our highways into pastures and corn fields, and procuring a road through the air. The highways, like the coin, are highly useful, but neither yield any revenue. Some people might be alarmed at the specie leaving the country, and might consider that as a disadvantageous trade which required us to part with it ; indeed the law so considers it by its enactments against the exportation of specie ; but a very little reflection will convince us that it is our choice, and not our necessity, that sends it abroad ; and that it is highly beneficial to us to exchange that commodity which is superfluous, for others which may be made productive.

§ 3. The exportation of the specie may at all times be safely left to the discretion of individuals ; it will not be exported more than any other commodity, unless its exportation should be advantageous to the country. If it be advantageous to export it, no laws can effectually prevent its exportation. Happily, in this case, as well as in most others in commerce, where there is free competition, the interests of the individual and that of the community are never at variance.[1]

Were it possible to carry the law against melting, or exporting of coin, into strict execution, at the same time that the exportation of gold bullion was freely allowed, no advantage could accrue from it, but great injury must arise to those who might have to pay, possibly, two ounces or more of coined gold for one of uncoined gold. This would be a real depreciation of our currency, raising the prices of all other commodities in the same proportion as it increased that of gold bullion. The owner of money would in this case suffer an injury equal to what a proprietor of corn would suffer, were a law to be passed prohibiting him from selling his corn for more than half its market value. The law against the exportation of the coin has this tendency, but is so easily evaded, that gold in bullion has always been nearly of the same value as gold in coin.

§ 4. Thus, then, it appears that the currency of one country can never for any length of time be much more valuable, as far as equal quantities of the precious metals are concerned, than that of another ; that excess of

[1] [This of course does not take into account the mercantilist argument as to the importance of treasure to the power of a country.]

currency is but a relative term; that if the circulation of England were 10 millions, that of France 5 millions, that of Holland 4 millions, &c., &c., whilst they kept their proportions, though the currency of each country were doubled or trebled, neither country would be conscious of an excess of currency. The prices of commodities would every where rise, on account of the increase of currency, but there would be no exportation of money from either. But if these proportions be destroyed by England alone doubling her currency, while that of France, Holland, &c., &c., continued as before, we should then be conscious of an excess in our currency, and for the same reason the other countries would feel a deficiency in theirs, and part of our excess would be exported till the proportions of ten, five, four, &c., were again established.

If in France an ounce of gold were more valuable than in England, and would therefore in France purchase more of any commodity common to both countries, gold would immediately quit England for such purpose, and we should send gold in preference to any thing else, because it would be the cheapest exchangeable commodity in the English market; for if gold be dearer in France than in England, goods must be cheaper; we should not therefore send them from the dear to the cheap market, but, on the contrary, they would come from the cheap to the dear market, and would be exchanged for our gold.

§ 5. The Bank might continue to issue their notes, and the specie be exported with advantage to the country, while their notes were payable in specie on demand, because they could never issue more notes than the value of the coin which would have circulated had there been no bank.*

If they attempted to exceed this amount, the excess would be immediately returned to them for specie; because our currency, being thereby diminished in value, could be advantageously exported, and could not be retained in our circulation. These are the means, as I

* They might, strictly speaking, rather exceed that quantity, because as the Bank would add to the currency of the world, England would retain its share of the increase.

have already explained, by which our currency endeavours to equalize itself with the currencies of other countries. As soon as this equality was attained, all advantage arising from exportation would cease; but if the Bank, assuming that because a given quantity of circulating medium had been necessary last year, therefore the same quantity must be necessary this, or for any other reason, continued to re-issue the returned notes, the stimulus which a redundant currency first gave to the exportation of the coin would be again renewed with similar effects; gold would be again demanded, the exchange would become unfavourable, and gold bullion would rise, in a small degree, above its Mint price, because it is legal to export bullion, but illegal to export the coin, and the difference would be about equal to the fair compensation for the risk.

In this manner, if the Bank persisted in returning their notes into circulation, every guinea might be drawn out of their coffers.

If, to supply the deficiency of their stock of gold, they were to purchase gold bullion at the advanced price, and have it coined into guineas, this would not remedy the evil; guineas would be still demanded, but, instead of being exported, would be melted, and sold to the Bank as bullion at the advanced price. "The operations of the Bank," observed Dr Smith, alluding to an analogous case, "were, upon this account, somewhat like the web of Penelope,—the work that was done in the day was undone in the night." The same sentiment is expressed by Mr Thornton[1]:—"Finding the guineas in their coffers to lessen every day, they must naturally be supposed to be desirous of replacing them by all effectual and not extravagantly expensive means. They will be disposed, to a certain degree, to buy gold, though at a losing price, and to coin it into new guineas; but they will have to do this at the very moment when many are privately melting what is coined. The one party will be melting and selling while the other is buying and coining. And each of these two contending businesses

[1] [Henry Thornton, *An Inquiry into the Nature and Effects of the Paper Credit of Great Britain.*]

will now be carried on, not on account of an actual exportation of each melted guinea to Hamburgh, but the operation, or at least a great part of it, will be confined to London, the coiners and the melters living on the same spot, and giving constant employment to each other.

"The Bank," continues Mr Thornton, "if we suppose it, as we now do, to carry on this sort of contest with the melters, is obviously waging a very unequal war; and even though it should not be tired early, it will be likely to be tired sooner than its adversaries."

The Bank would be obliged, therefore, ultimately to adopt the only remedy in their power to put a stop to the demand for guineas. They would withdraw part of their notes from circulation, till they should have increased the value of the remainder to that of gold bullion, and, consequently, to the value of the currencies of other countries. All advantage from the exportation of gold bullion would then cease, and there would be no temptation to exchange bank notes for guineas.

§ 6. In this view of the subject, then, it appears that the temptation to export money in exchange for goods, or what is termed an unfavourable balance of trade, never arises but from a redundant currency.[1] But Mr Thornton, who has considered this subject very much at large, supposes that a very unfavourable balance of trade may be occasioned to this country by a bad harvest, and the consequent importation of corn; and that there may be at the same time an unwillingness in the country to which we are indebted to receive our goods in payment; the balance due to the foreign country must therefore be paid out of that part of our currency consisting of coin, and that hence arises the demand for gold bullion, and its increased price. He considers the Bank as affording considerable accommodation to the merchants, by supplying with their notes the void occasioned by the exportation of the specie.

As it is acknowledged by Mr Thornton, in many parts

[1] [As the subsequent argument shows, Ricardo is not dealing with a temporary export of bullion. The phrase "redundant currency" is open to misunderstanding.]

of his work, that the price of gold bullion is rated in gold coin, and as it is also acknowledged by him that the law against melting gold coin into bullion, and exporting it, is easily evaded, it follows, that no demand for gold bullion, arising from this or any other cause, can raise the money price of that commodity. The error of this reasoning proceeds from not distinguishing between an increase in the value of gold, and an increase in its money price.

If there were a great demand for corn, its money price would advance, because, in comparing corn with money, we in fact compare it with another commodity; and, for the same reason, when there is a great demand for gold, its corn price will increase; but in neither case will a bushel of corn be worth more than a bushel of corn, or an ounce of gold more than an ounce of gold. An ounce of gold bullion could not, whatever the demand might be, whilst its price was rated in gold coin, be of more value than an ounce of coined gold, or 3*l.* 17s. 10½d.

If this argument should not be considered as conclusive, I should urge that a *void* in the currency, as here supposed, can only be occasioned by the annihilation or limitation of paper currency, and then it would speedily be filled by importations of bullion, which its increased value, in consequence of the diminution of circulating medium, would infallibly attract to the advantageous market. However great the scarcity of corn might be, the exportation of money would be limited by its increasing scarcity. Money is in such general demand, and, in the present state of civilization, is so essential to commercial transactions, that it can never be exported to excess; even in a war, such as the present,[1] when our enemy endeavours to interdict all commerce with us, the value which the currency would bear from its increasing scarcity would prevent the exportation of it from being carried so far as to occasion a void in the circulation.

Mr Thornton has not explained to us why any unwillingness should exist in the foreign country to receive

[1] [Accompanied as it was by the Decrees and Orders in Council.]

our goods in exchange for their corn; and it would be necessary for him to show, that if such an unwillingness were to exist, we should agree to indulge it so far as to consent to part with our coin.

If we consent to give coin in exchange for goods, it must be from choice, not necessity. We should not import more goods than we export, unless we had a redundancy [1] of currency, which it therefore suits us to make a part of our exports. The exportation of the coin is caused by its cheapness, and is not the effect, but the cause of an unfavourable balance: we should not export it, if we did not send it to a better market, or if we had any commodity which we could export more profitably. It is a salutary remedy for a redundant currency; and as I have already endeavoured to prove that redundancy or excess is only a relative term, it follows that the demand for it abroad arises only from the comparative deficiency of the currency of the importing country, which there causes its superior value.

It resolves itself entirely into a question of interest. If the sellers of the corn to England, to the amount, I will suppose, of a million, could import goods which cost a million in England, but would produce, when sold abroad, more than if the million had been sent in money, goods would be preferred; if otherwise, money would be demanded.

It is only after a comparison of the value in their markets and in our own of gold and other commodities, and because gold is cheaper in the London market than in theirs, that foreigners prefer gold in exchange for their corn. If we diminish the quantity of currency, we give an additional value to it: this will induce them to alter their election, and prefer the commodities. If I owed a debt in Hamburgh of 100*l.*, I should endeavour to find out the cheapest mode of paying it. If I send money, the expense attending its transportation being, I will suppose, 5*l.*, to discharge my debt will cost me

[1] [In the use of such terms as redundant, superabundant, Ricardo, it must be borne in mind, is referring to the value of money in this country as compared with its value in other countries.]

105*l*. If I purchase cloth here, which, with the expenses attending its exportation, will cost me 106*l*., and which will in Hamburgh sell for 100*l*., it is evidently more to my advantage to send the money. If the purchase and expenses of sending hardware to pay my debt will take 107*l*., I should prefer sending cloth to hardware, but I would send neither in preference to money, because money would be the cheapest exportable commodity in the London market. The same reasons would operate with the exporter of the corn, if the transaction were on his own account. But if the Bank, "fearful for the safety of their establishment," and knowing that the requisite number of guineas would be withdrawn from their coffers at the Mint price, should think it necessary to diminish the amount of their notes in circulation, the proportion between the value of the money, of the cloth, and of the hardware, would no longer be as 105, 106, and 107; but the money would become the most valuable of the three, and therefore would be less advantageously employed in discharging the foreign debts.

If, which is a much stronger case, we agreed to pay a subsidy to a foreign power, money would not be exported whilst there were any goods which could more cheaply discharge the payment. The interest of individuals would render the exportation of the money unnecessary.*

§ 7. Thus, then, specie will be sent abroad to discharge a debt only when it is superabundant; only when it is the cheapest exportable commodity. If the Bank were at such a time paying their notes in specie, gold would be demanded for that purpose. It would be obtained there at its Mint price, whereas its price as bullion would be

* This is strongly corroborated by the statement of Mr Rose in the House of Commons, that our exports exceeded our imports by (I believe) 16 millions. In return for those exports no bullion could have been imported, because it is well known that the price of bullion having been, during the whole year, higher abroad than in this country, a large quantity of our gold coin has been exported. To the value of the balance of exports, therefore, must be added the value of the bullion exported. A part of the amount may be due to us from foreign nations, but the remainder must be precisely equal to our foreign expenditure, consisting of subsidies to our allies, and the maintenance of our fleets and armies on foreign stations.

something above its value as coin, because bullion could, and coin could not, be legally exported.

It is evident, then, that a depreciation of the circulating medium is the necessary consequence of its redundance; and that in the common state of the national currency this depreciation is counteracted by the exportation of the precious metals.*

Such, then, appear to me to be the laws that regulate the distribution of the precious metals throughout the world, and which cause and limit their circulation from one country to another, by regulating their value in each. But before I proceed to examine on these principles the main object of my inquiry, it is necessary that I should show what is the standard measure of value in this country, and of which, therefore, our paper currency ought to be the representative, because it can only be by a comparison to this standard that its regularity, or its depreciation, may be estimated.

* It has been observed, in a work of great and deserved repute, the *Edinburgh Review*, Vol. i. p. 183, that an increase in the paper currency will only occasion a rise in the *paper* or *currency* price of commodities, but will not cause an increase in their bullion price.

This would be true at a time when the currency consisted wholly of paper not convertible into specie, but not while specie formed any part of the circulation. In the latter case the effect of an increased issue of paper would be to throw out of circulation an equal amount of specie; but this could not be done without adding to the quantity of bullion in the market, and thereby lowering its value, or, in other words, *increasing the bullion price of commodities*. It is only in consequence of this fall in the value of the metallic currency, and of bullion, that the temptation to export them arises; and the penalties on melting the coin is the sole cause of a small difference between the value of the coin and of bullion, or a small excess of the market above the Mint price. But exporting of bullion is synonymous with an unfavourable balance of trade. From whatever cause an exportation of bullion, in exchange for commodities, may proceed, it is called (I think very incorrectly) an unfavourable balance of trade.

When the circulation consists wholly of paper, any increase in its quantity will raise the *money* price of bullion without lowering its *value*, in the same manner, and in the same proportion, as it will raise the prices of other commodities, and for the same reason will lower the foreign exchanges; but this will only be a *nominal*, not a *real* fall, and will not occasion the exportation of bullion, because the real value of bullion will not be diminished, as there will be no increase to the quantity in the market.

§ 8. No permanent* measure of value can be said to exist in any nation while the circulating medium consists of two metals, because they are constantly subject to vary in value with respect to each other. However exact the conductors of the Mint may be, in proportioning the relative value of gold to silver in the coins, at the time when they fix the ratio, they cannot prevent one of these metals from rising, while the other remains stationary, or falls in value. Whenever this happens, one of the coins will be melted to be sold for the other. Mr Locke, Lord Liverpool, and many other writers, have ably considered this subject, and have all agreed, that the only remedy for the evils in the currency proceeding from this source, is the making one of the metals only the standard measure of value. Mr Locke considered silver as the most proper metal for this purpose, and proposed that gold coins should be left to find their own value, and pass for a greater or lesser number of shillings, as the market price of gold might vary with respect to silver.

Lord Liverpool,[1] on the contrary, maintained that gold was not only the most proper metal for a general measure of value in this country, but that, by the common consent of the people, it had become so, was so considered by foreigners, and that it was best suited to the increased commerce and wealth of England.

He, therefore, proposed, that gold coin only should be a legal tender for sums exceeding one guinea, and silver coins for sums not exceeding that amount. As the law now stands, gold coin is a legal tender for all sums;

* Strictly speaking, there can be no permanent measure of value. A measure of value should itself be invariable; but this is not the case with either gold or silver, they being subject to fluctuations as well as other commodities. Experience has indeed taught us, that though the variations in the *value* of gold or silver may be considerable, on a comparison of distant periods, yet, for short spaces of time, their value is tolerably fixed. It is this property, among other excellences, which fits them better than any other commodity for the uses of money. Either gold or silver may therefore, in the point of view in which we are considering them, be called a measure of value.

[1] [*A Treatise on the Coins of the Realm in a Letter to the King*, 1805, esp. 141, &c.]

but it was enacted in the year 1774, "That no tender in payment of money made in the silver coin of this realm, of any sum exceeding the sum of twenty-five pounds at any one time, shall be reputed in law, or allowed to be legal tender within Great Britain or Ireland, for more than according to its value by weight, after the rate of 5s. 2d. for each ounce of silver." The same regulation was revived in 1798, and is now in force.

For many reasons given by Lord Liverpool, it appears, proved beyond dispute, that gold coin has been for near a century the principal measure of value; but this is, I think, to be attributed to the inaccurate determination of the Mint proportions. Gold has been valued too high; no silver, therefore, can remain in circulation which is of its standard weight.

If a new regulation were to take place, and silver to be valued too high, or (which is the same thing) if the market proportions between the prices of gold and silver were to become greater than those of the Mint, gold would then disappear, and silver become the standard currency.

This may require further explanation. The relative value of gold and silver in the coins is as $15\frac{9}{124}$ to 1. An ounce of gold which is coined into 3*l*. 17s. $10\frac{1}{2}$d. of gold coin, is worth, according to the Mint regulation, $15\frac{9}{142}$ ounces of silver, because that weight of silver is also coined into 3*l*. 17s. $10\frac{1}{2}$d. of silver coin. Whilst the relative value of gold to silver is in the market under 15 to 1, which it has been for a great number of years till lately, gold coin would necessarily be the standard measure of value, because neither the Bank nor any individual would send $15\frac{9}{124}$ ounces of silver to the Mint to be coined into 3*l*. 17s. $10\frac{1}{2}$d., when they could sell that quantity of silver in the market for more than 3*l*. 17s. $10\frac{1}{2}$d. in gold coin; and this they could do by the supposition, that less than 15 ounces of silver would purchase an ounce of gold.

But if the relative value of gold to silver be more than the Mint proportion of $15\frac{9}{124}$ to 1, no gold would then be sent to the Mint to be coined, because as either of the metals are a legal tender to any amount, the possessor of an ounce of gold would not send it to the Mint to be coined into 3*l.* 17s. 10½d. of gold coin, whilst he could sell it, which he could do in such a case, for more than 3*l.* 17s. 10½d. of silver coin. Not only would not gold be carried to the Mint to be coined, but the illicit trader would melt the gold coin, and sell it as bullion for more than its nominal value in the silver coin. Thus, then, gold would disappear from circulation, and silver coin become the standard measure of value. As gold has lately experienced a considerable rise compared with silver (an ounce of standard gold, which, on an average of many years, was of equal value to 14¾ ounces of standard silver, being now in the market of the same value as 15½ ounces), this would be the case now were the Bank restriction bill repealed, and the coinage of silver freely allowed at the Mint, in the same manner as that of gold; but in an act of Parliament of 39 Geo. III. is the following clause:—

"Whereas inconvenience may arise from any coinage of silver until such regulations may be formed as shall appear necessary; and whereas from the present low price of silver bullion, owing to temporary circumstances, a small quantity of silver bullion has been brought to the Mint to be coined, and there is reason to suppose that a still further quantity may be brought; and it is, therefore, necessary to suspend the coining of silver for the present; be it therefore enacted, That from and after the passing of this act, no silver bullion shall be coined at the Mint, nor shall any silver coin that may have been coined there be delivered, any law to the contrary notwithstanding." This law is now in force.

It would appear, therefore, to have been the intention of the legislature to establish gold as the standard of currency in this country. Whilst this law is in force, silver coin must be confined to small payments only, the quantity in circulation being barely sufficient for that purpose. It might be for the interest of a debtor to pay his large debts in silver coin if he could get silver bullion coined into money; but being prevented by the above law from doing so, he is necessarily obliged to discharge his debt with gold coin, which he could obtain at the Mint with gold bullion to any amount. Whilst this law is in force, gold must always continue to be the standard of currency.

Were the market value of an ounce of gold to become equal to thirty ounces of silver, gold would nevertheless be the measure of value, whilst this prohibition continued in force. It would be of no avail, that the possessor of 30 ounces of silver should know that he once could have discharged a debt of 3*l.* 17s. 10½d. by procuring $15\frac{9}{124}$ ounces of silver to be coined at the Mint, as he would in this case have no other means of discharging his debt but by selling his 30 oz. of silver at the market value, that is to say, for one ounce of gold, or 3*l.* 17s. 10½d. of gold coin.

The public has sustained, at different times, very serious loss from the depreciation of the circulating medium, arising from the unlawful practice of clipping the coins.

In proportion as they become debased, so the prices of every commodity for which they are exchangeable rise in nominal value, not excepting gold and silver bullion: accordingly we find, that before the recoinage in the reign of King William the Third, the silver currency had become so degraded, that an ounce of silver, which ought to be contained in 62 pence, sold for 77 pence; and a guinea, which was valued at the Mint at 20 shillings, passed in all contracts for 30 shillings. This evil was then remedied by the recoinage. Similar effects followed from the debasement of the gold currency, which were again corrected in 1774 by the same means.

§ 9. Our gold coins have, since 1774, continued nearly at their standard purity; but our silver currency has again become debased. By an assay at the Mint in 1798, it appears that our shillings were found to be 24 per cent., and our sixpences 38 per cent., under their Mint value; and I am informed, that by a late experiment they were found considerably more deficient. They do not, therefore, contain as much pure silver as they did in the reign of King William. This debasement, however, did not operate previously to 1798, as on the former occasion. At that time both gold and silver bullion rose in proportion to the debasement of the silver coin. All foreign exchanges were against us full 20 per cent., and many of them still more. But although the debasement of the silver coin had continued for many years, it had neither, previously to 1798, raised the price of gold nor silver, nor had it produced any effect on the exchanges. This is a convincing proof, that gold coin was, during that period, considered as the standard measure of value. Any debasement of the gold coin would then have produced the same effects on the prices of gold and silver bullion, and on the foreign exchanges, which were formerly caused by the debasement of the silver coins.*

While the currency of different countries consists of the precious metals, or of a paper money which is at all times exchangeable for them; and while the metallic currency is not debased by wearing or clipping, a comparison of the weight and degree of fineness of their coins will enable us to ascertain their par of exchange. Thus the par of exchange between Holland and England is stated to be about eleven florins, because the pure silver contained in eleven florins is equal to the pure silver contained in twenty standard shillings.

This par is not, nor can it be, absolutely fixed; because gold coin being the standard of commerce in England, and silver coin in Holland, a pound sterling, or $\frac{20}{21}$ of a guinea, may at different times be more or less valuable than twenty standard shillings, and therefore more or less valuable than its equivalent of eleven florins. Estimating the par either by silver or by gold will be sufficiently exact for our purpose.

If I owe a debt in Holland, by knowing the par of exchange, I also know the quantity of our money which will be necessary to discharge it.

* When the gold coin was debased, previously to the recoinage in 1774, gold and silver bullion rose above their Mint prices, and fell immediately on the gold coin attaining its present perfection. The exchanges were, owing to the same causes, from being unfavourable rendered favourable.

If my debt amount to 1,100 florins, and gold have not varied in value, 100*l*. in our pure gold coin will purchase as much Dutch currency as is necessary to pay my debt. By exporting the 100*l*. therefore in coin, or (which is the same thing) paying a bullion merchant the 100*l*. in coin, and allowing him the expenses attending its transportation, such as freight, insurance, and his profit, he will sell me a bill which will discharge my debt ; at the same time he will export the bullion to enable his correspondent to pay the bill when it shall become due.

§ 10. These expenses, then, are the utmost limits of an unfavourable exchange. However great my debt may be, though it equalled the largest subsidy ever given by this country to an ally ; while I could pay the bullion merchant in coin of standard value, he would be glad to export it, and to sell me bills. But if I pay him for his bill in a debased coin, or in a depreciated paper-money, he will not be willing to sell me his bill at this rate ; because if the coin be debased it does not contain the quantity of pure gold or silver which ought to be contained in 100*l*., and he must therefore export an additional number of such debased pieces of money to enable him to pay my debt of 100*l*., or its equivalent, 1,100 florins. If I pay him in paper-money, as he cannot send it abroad, he will consider whether it will purchase as much gold or silver bullion as is contained in the coin for which it is a substitute ; if it will do this, paper will be as acceptable to him as coin ; but if it will not, he will expect a further premium for his bill, equal to the depreciation of the paper.

While the circulating medium consists, therefore, of coin undebased, or of paper-money immediately exchangeable for undebased coin, the exchange can never be more above, or more below par, than the expenses attending the transportation of the precious metals. But when it consists of a depreciated paper-money, it necessarily will fall according to the degree of the depreciation.

The exchange will, therefore, be a tolerably accurate criterion by which we may judge of the debasement of the currency, proceeding either from a clipped coinage or a depreciated paper-money.

It is observed by Sir James Stuart, "That if the foot measure was altered at once over all England, by adding to it or taking from it any proportional part of its standard length, the alteration would be best discovered by comparing the new foot with that of Paris, or of any other country which had suffered no alteration.

"Just so, if the pound sterling, which is the English unit, shall be found any how changed, and if the variation it has met with be difficult to ascertain because of a complication of circumstances, the best way to discover it will be to compare the former and the present value of it with the money of other nations which has suffered no variation. This the exchange will perform with the greatest exactness." [1]

The Edinburgh reviewers, in speaking of Lord King's pamphlet,[2] observe, that "it does not follow because our imports always consist partly of bullion that the balance of trade is therefore permanently in our favour. Bullion, they say, "is a commodity for which, as for every other, there is a varying demand, and which, exactly like any other, may enter the catalogue either of imports or exports; and this exportation or importation of bullion will not affect the course of exchange in a different way from the exportation or importation of any other commodities."

No person ever exports or imports bullion without first considering the rate of exchange. It is by the rate of exchange that he discovers the relative value of bullion in the two countries between which it is estimated. It is therefore consulted by the bullion merchant in the same manner as the price-current is by other merchants, before they determine on the exportation or importation of other commodities. If eleven florins in Holland contain an equal quantity of pure silver as 20 standard shillings, silver bullion, equal in weight to 20 standard

[1] [*An Inquiry into the Principles of Political Economy*, Book III, Chapter II., edition 1787, Vol. i. p. 534. Elsewhere he says, "Exchange, therefore, in my humble opinion, is one of the best measures for valuing a pound sterling, present currency" (p. 570).]

[2] [*Thoughts on the Restriction of Payments in Specie*, 1803.]

shillings, can never be exported from London to Amsterdam whilst the exchange is at par, or unfavourable to Holland. Some expense and risk must attend its exportation, and the very term *par* expresses that a quantity of silver bullion, equal to that weight and purity, is to be obtained in Holland by the purchase of a bill of exchange, free of all expense. Who would send bullion to Holland at an expense of 3 or 4 per cent. when, by the purchase of a bill at par, he in fact obtains an order for the delivery to his correspondent in Holland of the same weight of bullion which he was about to export?

It would be as reasonable to contend that, when the price of corn is higher in England than on the Continent, corn would be sent, notwithstanding all the charges on its exportation, to be sold in the cheaper market.

Having already noticed the disorders to which a metallic currency is exposed, I will proceed to consider those which, though not caused by the debased state of either the gold or silver coins, are nevertheless more serious in their ultimate consequences.

§ 11. Our circulating medium is almost wholly composed of paper, and it behoves us to guard against the depreciation of the paper currency with at least as much vigilance as against that of the coins. This we have neglected to do.

Parliament by restricting the Bank from paying in specie, have enabled the conductors of that concern to increase or decrease at pleasure the quantity and amount of their notes; and the previously existing checks against an over issue having been thereby removed, those conductors have acquired the power of increasing or decreasing the value of the paper currency.

§ 12. In tracing the present evils to their source, and proving their existence by an appeal to the two unerring tests I have before mentioned, namely, the rate of exchange and the price of bullion, I shall avail myself of the account given by Mr Thornton of the conduct of the Bank before the restriction, to show how clearly they acted on the principle which he has expressly acknowledged, viz. that the value of their notes is dependent on their amount, and that they ascertained the variation in their value by the tests I have just referred to.

Mr Thornton tells us, "That, if at any time the exchanges of the country become so unfavourable as to produce a material excess of the market above the Mint price of gold, the directors of the Bank, as appears by the evidence of some of their body given to parliament, were disposed to resort to a reduction of their paper, as a means of diminishing or removing the excess, and of *thus providing for the security of their establishment.* They, moreover, have at all times," he says, "been accustomed to observe some limit as to the quantity of their notes for the same prudential reasons." And in another place: "When the price which our coin will fetch in foreign countries is such as to tempt it out of the kingdom, the directors of the Bank naturally diminish, in some degree, the quantity of their paper *through an anxiety for the safety of their establishment.* By diminishing their paper, they raise its value; and in raising its value, they raise also the value in England of the current coin which is exchanged for it. Thus, the value of our gold coin conforms itself to the value of the current paper, and the current paper is rendered by the Bank directors of that value which it is necessary that it should bear in order to prevent large exportations,—a value sometimes rising a little above, and sometimes falling a little below, the price which our coin bears abroad."

The necessity which the Bank felt itself under to guard the safety of its establishment, therefore, always prevented, before the restriction from paying in specie, a too lavish issue of paper-money.

Thus we find that, for a period of twenty-three years previously to the suspension of cash payments in 1797, the average price of gold bullion was 3*l*. 17s. 7¾d. per oz., about 2¾d. under the Mint price; and for sixteen years previously to 1774, it never was much above 4*l*. per oz. It should be remembered, that during these sixteen years our gold coin was debased by wearing, and it is therefore probable that 4*l*. of such debased money did not weigh as much as the ounce of gold for which it was exchanged.

Dr A. Smith [1] considers every permanent excess of the market above the Mint price of gold, as referable to the state of the coins. While the coin was of its standard weight and purity, the market price of gold bullion, he thought, could not greatly exceed the Mint price.

Mr Thornton contends that this cannot be the only cause. "We have," he says, "lately experienced fluctuations in our exchanges, and correspondent variations in the market, compared with the Mint price of gold, amounting to no less than 8 or 10 per cent.; the state of our coinage continuing in all respects the same." Mr Thornton should have reflected, that at the time he wrote, specie could not be demanded at the Bank in exchange for notes; that this was a cause for the depreciation of the currency which Dr Smith could never have anticipated. If Mr Thornton had proved that there had been a fluctuation of 10 per cent. in the price of gold, while the Bank paid their notes in specie, and the coin was undebased, he would then have convicted Dr Smith of "having treated this important subject in a defective and unsatisfactory manner." *

* An excess in the market above the Mint price of gold or silver bullion, may, whilst the coins of both metals are legal tender, and there is no prohibition against the coinage of either metal, be caused by a variation in the relative value of those metals; but an excess of the market above the Mint price proceeding from this cause will be at once perceived by its affecting only the price of one of the metals. Thus, gold would be at or below, while silver was above, its Mint price, or silver at or below its Mint price, whilst gold was above.

In the latter end of 1795, when the Bank had considerably more notes in circulation than either the preceding or the subsequent year, when their embarrassments had already commenced, when they appear to have resigned all prudence in the management of their concerns, and to have constituted Mr Pitt sole director, the price of gold bullion did for a short time rise to 4*l.* 3s., or 4*l.* 4s. per oz.; but the directors were not without their fears for the consequences. In a remonstrance sent by them to Mr Pitt, dated October 1795, after stating, "that the demand for gold not appearing likely soon to cease," and "that it had excited great apprehension in the court of directors," they

[1] [*Wealth of Nations.* See especially Book I., Chapter V.; Book IV., Chapter VI.]

But as all checks against the over-issues of the Bank are now removed by the act of parliament, which restricts them from paying their notes in specie, they are no longer bound by "*fears for the safety of their establishment,*" to limit the quantity of their notes to that sum which shall keep them of the same value as the coin which they represent. Accordingly, we find that gold bullion has risen from 3*l.* 17s. 7¾d., the average price previously to 1797, to 4*l.* 10s., and has been lately as high as 4*l.* 13s. per oz.

§ 13. We may, therefore, fairly conclude, that this difference in the relative value, or, in other words, that this depreciation in the actual value of bank notes has been caused by the too abundant quantity which the Bank has sent into circulation. The same cause which has produced a difference of from 15 to 20 per cent. in bank notes when compared with gold bullion, may increase it to 50 per cent. There can be no limit to the depreciation which may arise from a constantly increasing quantity of paper. The stimulus which a redundant currency gives to the exportation of the coin has acquired new force, but cannot, as formerly, relieve itself. We have paper-money only in circulation, which is necessarily confined to ourselves. Every increase in its quantity degrades it below the value of gold and silver bullion, below the value of the currencies of other countries.

The effect is the same as that which would have been produced from clipping our coins.

If one-fifth were taken off from every guinea, the market price of gold bullion would rise one-fifth above

observe, "The present price of gold being 4*l.* 3s. to 4*l.* 4s.* per ounce, and our guineas being to be purchased at 3*l.* 17s. 10½d., clearly demonstrates the grounds of our fears; *it being only necessary to state those facts to the Chancellor of the Exchequer.*" It is remarkable that no price of gold above the Mint price is quoted during the whole year in Wetenhall's list. In December it is there marked 3*l.* 17s. 6d.

* It is difficult to determine on what authority the directors made this assertion, as by a return lately made to parliament it appears that during the year 1795 they did not purchase gold bullion at a price higher than 3*l.* 17s. 6d.

the Mint price. Forty-four guineas and a half (the number of guineas weighing a pound, and therefore called the Mint price), would no longer weigh a pound, therefore a fifth more than that quantity, or about 56*l.* would be the price of a pound of gold, and the difference between the market and the Mint price, between 56*l.* and 46*l.* 14s. 6d. would measure the depreciation.

If such debased coin were to continue to be called by the name of guineas, and if the value of gold bullion and all other commodities were rated in the debased coin, a guinea fresh from the Mint would be said to be worth 1*l.* 5s., and that sum would be given for it by the illicit trader ; but it would not be the value of the new guinea which had increased, but that of the debased guineas which had fallen. This would immediately be evident, if a proclamation were issued, prohibiting the debased guineas from being current but by weight at the Mint price of 3*l.* 17*s.* 10½d. ; this would be constituting the new and heavy guineas the standard measure of value, in lieu of the clipped and debased guineas. The latter would then pass at their true value, and be called 17 or 18 shillings-pieces. So if a proclamation to the same effect were now enforced, bank notes would not be less current, but would pass only for the value of the gold bullion which they would purchase. A guinea would then no longer be said to be worth 1*l.* 5s., but a pound note would be current only for 16 or 17 shillings. At present gold coin is only a commodity, and bank notes are the standard measure of value, but in that case gold coin would be that measure, and bank notes would be the marketable commodity.

" It is," says Mr Thornton, " the maintenance of our general exchanges, or, in other words, it is the agreement of the Mint price with the bullion price of gold, which seems to be the true proof that the circulating paper is not depreciated."

When the motive for exporting gold occurs, while the Bank do not pay in specie, and gold cannot therefore be obtained at its Mint price, the small quantity that can be procured will be collected for exportation, and bank notes will be sold at a discount for gold in proportion to their excess. In saying, however, that gold is at a high price, we are mistaken; it is not gold, it is paper which has changed its value. Compare an ounce of gold, or 3*l*. 17s. 10½d. to commodities, it bears the same proportion to them which it has before done; and if it do not, it is referable to increased taxation, or to some of those causes which are so constantly operating on its value. But if we compare the substitute of an ounce of gold, 3*l*. 17s. 10½d. in bank notes, with commodities, we shall then discover the depreciation of the bank notes. In every market of the world I am obliged to part with 4*l*. 10s. in bank notes to purchase the same quantity of commodities which I can obtain for the gold that is in 3*l*. 17s. 10½d. of coin.

It is often asserted, that a guinea is worth at Hamburgh 26 or 28 shillings; but we should be very much deceived if we should therefore conclude that a guinea could be sold at Hamburgh for as much silver as is contained in 26 or 28 shillings. Before the alteration in the relative value of gold and silver, a guinea would not sell at Hamburgh for as much silver coin as is contained in 21 standard shillings; it will at the present market price sell for a sum of silver currency, which, if imported and carried to our Mint to be coined, will produce in our standard silver coin 21s. 5d.*

It is nevertheless true, that the same quantity of silver will, at Hamburgh, purchase a bill payable in London, in bank notes, for 26 or 28 shillings. Can there be a more satisfactory proof of the depreciation of our circulating medium?

§ 14. It is said, that, if the Restriction-bill were not in force, every guinea would leave the country.†

This is, no doubt, true; but if the Bank were to diminish the quantity of their notes until they had increased their value 15 per cent., the restriction might be safely removed, as there would then be no temptation to

* The relative value of gold and silver is, on the Continent, nearly the same as in London.

† It must be meant that every guinea in the Bank would leave the country; the temptation of 15 per cent. is amply sufficient to send those out which can be collected from the circulation.

export specie. However long it may be deferred, however great may be the discount on their notes, the Bank can never resume their payments in specie, until they first reduce the amount of their notes in circulation to these limits.

The law is allowed by all writers on political economy to be a useless barrier against the exportation of guineas: it is so easily evaded, that it is doubted whether it has had the effect of keeping a single guinea more in England than there would have been without such law. Mr Locke, Sir J. Stuart, Dr A. Smith, Lord Liverpool, and Mr Thornton, all agree on this subject. The latter gentleman observes, "that the state of the British law unquestionably serves to discourage and limit, though not effectually to hinder, that exportation of guineas which is encouraged by an unfavourable balance of trade, and perhaps scarcely lessens it when the profit on exportation becomes very great." Yet, after every guinea that can in the present state of things be procured by the illicit trader has been melted and exported, he will hesitate before he openly buys guineas with bank notes at a premium, because, though considerable profit may attend such speculation, he will thereby render himself an object of suspicion. He may be watched, and prevented from effecting his object. As the penalties of the law are severe, and the temptation to informers great, secrecy is essential to his operations. When guineas can be procured by merely sending a bank note for them to the Bank, the law will be easily evaded; but when it is necessary to collect them openly and from a widely diffused circulation, consisting almost wholly of paper, the advantage attending it must be very considerable before any one will encounter the risk of being detected.

When we reflect that above 60 millions sterling have been coined into guineas during his present Majesty's reign, we may form some idea of the extent to which the exportation of gold must have been carried.—But repeal the law against the exportation of guineas, permit them to be openly sent out of the country, and what can prevent an ounce of standard gold in guineas from selling at as good a price for bank notes as an ounce of

Portuguese gold coin, or standard gold in bars, when it is known to be equal to them in fineness? And if an ounce of standard gold in guineas would sell in the market, as standard bars do now, at 4*l.* 10s. per oz., or, as they have lately done, at 4*l.* 13s. per oz., what shopkeeper would sell his goods at the same price either for gold or bank notes indifferently? If the price of a coat were 3*l.* 17s. 10½d. or an ounce of gold, and if at the same time an ounce of gold would sell for 4*l.* 13s., it is conceivable that it would be a matter of indifference to the tailor whether he were paid in gold or in bank notes?

It is only because a guinea will not purchase more than a pound-note and a shilling that many hesitate to allow that bank notes are at a discount. The *Edinburgh Review* supports the same opinion; but, if my reasoning be correct, I have shown such objections to be groundless.

§ 15. Mr Thornton has told us that an unfavourable trade will account for an unfavourable exchange; but we have already seen that an unfavourable trade, if such be an accurate term, is limited in its effects on the exchange. That limit is probably 4 or 5 per cent. This will not account for a depreciation of 15 to 20 per cent. Moreover, Mr Thornton has told us, and I entirely agree with him, "that it may be laid down as a general truth, that the commercial exports and imports of a state naturally proportion themselves in some degree to each other, and that the balance of trade, therefore, cannot continue for a very long time to be either highly favourable or highly unfavourable to a country." Now, the low exchange, so far from being temporary, existed before Mr Thornton wrote in 1802, and has since been progressively increasing, and is now from 15 to 20 per cent. against us. Mr Thornton must therefore, according to his own principles, attribute it to some more permanent cause than an unfavourable balance of trade, and will, I doubt not, whatever his opinion may formerly have been, now agree that it is to be accounted for only by the depreciation of the circulating medium.

§ 16. It can, I think, no longer be disputed that bank notes are at a discount. While the price of gold bullion is 4*l.* 10s. per oz., or, in other words, while any man will consent to give that which professes to be an obligation to pay nearly an ounce and a sixth of an ounce of gold for an ounce, it cannot be contended that 4*l.* 10s. in notes and 4*l.* 10s. in gold coin are of the same value.

An ounce of gold is coined into 3*l.* 17s. 10½d.; by possessing that sum, therefore, I have an ounce of gold, and would not give 4*l.* 10s. in gold coin, or notes which I could immediately exchange for 4*l.* 10s., for an ounce of gold.

It is contrary to common sense to suppose that such could be the market value, unless the price were estimated in a depreciated medium.

§ 17. If the price of gold were estimated in *silver*, indeed, the price might rise to 4*l.*, 5*l.*, or 10*l.* an ounce, and it would of itself be no proof of the depreciation of paper currency, but of an alteration in the relative value of gold and silver. I have, however, I think, proved that silver is not the standard measure of value, and therefore not the medium in which the value of gold is estimated. But if it were, as an ounce of gold is only worth in the market 15½ ounces of silver, and as 15½ ounces of silver is precisely equal in weight, and is therefore coined into 80 shillings, an ounce of gold ought not to sell for more than 4*l.*

Those, then, who maintain that silver is the measure of value, cannot prove that any demand for gold which may have taken place, from whatever cause it may have proceeded, can have raised its price above 4*l.* per oz. All above that price must, on their own principles, be called a depreciation in the value of bank notes. It therefore follows, that if bank notes be the representative of silver coin, then an ounce of gold, selling as it now does for 4*l.* 10s., sells for an amount of notes which represent 17½ ounces of silver, whereas, in the bullion market, it can only be exchanged for 15½ ounces. Fifteen ounces and a half of silver bullion are therefore of equal value with an engagement of the Bank to pay to *bearer* seventeen ounces and a half.

The market price of silver is at the present time 5s. 9½d. per oz., estimated in bank notes, the Mint pric

E

being only 5s. 2d., consequently, the standard silver in 100*l.* is worth more than 112*l.* in bank notes.

§ 18. But bank notes, it may be said, are the representatives of our debased silver coin, and not of our standard silver. This is not true, because the law which I have already quoted declares silver to be a legal tender for sums only not exceeding 25*l.*, except by weight. If the Bank insisted on paying the holder of a bank note of 1000*l.* in silver coin, they would be bound either to give him standard silver of full weight, or debased silver of an equal value, with the exception of 25*l.*, which they might pay him in debased coin. But the 1000*l.*, so consisting of 975*l.* pure money, and 25*l.* debased, is worth more than 1,112*l.* at the present market value of silver bullion.

§ 19. It is said that the amount of bank notes has not increased in a greater proportion than the augmentation of our trade required, and therefore cannot be excessive. This assertion would be difficult to prove, and if true, no argument but what is delusive could be founded on it. In the first place, the daily improvements which we are making in the art of economizing the use of circulating medium by improved methods of banking, would render the same amount of notes excessive now which were necessary for the same state of commerce at a former period. Secondly, there is a constant competition between the Bank of England and the country banks to establish their notes, to the exclusion of those of their rivals, in every district where the country banks are established.

As the latter have more than doubled in number within very few years, is it not probable that their activity may have been crowned with success, in displacing with their own notes many of those of the Bank of England ?

If this have happened, the same amount of Bank of England notes would now be excessive, which, with a less extended commerce, was before barely sufficient to keep our currency on a level with that of other countries. No just conclusion can, therefore, be drawn from the actual amount of bank notes in circulation, though the fact, if examined, would, I have no doubt, be found to be that the increase in the amount of bank notes, and the high price of gold, have usually accompanied each other.

It is doubted whether 2 or 3 millions of bank notes (the sum which the Bank is supposed to have added to the circulation, over and above the amount which it will easily bear) could have had such effects as are ascribed to them; but it should be recollected, that the Bank regulate the amount of the circulation of all the country banks, and it is probable that, if the Bank increase their issues 3 millions, they enable the country banks to add more than 3 millions to the general circulation of England.

The money of a particular country is divided amongst its different provinces by the same rules as the money of the world is divided amongst the different nations of which it is composed. Each district will retain in its circulation such a proportionate share of the currency of the country as its trade, and consequently its payments, may require, compared to the trade of the whole; and no increase can take place in the circulating medium of one district, without being generally diffused, or calling forth a proportionable quantity in every other district. It is this which keeps a country bank note always of the same value as a Bank of England note. If in London, where Bank of England notes only are current, 1 million be added to the amount in circulation, the currency will become cheaper there than elsewhere, or goods will become dearer. Goods, will therefore, be sent from the country to the London market to be sold at the high prices, or, which is much more probable, the country banks will take advantage of the relative deficiency in the country currency, and increase the amount of their notes in the same proportion as the Bank of England had done; prices would then be generally, and not partially, affected.

In the same manner, if Bank of England notes be diminished 1 million, the comparative value of the currency of London will be increased, and the prices of goods diminished. A Bank of England note will then be more valuable than a country bank note, because it will be wanted to purchase goods in the cheap market; and as the country banks are obliged to give Bank of England notes for their own when demanded, they would be called upon for them till the quantity of country paper should be reduced to the same proportion which it before bore to the London paper, producing a corresponding fall in the prices of all goods for which it was exchangeable.

§ 20. The country banks could never increase the amount of their notes, unless to fill up a relative deficiency in the country currency, caused by the increased issues of the Bank of England.* If they attempted it, the same check which compelled the Bank of England to withdraw part of their notes from circulation when they used to pay them on demand in specie, would oblige the country banks to adopt the same course. Their notes would, on account of the increased quantity, be rendered of less value than the Bank of England notes, in the same manner as Bank of England notes were rendered of less value than the guineas which they represented. They would therefore be exchanged for Bank of England notes until they were of the same value.

The Bank of England is the great regulator of the country paper. When they increase or decrease the amount of their notes, the country banks do the same; and in no case can country banks add to the general circulation unless the Bank of England shall have previously increased the amount of their notes.

§ 21. It is contended, that the rate of interest, and not the price of gold or silver bullion, is the criterion by which we may always judge of the abundance of paper money; that if it were too abundant, interest would fall, and if not sufficiently so, interest would rise. It can, I think, be made manifest, that the rate of interest is not regulated by the abundance or scarcity of money, but by the abundance or scarcity of that part of capital not consisting of money.

"Money," observes Dr A. Smith, "the great wheel of circulation, the great instrument of commerce, like all other instruments of trade, though it makes a part, and

* They might, on some occasions, displace Bank of England notes, but that consideration does not affect the question which we are now discussing.

a very valuable part of the capital, makes no part of the revenue of the society to which it belongs; and though the metal pieces of which it is composed, in the course of their annual circulation, distribute to every man the revenue which properly belongs to him, they make themselves no part of that revenue.

"When we compute the quantity of industry which the circulating capital of any society can employ, we must always have regard to those parts of it only which consist in provisions, materials, and finished work: the other, which consists in money, and which serves only to circulate those three, must always be deducted. In order to put industry into motion, three things are requisite:—materials to work upon, tools to work with, and the wages or recompense for the sake of which the work is done. Money is neither a material to work upon nor a tool to work with; and though the wages of the workman are commonly paid to him in money, his real income, like that of all other men, consists not in money, but in money's worth; not in the metal pieces, but what can be got for them."

And in other parts of his work, it is maintained that the discovery of the mines in America, which so greatly increased the quantity of money, did not lessen the interest for the use of it; the rate of interest being regulated by the profits on the employment of capital, and not by the number or quality of the pieces of metal which are used to circulate its produce.

Mr Hume [1] has supported the same opinion. The

[1] [Essay XXV., *Of Money*. See such passages as—

"It is indeed evident, that money is nothing but the representation of labour and commodities, and serves only as a method of rating or estimating them."

"It is none of the wheels of trade; it is the oil which renders the motions of the wheels more smooth and easy."

But the whole essay is important.

Again, in a note to Essay XXVII., *Of the Balance of Trade*, Hume writes, "It must be carefully remarked, that throughout this discourse where ever I speak of the level of money, I mean always its proportional level to the commodities, labour, industry, and skill which is in the several states. And I assert that where these advantages are double, triple, quadruple, to what they are value of the circulating medium of every country bears some proportion to the value of the commodities which it circulates. In some countries this proportion is much greater than in others, and varies, on some occasions, in the same country. It depends upon the rapidity of circulation, upon the degree of confidence and credit existing between traders, and, above all, on the judicious operations of banking. In England, so many means of economizing the use of circulating medium have been adopted, that its value, compared with the value of the commodities which it circulates, is probably (during a period of confidence *) reduced to as small a proportion as is practicable. What that proportion may be has been variously estimated.

No increase or decrease of its quantity, whether consisting of gold, silver, or paper money, can increase or decrease its value above or below this proportion. If the mines cease to supply the annual consumption of the precious metals, money will become more valuable, and a smaller quantity will be employed as a circulating medium. The diminution in the quantity will be proportioned to the increase of its value. In like manner, if new mines be discovered, the value of the precious metals will be reduced, and an increased quantity used in the circulation; so that, in either case the relative value of money to the commodities which it circulates will continue as before.

If, whilst the Bank paid their notes on demand in specie, they were to increase their quantity, they would produce little permanent effect on the value of the currency, because nearly an equal quantity of the coin would be withdrawn from circulation and exported.

If the Bank were restricted from paying their notes in specie, and all the coin had been exported, any excess of their notes would depreciate the value of the circulating medium in proportion to the excess. If 20 millions had

* In the following observations, I wish it to be understood as supposing always the same degree of confidence and credit to exist.

---

in the neighbouring states, the money infallibly will also be double, triple, and quadruple."]

been the circulation of England before the restriction, and 4 millions were added to it, the 24 millions would be of no more value than the 20 were before, provided commodities had remained the same, and there had been no corresponding exportation of coins; and if the Bank were successively to increase it to 50 or 100 millions, the increased quantity would be all absorbed in the circulation of England, but would be, in all cases, depreciated to the value of the 20 millions.

§ 22. I do not dispute, that if the Bank were to bring a large additional sum of notes into the market, and offer them on loan, but that they would for a time affect the rate of interest. The same effects would follow from the discovery of a hidden treasure of gold or silver coin. If the amount were large, the Bank, or the owner of the treasure, might not be able to lend the notes or the money at 4, nor perhaps above 3 per cent.; but having done so, neither the notes, nor the money, would be retained unemployed by the borrowers; they would be sent into every market, and would everywhere raise the prices of commodities, till they were absorbed in the general circulation. It is only during the interval of the issues of the Bank, and their effect on prices, that we should be sensible of an abundance of money; interest would, during that interval, be under its natural level; but as soon as the additional sum of notes or of money became absorbed in the general circulation, the rate of interest would be high, and new loans would be demanded with as much eagerness as before the additional issues.

The circulation can never be over full. If it be one of gold and silver, any increase in its quantity will be spread over the world. If it be one of paper, it will diffuse itself only in the country where it is issued. Its effects on prices will then be only local and nominal, as a compensation by means of the exchange will be made to foreign purchasers.

To suppose that any increased issues of the Bank can have the effect of permanently lowering the rate of interest, and satisfying the demands of all borrowers, so that there will be none to apply for new loans, or that a productive gold or silver mine can have such an effect, is to attribute a power to the circulating medium which it can never possess. Banks would, if this were possible, become powerful engines indeed. By creating paper money, and lending it at 3 or 2 per cent. under the present market rate of interest, the Bank would reduce the profits on trade in the same proportion ; and if they were sufficiently patriotic to lend their notes at an interest no higher than necessary to pay the expenses of their establishment, profits would be still further reduced ; no nation, but by similar means, could enter into competition with us, we should engross the trade of the world. To what absurdities would not such a theory lead us ! Profits can only be lowered by a competition of capitals not consisting of circulating medium. As the increase of bank notes does not add to this species of capital, as it neither increases our exportable commodities, our machinery, or our raw materials, it cannot add to our profits nor lower interest.*

When any one borrows money for the purpose of entering into trade, he borrows it as a medium by which he can possess himself of " materials, provisions, &c.," to carry on that trade ; and it can be of little consequence to him, provided he obtain the quantity of materials, &c., necessary, whether he be obliged to borrow a thousand, or ten thousand pieces of money. If he borrow ten thousand, the produce of his manufacture will be ten times the nominal value of what it would have been, had one thousand been sufficient for the same purpose. The capital actually employed in the country is necessarily limited to the amount of the " materials, provisions, &c.," and might be made equally productive, though not with equal facility, if trade were carried on wholly by barter. The successive possessors of the

* I have already allowed that the Bank, as far as they enable us to turn our coin into " materials, provisions, &c.," have produced a national benefit, as they have thereby increased the quantity of productive capital ; but I am here speaking of an excess of their notes, of that quantity which adds to our circulation without effecting any corresponding exportation of coin, and which, therefore, degrades the notes below the value of the bullion contained in the coin which they represent.

circulating medium have the command over this capital: but however abundant may be the quantity of money or of bank notes; though it may increase the nominal prices of commodities; though it may distribute the productive capital in different proportions; though the Bank, by increasing the quantity of their notes, may enable A to carry on part of the business formerly engrossed by B and C, nothing will be added to the real revenue and wealth of the country. B and C may be injured, and A and the Bank may be gainers, but they will gain exactly what B and C lose. There will be a violent and an unjust transfer of property, but no benefit whatever will be gained by the community.

For these reasons I am of opinion that the funds are not indebted for their high price to the depreciation of our currency. Their price must be regulated by the general rate of interest given for money. If before the depreciation I gave thirty years' purchase for land, and twenty-five for an annuity in the stocks, I can, after the depreciation, give a larger sum for the purchase of land, without giving more years' purchase, because the produce of the land will sell for a greater nominal value in consequence of the depreciation; but as the annuity in the funds is paid in the depreciated medium, there can be no reason why I should give a greater nominal value for it after than before the depreciation.

If guineas were degraded by clipping to half their present value, every commodity as well as land would rise to double its present nominal value; but as the interest of the stocks would be paid in the degraded guineas, they would, on that account, experience no rise.

§ 23. The remedy which I propose for all the evils in our currency, is that the Bank should gradually decrease the amount of their notes in circulation until they shall have rendered the remainder of equal value with the coins which they represent, or, in other words, till the prices of gold and silver bullion shall be brought down to their Mint price. I am well aware that the total failure of paper credit would be attended with the most disastrous consequences to the trade and commerce of the country, and even its sudden limitation would occasion so much ruin and distress, that it would be highly inexpedient to have recourse to it as the means of restoring our currency to its just and equitable value.

If the Bank were possessed of more guineas than they had notes in circulation they could not, without great injury to the country, pay their notes in specie, while the price of gold bullion continued greatly above the Mint price, and the foreign exchanges unfavourable to us. The excess of our currency would be exchanged for guineas at the Bank, and exported, and would be suddenly withdrawn from circulation. Before, therefore, they can safely pay in specie, the excess of notes must be gradually withdrawn from circulation. If gradually done, little inconvenience would be felt; so that the principle were fairly admitted, it would be for future consideration whether the object should be accomplished in one year or in five. I am fully persuaded that we shall never restore our currency to its equitable state, but by this preliminary step, or by the total overthrow of our paper credit.

If the Bank directors had kept the amount of their notes within reasonable bounds; *if they had acted up to the principle which they have avowed to have been that which regulated their issues when they were obliged to pay their notes in specie, namely, to limit their notes to that amount which should prevent the excess of the market above the Mint price of gold, we should not have been exposed to all the evils of a depreciated, and perpetually varying currency.*

Though the Bank derive considerable advantage from the present system, though the price of their capital stock has nearly doubled since 1797, and their dividends have proportionally increased, I am ready to admit with Mr Thornton, that the directors, as monied men, sustain losses in common with others by a depreciation of the currency, much more serious to them than any advantages which they may reap from it as proprietors of Bank stock. I do, therefore, acquit them of being influenced by interested motives, but their mistakes, if they are such, are in their effects quite as pernicious to the community.

§ 24. The extraordinary powers with which they are intrusted enable them to regulate at their pleasure the price at which those who are possessed of a particular kind of property, called money, shall dispose of it. The Bank directors have imposed upon these holders of money all the evils of a maximum. To-day it is their pleasure that 4*l.* 10s. shall pass for 3*l.* 17s. 10½d., to-morrow they may degrade 4*l.* 15s. to the same value, and in another year 10*l.* may not be worth more. By what an insecure tenure is property consisting of money or annuities paid in money held! What security has the public credit that the interest on the public debt, which is now paid in a medium depreciated 15 per cent., may not hereafter be paid in one degraded 50 per cent.? The injury to private creditors is not less serious. A debt contracted in 1797 may now be paid with 85 per cent. of its amount; and who shall say that the depreciation will go no further?

§ 25. The following observations of Dr Smith on this subject are so important, that I cannot but recommend them to the serious attention of all thinking men.

"The raising the denomination of the coin has been the most usual expedient by which a real public bankruptcy has been disguised under the appearance of a pretended payment. If a sixpence, for example, should, either by act of parliament, or royal proclamation, be raised to the denomination of a shilling, and twenty sixpences to that of a pound sterling, the person who under the old denomination had borrowed twenty shillings, or near four ounces of silver, would, under the new, pay with twenty sixpences, or with something less than two ounces. A national debt of about 120 millions, nearly the capital of the funded debt of Great Britain, might in this manner be paid with about 64 millions of our present money. It would indeed be a pretended payment only, and the creditors of the public would be defrauded of ten shillings in the pound of what was due to them. The calamity, too, would extend much further than to the creditors of the public, and those of every private person would suffer a proportionable loss; and this without any advantage, but in most cases with a great additional loss to the creditors of the public. If the creditors of the public, indeed, were generally much in debt to other people, they might in some measure compensate their loss by paying their creditors in the same coin in which the public had paid them. But in most countries the creditors of the public are the greater part of them wealthy people, who stand more in the relation of creditors than in that of debtors towards the rest of their fellow citizens. A pretended payment of this kind, therefore, instead of alleviating, aggravates in most cases the loss of the creditors of the public; and without any advantage to the public, extends the calamity to a great number of other innocent people. It occasions a general and most pernicious subversion of the fortunes of private people; enriching in most cases the idle and profuse debtor at the expense of the industrious and frugal creditor, and transporting a great part of the national capital from the hands which are likely to increase and improve it, to whose which are likely to dissipate and destroy it. When it becomes necessary for a state to declare itself bankrupt, in the same manner as when it becomes necessary for an individual to do so, a fair, open, and avowed bankruptcy is always the measure which is both least dishonourable to the debtor, and least hurtful to the creditor. The honour of a state is surely very poorly provided for, when, in order to cover the disgrace of a real bankruptcy, it has recourse to a juggling trick of this kind, so easily seen through, and at the same time so extremely pernicious."

These observations of Dr Smith on a debased money are equally applicable to a depreciated paper currency. He has enumerated but a few of the disastrous consequences which attend the debasement of the circulating medium, but he has sufficiently warned us against trying such dangerous experiments. It will be a circumstance ever to be lamented, if this great country, having before its eyes the consequences of a forced paper circulation in America and France, should persevere in a system pregnant with so much disaster. Let us hope that she will be more wise. It is said, indeed, that the cases are dissimilar; that the Bank of England is independent of Government. If this were true, the evils of a superabundant circulation would not be less felt; but it may be questioned whether a bank lending many millions more to Government than its capital and savings, can be called independent of that Government.

When the order of council for suspending the cash payments became necessary in 1797, the run upon the Bank was, in my opinion, caused by political alarm alone and not by a superabundant, or a deficient quantity (as some have supposed) of their notes in circulation.*

This is a danger to which the Bank, from the nature of its institution, is at all times liable. No prudence on the part of the directors could perhaps have averted it: but if their loans to Government had been more limited; if the same amount of notes had been issued to the public through the medium of discounts; they would have been able, in all probability, to have continued their payments till the alarm had subsided. At any rate, as the debtors to the Bank would have been obliged

* At that period the price of gold kept steadily under its Mint price.

["The circumstances which occurred in the beginning of the year 1797 were very similar to those of 1793;—an alarm of invasion, a run upon the country banks for gold, the failure of some of them, and a run upon the Bank of England, forming a crisis like that of 1793, for which perhaps an effectual remedy might have been provided, if the Bank of England had had courage to extend instead of restricting its accommodations and issue of notes. Some few persons, it appears from the Report of the Secret Committee of the Lords, were of this opinion at the time; and the late Governor and Deputy Governor of the Bank stated to your Committee (Mai. p. 110) that they and many of the directors are now satisfied from the experience of the year 1797, that the diminution of their notes in that emergency increased the public distress: an opinion in the correctness of which your Committee entirely concur" (Bullion Rep. p. 27).

The Secret Committee report the opinion referred to, though without any definite finding of their own as they considered it "their duty to call the attention of the House to a point of so great importance and refer the House to the arguments stated more at large in the evidence." (Report of Secret Committee 1797, pp. 149, 150.) The point in question is dealt with at considerable length in the evidence of Mr Henry Thornton and Mr Boyd.]

to discharge their debts in the space of sixty days, that being the longest period for which any bill discounted by the Bank has to run, the directors would in that time, if necessary, have been enabled to redeem every note in circulation. It was then owing to the too intimate connexion between the Bank and Government,[1] that the restriction became necessary; it is to that cause, too, that we owe its continuance.

To prevent the evil consequences which may attend the perseverance in this system, we must keep our eyes steadily fixed on the repeal of the restriction bill.

The only legitimate security which the public can possess against the indiscretion of the Bank is to oblige them to pay their notes on demand in specie; and this can only be effected by diminishing the amount of bank notes in circulation till the nominal price of gold be lowered to the Mint price.

Here I will conclude, happy if my feeble efforts should awaken the public attention to a due consideration of the state of our circulating medium. I am well aware that I have not added to the stock of information with which the public has been enlightened by many able writers on the same important subject. I have had no such ambition. My aim has been to introduce a calm and dispassionate inquiry into a question of great importance to the State, and the neglect of which may be attended with consequences which every friend of his country would deplore.

[1] [The diminution of the advances to the Government is referred to (but see Mr Bosanquet's evidence before the Lords' Secret Committee 1797, pp. 22—23). On the other hand some witnesses were of opinion that a decrease in them might have led the Bank to lessen the number of notes; but this is hardly probable, having regard to the number of notes in regular use prior to 1793. The arguments of these was that *so far as the circulation in number of notes was concerned and the consequential effects*, it did not matter whether they were issued because of advances to the Government or in discounts to merchants. This is distinct from the consideration as to the effects produced by a restriction in private discounts owing to advances to the Government.]

APPENDIX

OBSERVATIONS ON SOME PASSAGES IN AN ARTICLE IN THE EDINBURGH REVIEW, ON THE DEPRECIATION OF PAPER CURRENCY; ALSO SUGGESTIONS FOR SECURING TO THE PUBLIC A CURRENCY AS INVARIABLE AS GOLD, WITH A VERY MODERATE SUPPLY OF THAT METAL.

THE public having called for a new edition of this pamphlet, I avail myself of the occasion to consider the observations which the Edinburgh Reviewers, in the last number of their publication, have done me the honour to make on some of the passages contained in it. I am induced to do this from the conviction that discussion on every point connected with this important subject will hasten the remedy against the existing abuse, and will tend to secure us against the risk of its recurrence in future.

In the article on the depreciation of money, the Reviewers observe, "The great fault of Mr Ricardo's performance is the partial view which he takes of the causes which operate upon the course of exchange. He attributes," they say, "a favourable or an unfavourable exchange *exclusively* to a redundant or deficient currency, and overlooks the varying desires and wants of different societies as an original cause of a temporary excess of imports above exports, or exports above imports." They then comment on the passage in which I have maintained that a bad harvest will not occasion the export of money, unless money is relatively cheap in the exporting country, and conclude their observations by giving it as their decided opinion, that the exportation of money in the supposed case of a bad harvest, "is not occasioned by its cheapness. It is not, as Mr Ricardo endeavours to persuade us, the cause of the unfavourable balance instead of the effect. It is not merely a salutary remedy for a redundant currency: but it is owing precisely to the cause mentioned by Mr Thornton—the unwillingness of the creditor nation to receive a great additional quantity of goods not wanted for immediate consumption without being bribed to it by excessive cheapness; and its willingness to receive bullion—the currency of the commercial world—without any such bribe. *It is unquestionably true, as stated by Mr Ricardo, that no nation will pay a debt in the precious metals if it can do it cheaper by commodities*; but the prices of commodities are liable to great depressions from a glut in the market; whereas the precious metals, on account of their having been constituted by the universal consent of society the general medium of exchange and instrument of commerce, will pay a debt of the largest amount at its nominal estimation, according to the quantity of bullion contained in the respective currencies of the countries in question, and, whatever variations between the quantity of currency and commodities may be stated to take place subsequent to the commencement of these transactions, it cannot be for a moment doubted that the cause of them is to be found in the wants and desires of one of the two nations, and not in any original redundancy or deficiency of currency in either of them."

They agree with me, "that no nation will pay a debt in the precious metals, if it can do it cheaper by commodities, *but the prices of commodities,*" they say, "*are liable to great depressions from a glut in the market;*" of course they must mean in the foreign market, and then the words express the opinion which they are endeavouring to controvert, viz. that when goods cannot be sent out so advantageously as money, money will be exported,—which is another way of saying that money will never be exported, unless it is relatively redundant with commodities, as compared with other countries. Yet, immediately after, they contend, that the exportation of the "precious metals is the *effect of a balance of trade,** originating in causes which may exist without any relation whatever to redundancy or deficiency of currency." These opinions appear to me directly contradictory. If, however, the precious metals can be exported from a country in exchange for commodities, although they should be as dear in the exporting as in the importing country, what are the effects which will follow from such improvident exportation?

"A comparative deficiency in one country, and redundancy in the other," say the Reviewers, p. 343, "and this state of things could not fail to have a speedy effect in changing the direction of the balance of payments, and in restoring that equilibrium of the precious metals, which had been for a time disturbed by the naturally unequal wants and necessities of the countries which trade with each other." Now it would have been well if the Reviewers had told us at what point this re-action would commence,—as at the first view it appears that the same law which will permit money to be exported from a country, when it is no cheaper than in the importing country, may also allow it to be exported when it is actually dearer. It is self-interest which regulates all the speculations of trade, and where that can be clearly and satisfactorily ascertained, we should not know where to stop if we admitted any other rule of action. They should have explained to us therefore, why, if the demand for the commodity imported should continue, the country importing might not be entirely exhausted of its coin and bullion. What is under

* We are here speaking of a *balance of trade* abstracted from a *balance of payments*. A balance of trade may be favourable whilst a balance of payments is unfavourable. It is the balance of payments only which operates on the exchange.

such circumstances to check the exportation of the currency? The Reviewers say, because " a country with a diminished quantity of bullion would evidently soon be limited in its powers of paying with the precious metals." Why soon? Is it not admitted " that excess and deficiency of currency are only relative terms; that the circulation of a country can never be superabundant," (and therefore can never be deficient), " except in relation to other countries." Does it not follow from these admissions, that if the balance of trade may become unfavourable to a country, though its currency be not relatively superabundant, that there is no check against the exportation of its coin, whilst any amount of money remains in circulation; as the diminished sum (by acquiring a new value), will as readily and as effectually make the required payments as the larger sum did before? A succession of bad harvests might, on this principle, drain a country of its money, whatever might be its amount, although it consisted exclusively of the precious metals. The observation that its diminished value in the importing country, and its increasing value in the exporting country, would make it revert again to the old channel, does not answer the objection. When will this happen? and in exchange for what will it be returned? The answer is obvious—for commodities. The ultimate result then of all this exportation and importation of money, is that one country will have imported one commodity in exchange for another, and the coin and bullion will in both countries have regained their natural level. Is it to be contended that these results would not be foreseen, and the expense and trouble attending these needless operations effectually prevented, in a country where capital is abundant, where every possible economy in trade is practised, and where competition is pushed to its utmost limits? Is it conceivable that money should be sent abroad for the purpose merely of rendering it dear in this country and cheap in another, and by such means to insure its return to us?

It is particularly worthy of observation that so deep-rooted is the prejudice which considers coin and bullion as things essentially differing in all their operations from other commodities, that writers greatly enlightened upon the general truth of political economy seldom fail, after having requested their readers to consider money and bullion merely as commodities subject to " the same general principle of supply and demand which are unquestionably the foundation on which the whole superstructure of political economy is built; " to forget this recommendation themselves, and to argue upon the subject of money, and the laws which regulate its export and import, as quite distinct and different from those which regulate the export and import of other commodities. Thus the Reviewers, if they had been speaking of coffee or of sugar, would have denied the possibility of those articles being exported from England to the Continent, unless they were dearer there than here. It would have been in vain to have urged to them, that our harvest had been bad, and that we were in want of corn; they would confidently and undeniably have proved that to whatever degree the scarcity of corn might have existed, it would not have been possible for England to send, or for France (for example) to be willing to receive, coffee or sugar in return for corn, whilst coffee or sugar cost more money in England than in France. What! they would have said, do you believe it possible for us to send a parcel of coffee to France to sell there for 100*l*. when that coffee cost here 105*l*.—when by sending 100*l*. of the 105*l*. we should equally discharge the debt contracted for the imported corn? And, I say, do you believe it possible that we shall agree to send, or France agree to receive (if the transaction is on her account) 100*l*. in money, when 95*l*. invested in coffee and exported will be equally valuable as the 100*l*. when it arrives in France? But coffee is not wanted in France, there is a glut of it;—allowed, but money is wanted still less, and the proof is, that a hundred pounds' worth of coffee will sell for more than a hundred pounds' worth of money. The only proof which we can possess of the relative cheapness of money in two places, is by comparing it with commodities. Commodities measure the value of money in the same manner as money measures the value of commodities. If, then, commodities will purchase more money in England than in France, we may justly say that money is cheaper in England, and that it is exported to *find* its level, not to *destroy* it. After comparing the relative value of coffee, sugar, ivory, indigo, and all other exportable commodities in the two markets, if I persist in sending money, what further proof can be required of money being actually the cheapest of all these commodities in the English market, in relation to the foreign markets, and therefore the most profitable to be exported? What further evidence is necessary of the relative redundance and cheapness of money between France and England, than that in France it will purchase more corn, more indigo, more coffee, more sugar, more of every exportable commodity than in England?

I may, indeed, be told that the Reviewers' supposition is not that coffee, sugar, indigo, ivory, &c., &c., are cheaper than money, but that these commodities and money are equally cheap in both countries, that is to say, that one hundred pounds sent in money, or invested in coffee, sugar, indigo, ivory, &c., &c., will be of equal value in France. If the value of all these commodities were so nicely poised, what would determine an exporter to send the one in preference to the other in exchange for corn, in relation to which they are all cheaper in England? If he sends money, and thereby destroys the natural level, we are told by the Reviewers that money would on account of its increasing quantity in France and its decreasing quantity in England, become cheaper in France than in England, and would be re-imported in exchange for goods, till the level were restored. But, would not the same effects take place if coffee or any of the other commodities were exported, whilst they were equally valuable in relation to money in both countries? Would not the equilibrium between supply and demand be destroyed, and would not the diminished value of coffee, &c., in consequence of their increased quantity in France and their increased value in England, from their diminished quantity, produce their re-importation into England? Any of *these* commodities might be exported without producing much inconvenience from their enhanced price; whereas money, which circulates all other commodities, and the increase or diminution of which, even in a moderate proportion, raises or falls prices in an extravagant degree, could not be exported without the most serious consequences. Here, then, we see the defective principle of the Reviewers. On my system, however, there would be no difficulty in determining the mode in which, in a case so extremely improbable as that of an equal value in both countries for *all* commodities, money included, and corn alone excepted, the returns would be made so as to preserve the relative amount and the relative value of their respective currencies.

If the circulating medium of England consisted wholly of the precious metals, and were a fiftieth part of the value of the commodities which it circulated, the whole amount of money which would, under the circumstances supposed, be exported in exchange for corn, would be a fiftieth part of the value of such corn: for the rest we should export commodities, and thus would the proportion between money and commodities be equally preserved in both countries. England, in consequence of a bad harvest, would come under the case mentioned at page 4—of a country having been deprived of a part of its commodities, and therefore requiring a diminished amount of circulating medium. The currency, which was before equal to her payments, would now become superabundant, and relatively cheap, in the proportion of one fiftieth part of her diminished production; the exportation of this sum, therefore, would restore the value of her currency to the value of the currencies of other countries. Thus, it appears to be satisfactorily proved, that a bad harvest operates on the exchange in no other way than by causing the currency, which was before at its just level, to become redundant, and thus is the principle that an unfavourable exchange may always be traced to a relatively redundant currency most fully exemplified.

If we can suppose that, after an unfavourable harvest, when England has occasion for an unusual importation of corn, another nation is possessed of a superabundance of that article, "*but has no wants for any commodity whatever*," it would unquestionably follow that such nation would not export its corn in exchange for commodities; but neither would it export corn for money, as that is a commodity which no nation ever wants absolutely, but relatively, as is expressly admitted by the Reviewers. The case is, however, impossible, because a nation possessed of every commodity necessary for the consumption and enjoyment of all its inhabitants who have wherewithal to purchase them, will not let the corn which it has over and above what it can consume, rot in its granaries. Whilst the desire of accumulation is not extinguished in the breast of man, he will be desirous to realise the excess of his productions, above his own consumption, into the form of capital. This he can only do by employing, himself, or by loans to others enabling them to employ an additional number of labourers, as it is by labour only that revenue is realised into capital. If his revenue be corn, he will be disposed to exchange it for fuel, meat, butter, cheese, and other commodities in which the wages of labour are usually expended, or, which is the same thing, he will sell his corn for money, pay the wages of his labourers in money, and thereby create a demand for those commodities which may be obtained from other countries in exchange for the superfluous corn. Thus will be reproduced to him articles more valuable, which he may again employ in the same manner, adding to his own riches, and augmenting the wealth and resources of his country.

No mistake can be greater than to suppose *that a nation can ever be without wants for commodities of some sort.* It may possess too much of one or more commodities for which it may not find a market at home. It may have more sugar, coffee, tallow, than it can either consume or dispose of, but no country ever possessed a general glut of all commodities. It is evidently impossible. If a country possesses every thing necessary for the maintenance and comfort of man, and these articles be divided in the proportions in which they are usually consumed, they are sure, however abundant, to find a market to take them off. It follows, therefore, that whilst a country is in possession of a commodity for which there is no demand at home, it will be desirous of exchanging it for other commodities in the proportion in which they are consumed.

No nation grows corn, or any other commodity, with a view to realise its value in money (the case supposed, or involved in the case supposed, by the Reviewers), as this would be the most unprofitable object to which the labour of man could be devoted. Money is precisely that article which, till it is re-exchanged, never adds to the wealth of a country; accordingly we find, that to increase its amount is never the voluntary act of any country any more than it is that of any individual. Money is forced upon them only in consequence of the relatively less value which it possesses in those countries with which they have intercourse.

Whilst a country employs the precious metals for money, and has no mines of its own, it is a conceivable case that it may greatly augment the amount of the productions of its land and labour without adding to its wealth, because at the same time those countries which are in possession of the mines may possibly have obtained so enormous a supply of the precious metals as to have forced an increase of currency on the industrious country, equal in value to the whole of its increased productions. But by so doing the augmented currency, added to that which was before employed, will be of no more real value than the original amount of currency. Thus then will this industrious nation become tributary to those nations which are in possession of the mines, and will carry on a trade in which it gains nothing and loses every thing.

That the exchange is in a constant state of fluctuation with all countries I am not disposed to deny, but it does not generally vary to those limits at which remittances can be more advantageously made by means of bullion than by the purchase of bills. Whilst this is the case, it cannot be disputed that imports are balanced by exports. The varying demands of all countries may be supplied, and the exchanges of all deviate in some degree from par, if the currency of any one of them is either redundant or deficient, as compared with the rest. Suppose England to send goods to Holland, and not to find there any commodities which suit the English market; or, which is the same thing, suppose that we can purchase those commodities cheaper in France. In this case we confine our operation to the sale of goods in Holland, and the purchase of other goods in France. The currency of England is not disturbed by either transaction, as we shall pay France by a bill on Holland, and there will neither be an excess of imports nor of exports. The exchange may, however, be favourable to us with Holland, and unfavourable with France; and will be so, if the account be not balanced by the importation into France of goods from Holland, or from some country indebted to Holland. If there be no such importation, it can arise only from a relative redundancy of the circulation of Holland, as compared with that of France, and in payment of the bill it will suit both those countries that bullion should be transmitted. If the balance be settled by the transmission of goods, the exchange between all the three countries will be at par. If, by bullion, the exchange between Holland and England will be as much above par as that between France and England will be below the par, and the difference will be equal to the expenses attending the passage of bullion from Holland to France. It will make no difference in the result, if every nation of the world were concerned in the transaction. England having bought goods from France and sold goods to Holland, France might have purchased to the same amount from Italy; Italy may have done the same from Russia, Russia from Germany, and Germany within 100,000*l*. of the same amount from Holland; Germany might require this amount of bullion either to supply a deficient currency, or for the fabrication of plate. All these various transactions would be settled by bills of exchange, with the exception of the 100,000*l*., which would be either transmitted from an existing redundancy of coin or bullion in Holland, or it would be collected by Holland from the different currencies of Europe. It is not contended, as the Reviewers infer, "that a bad harvest, or the necessity of paying a subsidy in one country should be immediately and invariably accompanied by an unusual demand for muslins, hardware, and colonial produce," as the same effects would be produced if the country paying the subsidy, or suffering from a bad harvest, were to import less of other commodities than it had before been accustomed to do.

The Reviewers observe, page 345, " The same kind of error which we have here noticed pervades other parts of Mr. Ricardo's pamphlet, particularly the opening of his subject. He seems to think that when once the precious metals have been divided among the different countries of the earth, according to their relative wealth and commerce, that each having an equal necessity for the quantity actually in use, no temptation would be offered for their importation or exportation, till either a new mine or a new bank was opened; or till some marked change had taken place in their relative prosperity." And afterwards, at page 361, " We have already adverted to the error (confined, however, principally to Mr Ricardo, and from which the Report is entirely free) of denying the existence of a balance of trade or of payments not connected with some original redundancy or deficiency of currency." " But there is *another point* in which almost all the writers on this side of the question concur, where, notwithstanding, we cannot agree with them, and feel more inclined to the mercantile view of the subject. Though they acknowledge that bullion occasionally passes from one country to another, from causes connected with the exchange, yet they represent these transactions as quite inconsiderable in degree. Mr. Huskisson observes, ' that the operations in the trade of bullion originate almost entirely in the fresh supplies which are yearly poured in from the mines of the New World, and are chiefly confined to the distribution of those supplies through the different parts of Europe. If this supply were to cease altogether, the dealings in gold and silver, as objects of foreign trade, would be very few and those of short duration.' "

" Mr. Ricardo, in his reply to Mr Bosanquet, refers to this passage with particular approbation." Now, I am at a loss to discover in what this opinion of Mr. Huskisson differs from that which I had before given, and on which the Reviewers had been commenting.

The passages are in substance precisely the same, and must stand or fall together. If " we acknowledge that bullion occasionally passes from one country to another from causes connected with the exchange," we do not acknowledge that it would so pass till the exchange had fallen to such limits as would make the exportation of bullion profitable; and I am of opinion that if it should so fall, it is in consequence of the cheapness and redundance of currency, which " would originate almost entirely in the fresh supplies which are yearly poured in from the mines of the New World." This, then, is not *another point* in which the Reviewers differ with me, but the same.

If " it is well known that most States, in their usual relations of commercial intercourse, have an almost constantly favourable exchange with some countries, and an almost constantly unfavourable one with the others," to what cause can it be ascribed but to that mentioned by Mr Huskisson? " The fresh supplies of bullion which are yearly poured in (and in nearly the same direction) from the mines of the New World." Dr A. Smith does not seem to have been sufficiently aware of the powerful and uniform effects which this stream of bullion had on the foreign exchanges, and he was inclined much to overrate the uses of bullion in carrying on the various roundabout foreign trades which a country finds it necessary to engage in. In the early and rude transactions of commerce between nations, as in the early and rude transactions between individuals, there is little economy in the use of money and bullion; it is only in consequence of civilisation and refinement that paper is made to perform the same office between the commonwealth of nations, as it so advantageously performs between individuals of the same country. The Reviewers do not appear to me to be sufficiently aware of the extent to which the principle of economy in the use of the precious metals is extended between nations, indeed, they do not seem to acknowledge its force even when confined to a single nation, as from a passage in page 346, their readers would be induced to suppose their opinion to be, that there are frequent transfers of currency between the distant provinces of the same country; for they tell us that "there have been, and ever will be, a quantity of the precious metals in use destined to perform the same part with regard to the different nations connected with each other by commerce, which the currency of a particular country performs with regard to its distant provinces." Now, what part does the currency of a country perform with regard to the distant provinces?

I am well persuaded, that, in all the multiplicity of commercial transactions which take place between the distant provinces of this kingdom, the currency performs a very inferior part, imports being almost always balanced by exports,* and the proof is, that the local currency of the provinces (and they have no other) is seldom circulated at any considerable distance from the place where it is issued.

It appears to me that the Reviewers were induced to admit the erroneous doctrine of the merchants, *that money might be exported in exchange for commodities, although money were no cheaper in the exporting country*, because they could in no other way account for the rise of the exchange having, on some occasions, accompanied the increased amount of bank notes, as stated by Mr Pearse, the late deputy governor, and now governor of the Bank, in a paper delivered by him to the bullion committee. They say, "according to this view of the subject, it certainly is not easy to explain an improving exchange under an obviously increasing issue of notes: an event that not unfrequently happens, and was much insisted upon by the deputy governor of the Bank as a proof that our foreign exchanges had no connexion with the state of our currency."

These are circumstances, however, which are not absolutely

* Part of the produce of the provinces is exported without any return, as it constitutes the revenue of absentees, but this consideration can have no effect on the question of currency.

irreconcileable. Mr Pearse, as well as the Edinburgh Reviewer, appears to have wholly mistaken the principle advanced by those who are desirous of the repeal of the restriction bill. They do not contend, as they are understood to do, that the increase of *bank notes* will permanently lower the exchange, but that such an effect will proceed from a redundant currency. It remains, therefore, to be considered whether an increase of bank notes is necessarily at all times accompanied with a permanently increased currency, as, if I can make it appear that it is not, there will be no difficulty in accounting for a rise in the exchange with an increased amount of bank notes.

It will be readily admitted, that, whilst there is any great portion of coin in circulation, every increase of bank notes, though it will for a short time lower the value of the whole currency, paper as well as gold, yet that such depression will not be permanent, because the redundant and cheap currency will lower the exchange, and will occasion the exportation of a portion of the coin, which will cease as soon as the remainder of the currency shall have regained its value and restored the exchange to par. The increase of small notes, then, will ultimately be a substitution of one currency for another, of a paper for a metallic currency, and will not operate in the same way as an actual and permanent increase of circulation.* We are not, however, without a criterion by which we may determine the relative amount of currency at different periods, as distinguished from bank notes, on which, though we cannot infallibly rely, it will probably be a sufficiently accurate test to determine the question which we are now discussing. This criterion is the amount of notes of 5*l.* and upwards in circulation, which, we may reasonably calculate, always bear some tolerably regular proportion to the whole circulation. Thus, if since 1797 the bank notes of this description have increased from 12 to 16 millions, we may infer that the whole circulation has increased one-third, if the districts in which bank notes circulate have neither been enlarged nor contracted. The notes under 5*l.* will be issued in proportion as the metallic currency is withdrawn from circulation, and will be further augmented if there be also an augmentation of notes of a higher denomination.

If I am correct in this view of the subject, that the increase in the amount of our currency is to be inferred from the increased amount of bank notes of 5*l.* and upwards, and can by no means be proved by an increase of 1*l.* and 2*l.* notes which have been substituted in the place of the exported or hoarded guineas, I must wholly reject the calculations of Mr Pearse, because they

* That an increase of bank notes under 5*l.* should be considered as a substitute for the coins exported, rather than an actual increase of circulation, is often and justly maintained by those who oppose the reasoning of the bullion report; but when these same gentlemen want to establish their favourite theory, that there is no connexion between the amount of the circulation and the rate of exchange, they do not forget to bring to their aid these small notes which they had before discarded.

are made on the supposition that every increase of this description of notes is an increase of currency to that amount. When it is considered, that in 1797 there were no notes of 1*l.* and 2*l.* in circulation, but that their place was wholly filled with guineas; and that, since that period, there have been no less than 7 millions issued, partly to supply the place of our exported and hoarded guineas, and partly to keep up the proportion between the circulation for the larger and for the smaller payments, we shall observe to what errors such reasoning may lead. I can consider the paper in question of no authority whatever as opposed to the opinion which I have ventured to give, namely, that an unfavourable balance of trade, and a consequently low exchange, may in all cases be traced to a relatively redundant and cheap currency.* But if the reasoning of Mr Pearse were not incorrect as his *facts* are, he is no way warranted in the conclusions which he has drawn from them.

Mr. Pearse states the increase of bank notes from January 1808 to Christmas 1809, to have been from 17½ to 18 millions, or 500,000*l.*, the exchange with Hamburgh during the same period having fallen from 34s. 9g. to 28s. 6g. an increase in the amount of notes of less than 3 per cent., and a fall in the exchange of more than 18 per cent.

But from whence did Mr Pearse obtain this information, of 18 millions of bank notes *only* being in circulation at Christmas in 1809? After looking at every return with which I have been able to meet, of the amount of bank notes in circulation at the end of 1809, I cannot but conclude that Mr Pearse's statement is incorrect. Mr Mushet in his tables gives four returns of bank notes in the year. In the last, for the year 1809, he has stated the

amount of bank notes in circulation at . . .	19,742,998
In the Appendix to the Bullion Report, and in returns lately made to the House of Commons, the amount of bank notes in circulation appears to have been on December 12, 1809, . . .	19,727,520
On the 1st January, 1810, ...	20,669,320
On the 7th January, 1810, ...	19,528,030

For many months previously to December it was not lower. When I first discovered this inaccuracy I thought Mr Pearse might have omitted the bank post bills in both estimates, although they did not in December 1809, exceed 880,880*l.*; but on looking at the return of bank notes in circulation, including bank post bills in January 1808, I find Mr Pearse has stated it larger than I can any where find it: indeed his estimate exceeds the return made by the Bank for the 1st of January 1808, by

* It is not meant to be denied, that the sudden invasion of an enemy, or a convulsion in a country of any kind which renders the possession of property insecure may form an exception to this rule, but the exchange will in general be unfavourable to a country thus circumstanced.

nearly 900,000*l.*, so that from the 1st of January 1808 to the 12th of December 1809, the increase was from 16,619,240 to 19,727,520, a difference of more than 3 millions, instead of 500,000, as stated by Mr Pearse, and of 2 millions if Mr Pearse's statement for any time in January 1808, be correct.

Mr Pearse's statement, too, that from January 1803 to the end of 1807, the amount of bank notes had increased from 16½ to 18 millions, an increase of a million and a half, appears to me to exceed the fact by half a million. The increase of notes of 5*l.* and upwards, including bank post bills, did not, during that period, exceed 150,000*l.* It is material that these errors should be pointed out, that those who may, in spite of what I have urged, agree in principle with Mr Pearse, may see that the facts of the case do not warrant the conclusions which that gentleman has drawn from them, and, indeed, that all calculations founded on the particular amount of bank notes for a day, or for a week, when the general average has been for some time before, or some time after, greater or less, will be of little avail in overturning a theory which has every other proof of its truth. Such I consider the theory which asserts that the unlimited multiplication of a currency which is referable to no fixed standard may and must produce a permanent depression of the exchange, estimated with a country whose currency is founded on such standard.

Having considered the weight which ought to be attached to Mr Pearse's paper, I beg the reader's attention to the table which I have drawn out from the statements in the Bullion Report, and from the papers which have since been presented to the House of Commons. I request him to compare the amount of the circulation of the larger notes with the variations in the exchange, and I trust he will find no difficulty in reconciling the principle maintained by me with the actual facts of the case, particularly if he considers that the operations of an increased currency are not instantaneous, but require some interval of time to produce their full effect,—that a rise or fall in the price of silver, as compared with gold, alters the relative value of the currencies of England and Hamburgh, and therefore makes the currency of one or other relatively redundant and cheap ;—that the same effect is produced, as I have already stated, by an abundant or deficient harvest, either in this country or in those countries with which we trade, or by any other addition or diminution to their real wealth, which by altering the relative proportion between commodities and money alters the value of the circulating medium. With these corrections, I have no fear but that it will be found that Mr Pearse's objections may be refuted without having recourse to the abandonment of a principle which, if yielded, will establish the mercantile theory of exchange, and may be made to account for a drain of circulating medium, so great, that it can only be counteracted by locking up our money in the bank, and absolving the directors from the obligation of paying their notes in specie.

Mr Pearse's statement as presented to the Bullion Committee:*

	Total of Bank notes. *Millions.*		Rate of Hambro' Exchange. s. g.
27th February 1797 . .	8½		35 6
Rose gradually in 1797 and 1798 to	13		38 0
March 1799, ...	13½		37 7
After this period, great commercial distress, large importation of corn, heavy subsidies, and the Hambro' Exchange continued falling, and on the 2d January 1801, was as low as .			29 8
Between the end of the year 1799 to the end of 1802, an increased quantity of 1*l.* and 2*l.* notes were issued, swelling the sum total of *all* notes to . . .	13½ to 16½	Fluctuation	from 33 3 to 29 8
From January 1803 to the end of 1807, ...	16½ to 18	Fluctuation	from 32 10 to 35 10
From January 1808 to Christmas 1809, ...	17½ to 18	Fall	from 34 9 to 28 6

The rate of the Hambro' Exchange is taken from Lloyd's list.

The average amount of bank notes from the year 1797 to 1809 inclusive, in the following table, is copied from the Report of the Bullion Committee. The rates of exchange are extracted from a list presented by the Mint to parliament. There have been three returns made to parliament by the Bank of the amount of their notes in circulation in the year 1810;—the first for the 7th and 12th of each month; the second, a weekly return from the 19th January 1810 to 28th December; and the third also a weekly account from the 3d March to 29th December 1810. The average amount of notes above 5*l.*, including bank post bills, according to the first account, is

	£15,706,226	Of notes under 5*l.*	£6,560,674
Second, . .	16,192,110		6,758,895
Third, . .	16,358,230		6,614,721
	3)48,256,566		19,934,290
General average.	16,085,522		6,644,763

* I have omitted as much of Mr Pearse's paper as regarded the amount of bank notes in circulation before the restriction on bank payments, because whilst the public possessed the power of obtaining specie for their notes, the exchange could not but be momentarily lowered by the amount of the bank issues.

In the years marked thus * the value of silver as compared with gold exceeded the Mint valuation; this was the case particularly in the year 1801, when less than 14 oz. of silver could purchase an ounce of gold;—the Mint valuation is as 1 to 15.07; the present market value is as 1 to 16 nearly.

Average amount of Bank of England Notes in circulation in each of the following years:

	Notes of 5*l.* and upwards, including Bank Post Bills.	Notes under 5*l.*	Total.	Highest rate of Exchange with Hamburgh.		Lowest rate of Exchange with Hamburgh.	
1798	£11,527,250	£1,807,502	£13,334,752	38.2	Jan.	37.4	Dec.
*1799	12,408,522	1,653,805	14,062,327	37.7	Jan.	31.6	Oct.
*1800	13,598,666	2,243,266	15,841,932	32.5	May.	31.–	Feb.
*1801	13,454,367	2,715,182	16,169,594	31.8	Oct.	29.8	Jan.
*1802	13,917,977	3,136,477	17,054,454	34.–	Dec.	32.–	Feb.
1803	12,983,477	3,864,045	16,847,522	35.–	Dec.	34.–	Jan.
1804	12,621,348	4,723,672	17,345,020	36.–	June.	34.8	Feb.
*1805	12,697,352	4,544,580	17,241,932	35.8	March.	32.9	Nov.
*1806	12,844,170	4,291,230	17,135,400	34.8	Dec.	33.3	Jan.
*1807	13,221,988	4,183,013	17,405,001	34.10	March.	34.2	Sept.
*1808	13,402,160	4,132,420	17,534,580	35.3	July.	32.4	Dec.
1809	14,133,615	4,868,275	19,001,890	31.3	Jan.	28.6	Nov.
1810	16,085,522	6,644,763	22,730,285	31.2	June.	28.6	Dec.
1811				26.6	Jan.	24.–	March.

The Bank have made a return of the amount of their notes for eighteen days in this present year 1811. The average amount of notes of 5*l.* and upwards in circulation for those eighteen days, including bank post bills, is £16,286,950

And of those under 5*l.* 7,260,575

Total . . £23,547,525

"If," say the Reviewers, "considerable portions of the currency were taken from the idle, *and those who live upon fixed incomes*, and transferred to farmers, manufacturers, and merchants, the proportion between capital and revenue would be greatly altered to the advantage of capital; and in a short time the produce of the country would be greatly augmented." It is no doubt true "that it is not the *quantity*" of circulating medium which adds to the national wealth, "but the *different distribution* of it." If, therefore, we could be fully assured that the effects of the abundance, and the consequent depreciation of the currency, would diminish the powers of consumption in the idle and unproductive class, whilst it increased the number of the industrious and productive class, the effect would undoubtedly be to augment the national wealth, as it would realize into capital that which was before expended as revenue. But the question is, will it so operate? Will not a thousand pounds saved by the stockholder from his income and lent to the farmer, be equally productive as if it had been saved by the farmer himself? The Reviewers observe, "on every fresh issue of notes, not only is the quantity of the circulating medium increased, but the distribution of the whole mass is altered. A large proportion falls into the hands of those who consume and produce, and a smaller proportion into the hands of those who only consume." But is this necessarily so? They appear to take it for granted, that those who live on fixed incomes *must* consume the whole of their income and that no part of it can be saved and annually added to capital. But this is very far from being the true state of the case; and I would ask, do not the stockholders give as great a stimulus to the growth of the national wealth by saving half their incomes and investing it in the stocks, thereby liberating a capital which will ultimately be employed by those who consume and produce, as would be done if their incomes were depreciated 50 per cent. by the issues of bank notes, and the power of saving were in consequence entirely taken from them, although the Bank should lend to an industrious man an amount of notes equal in value to the diminished income of the stockholder? The difference, and the only difference appears to me to be this, that in the one case the interest on the money lent would be paid to the real owner of the property; in the other, it would ultimately be paid in the shape of increased dividends or bonuses to the Bank proprietors who had been enabled unjustly to possess themselves of it. If the creditor of the Bank employed his loan in less profitable speculations than the employer of the savings of the stockholders would have done, there would result a real loss to the country; so that a depreciation of currency may, as far as it is considered as a stimulus to production, be beneficial or otherwise.

I see no reason why it should diminish the idle and add to the productive class of society. At any rate the evil is certain. It must be accompanied with a degree of injustice to individuals which requires only to be understood to excite the censure and indignation of all those who are not wholly insensible to every honourable feeling.

With the sentiments of the remainder of the article I most cordially agree, and trust the efforts of the Reviewers will powerfully contribute to overturn the mass of error and prejudice which pervades the public mind on this most important subject.

It is often objected to the recommendation of the bullion committee, namely, that the Bank should be required to pay their notes in specie in two years, that, if adopted, the Bank would be exposed to considerable difficulty in providing themselves with the requisite amount of bullion for such purpose; and it cannot be denied, that, before the restriction bill can be repealed, the Bank would be in prudence bound to make ample provision for every demand which might by possibility be made on them. It is observed by the bullion committee, that the average amount of bank notes in circulation, including bank post bills, in the year 1809, was 19 millions. During the same period the average price of gold was 4*l.* 10s.,—exceeding its Mint price by nearly 17 per cent., and proving a depreciation of the currency of nearly 15 per cent. A diminution, therefore, of 15 per cent. in the amount of the Bank circulation in 1809, should, on the principles of the committee, raise it to par, and reduce the market price of gold to 3*l*. 17s. 10½d.; and till such reduction take place, there would be imminent danger to the Bank as well as to the public that the restriction bill should cease to operate. Now, admitting (which we are far from doing) the truth of your principles, say the advocates for the Bank; admitting that after such a reduction in the amount of bank notes, the value of the remainder would be so raised, that it would not be the interest of any person to demand specie at the Bank in exchange for notes, because no profit could be made by the exportation of bullion; what security would the Bank have that caprice or ill-will might not render the practice general of discontinuing the use of small notes altogether, and demanding guineas of the Bank in lieu of them? Not only, then, must the Bank reduce their circulation 15 per cent. on their issues of 19 millions,—not only must they provide bullion for 4 millions of 1*l*. and 2*l*. notes which would remain in circulation, but they must also furnish themselves with the means of meeting the demands which may be made on them to pay the small notes of all the country banks in the kingdom,—and all this within the short period of two years. It must be confessed, that, whether these apprehensions are likely or not likely to be realized, the Bank could not but make some provision for the worst that might happen; and though it is a situation in which their own indiscretion has involved them, it would be desirable, if possible, to protect them against the consequences of it.

If the same benefits to the public,—the same security against the depreciation of the currency, can be obtained by more gentle means, it is to be hoped that all parties who agree in principle will concur in the expediency of adopting them. Let the Bank of England be required by Parliament to pay (if demanded) all notes above 20*l*., and no other, at their option, either in specie, in gold standard bars, or in foreign coin (allowance being made for the difference in its purity) at the English Mint value of gold bullion, viz. 3*l*. 17s. 10½d. per ounce, such payments to commence at the period recommended by the committee.

This privilege of paying their notes as above described might be extended to the Bank for three or four years after such payments commenced, and, if found advantageous, might be continued as a permanent measure. Under such a system the currency could never be depreciated below its standard price, as an ounce of gold and 3*l*. 17s. 10½d. would be uniformly of the same value. By such regulations we should effectually prevent the amount of small notes necessary for the smaller payments from being withdrawn from circulation, as no one who did not possess to the amount of 20*l*. at least of such small notes could exchange them at the Bank, and even then bullion, and not specie, could be obtained for them. Guineas might indeed be procured at the Mint for such bullion, but not till after the delay of some weeks or months, the loss of interest for which time would be considered as an actual expense, an expense which no one would incur whilst the small notes could purchase as much of every commodity as the guineas which they represented. Another advantage attending the establishment of this plan, would be to prevent the useless labour which, under our system previously to 1797, was so unprofitably expended on the coinage of guineas, which, on every occasion of an unfavourable exchange (we will not inquire by what caused), were consigned to the melting pot, and, in spite of all prohibitions, exported as bullion. It is agreed by all parties that such prohibitions were ineffectual, and that whatever obstacles were opposed to the exportation of the coin, they were with facility evaded.

An unfavourable exchange can ultimately be corrected only by an exportation of goods,—by the transmission of bullion,—or *by a reduction in the amount of the paper circulation.* The facility, therefore, with which bullion would be obtained at the Bank cannot be urged as an objection to this plan, because an equal degree of facility actually existed before 1797, and must exist under any system of Bank payments. Neither ought it to be urged, because it is now no longer questioned by all those who have given the subject of currency much of their consideration, that not only is the law against the exportation of bullion, whether in coin or in any other form, ineffectual, but that it is also impolitic and unjust; injurious to ourselves only, and advantageous to the rest of the world.

The plan here proposed appears to me to unite all the advantages of every system of banking which has been hitherto adopted in Europe. It is in some of its features similar to the banks of deposit of Amsterdam and Hamburgh. In those establishments bullion is always to be purchased from the Bank at a fixed invariable price. The same thing is proposed for the Bank of England; but in the foreign banks of deposit, they have actually in their coffers, as much bullion as there are credits for bank money in their books; accordingly, there is an inactive capital as great as the whole amount of the commercial circulation. In our Bank, however, there would be an amount of bank money under the name of bank notes, as great as the demands of commerce could require, at the same time there would not be more inactive capital in the Bank coffers than that fund which the Bank should think it necessary to keep in bullion, to answer those demands which might occasionally be made on them. It should always be remembered, too, that the Bank would be enabled, by contracting their issues of paper, to diminish such demands at pleasure. In imitation of the Bank of Hamburgh, who purchase silver at a fixed price, it would be necessary for the Bank to fix a price *very little below* the Mint price, at which they would at all times purchase, with their notes, such gold bullion as might be offered to them.

The perfection of banking is to enable a country, by means of a paper currency, (always retaining its standard value), to carry on its circulation with the least possible quantity of coin or bullion. This is what this plan would effect. And with a silver coinage on just principles, we should possess the most economical and the most invariable currency in the world. The variations in the price of bullion, whatever demand there might be for it on the Continent, or whatever supply might be poured in from the mines in America, would be confined within the prices at which the Bank bought bullion, and the Mint price at which they sold it. The amount of the circulation would be adjusted to the wants of commerce with the greatest precision; and if the Bank were for a moment so indiscreet as to overcharge the circulation, the check which the public would possess would speedily admonish them of their error. As for the country Banks, they must, as now, pay their notes, when demanded, in Bank of England notes. This would be a sufficient security against the possibility of their being able too much to augment the paper circulation. There would be no temptation to melt the coin, and consequently the labour which has been so uselessly bestowed by one party in recoining what another party found it their interest to melt into bullion, would be effectually saved. The currency could neither be clipped nor deteriorated, and would possess a value as invariable as gold itself, the great object which the Dutch had in view, and which they most successfully accomplished by a system very like that which is here recommended.

REPLY

TO

MR BOSANQUET'S

PRACTICAL OBSERVATIONS

ON THE

REPORT

OF

THE BULLION COMMITTEE.

1811

REPLY

TO

MR BOSANQUET

CHAPTER I.

PRELIMINARY OBSERVATIONS—MR BOSANQUET'S OBJECTIONS TO THE CONCLUSIONS OF THE BULLION COMMITTEE BRIEFLY STATED.

§ 1. THE question concerning the depreciation of our currency has lately assumed peculiar interest, and has excited a degree of attention in the public mind, which promises the most happy results. To the Bullion Committee we are already most particularly indebted for a more just exposition of the true principles which should regulate the currency of nations, than has before appeared in any authoritative shape, in this or any other country. It could not, however, be expected that a reform, so important as that which the Committee recommend, could be effected without calling forth the warmest opposition, dictated by the erroneous principles of some, and by the interested views of others. Hitherto this opposition has been attended with the best effects; it has tended to prove more fully the correctness of the principles laid down by the Committee; it has called forth new champions in the field of argument; and discussion has daily produced new converts to the cause of truth. Of all the attacks on the report of the Committee, however, that of Mr Bosanquet has appeared to me the most formidable. He has not, as his predecessors have done, confined himself to declamation alone; and though he disclaims all reasoning and argument, he has brought forward, what he thought were irrefragable proofs of the discordance of the theory with former practice. It is these proofs which I propose to examine, and I am confident that it will be from a deficiency of ability in me, and not from any fault in the principles themselves, if I do not show that they are wholly unfounded. Mr Bosanquet commences, by availing himself of the vulgar charge, which has lately been so often countenanced, and in places too high, against theorists. He cautions the public against listening to their speculations before they have submitted them to the test of fact; and he kindly undertakes to to be their guide in the examination. If this country had hitherto carried on trade by barter, and it were, for the first time, going to establish a system by which the intervention of money should facilitate the operations of trade, there might be some foundation for calling the principles which might be offered to public attention wholly theoretical; because, however clearly dictated by the experience of the past, their practical effects would not have been witnessed. But, when the principles of a currency, long established, are well understood; when the laws which regulate the variations of the rate of exchange between countries have been known and observed for centuries, can that system be called wholly theoretical which appeals to those principles, and is willing to submit to the test of those laws?

To such an examination the report of the Committee is now submitted, and the public is called upon to believe that a theory which its adversary allows to be unassailable by reasoning and argument, is to be battered down by an appeal to facts. We are told, "that boldly as the principle is asseted, *and strongly as reason appears to sanction it*, that it is not generally true, and is at variance with fact." This is the test to which I have long wished to see this important question brought. I have long wished that those who refused their assent to principles which experience has appeared to sanction, would either state their own theory as to the cause of the present appearances in the state of our currency, or that they would point out those facts which they considered at variance with that which, from the firmest conviction, I have espoused.

To Mr Bosanquet, then, I feel considerably obliged. If, as I trust, I shall be able to obviate his objections; to prove them wholly untenable; to convince him that *his* statements are at variance with fact; that for his supposed proofs he is indebted to the wrong application of a principle, and not to any deficiency in the principle itself:—I shall confidently expect that he will abjure his errors, and become the foremost of our defenders.

§ 2. Mr Bosanquet has thus stated the principal positions of the Committee, to which he is induced to object:

1st, "That the variations of the exchange with foreign countries can never, for any considerable time, exceed the expense of transporting and insuring the precious metals from one country to the other.

2d, "That the price of gold bullion can never exceed the Mint price, unless the currency in which it is paid is depreciated below the value of gold.

3d, "That, so far as any inference is to be drawn from Custom-house returns of exports and imports, the state of the exchanges ought to be peculiarly favourable.

4th, "That the Bank, during the restriction, possesses exclusively the power of limiting the circulation of bank notes.

5th, "That the circulation of country bank notes depends upon, and is proportionate to, the issues from the bank.

Lastly, "That the paper currency is now excessive, and depreciated in comparison with gold, and that the high price of bullion and low rates of exchange are the consequences as well as the sign of such depreciation."

These principles being in all essential points the same as those which I have avowed, and on which Mr Bosanquet has attacked me, to avoid the necessity of speaking at one time of the opinion of the Bullion Committee, and at another of my own, I shall, in the future pages of this work, consider them as the principles of the Bullion Committee only, and shall take occasion to mention any shade of difference that may occur between theirs and mine.

CHAPTER II.

MR BOSANQUET'S ALLEGED FACTS, DRAWN FROM THE HISTORY OF THE STATE OF EXCHANGE, CONSIDERED.

SECTION I.

Exchange with Hamburgh.

§ 3. THE first position controverted is, "That the variations of the exchange with foreign countries can never, for any length of time, exceed the expense of transmitting and insuring the precious metals from one country to the other."

Can this be called a theoretical opinion, now brought forward for the first time? Has it not been sanctioned by the writings of Hume[1] and Smith? and has it not been undisputed even by practical men?

Mr ——, in his evidence before the Bullion Committee, observes, "that the extent to which the exchange can fall is the charge of transporting bullion, together with an adequate profit to the risk the transporting such specie is liable to."

Mr A. Goldsmid "never recollected the exchange to have differed more from par than 5 per cent. before the suspension of cash payments."

Mr Grefulhe stated, "that since he had been in business

[1] [Hume, speaking of the relation between the amount of money in a country and the state of its industry says, *Essay XXVII. of the Balance of Trade*, note; "The only circumstance that can obstruct the exactness of these proportions is the expense of transporting the commodities from one place to another; and this expense is sometimes unequal, &c."

Adam Smith deals with the matter in many parts of the Wealth of Nations; but see especially Book IV., Chapter I.]

he recollected no period prior to the suspension of the cash payments by the Bank, when the exchange was considerably below par."

The same opinions were given by many practical men before the Lords' Committee in 1797.

§ 4. But in opposition to all these opinions, Mr Bosanquet has facts which he boldly thinks will prove the unsoundness of the doctrine. "In the years 1764 to 1768," he observes, "prior to the recoinage, when the imperfect state of the coins occasioned gold to be 2 to 3 per cent. above the Mint price, the exchange with Paris was 8 to 9 per cent. against London, at the same time—the exchange with Hamburgh was, during the whole period, 2 to 6 per cent. in favour of London; here appears, then, a profit of 12 to 14 per cent. for the expense, in time of peace, of paying the debt to Paris with gold from Hamburgh, which must have exceeded the fact by at least 8 or 10 per cent.; and it is worthy of remark, that the average exchange with Hamburgh, for the years 1766 and 1767, of 5 per cent. in favour of London, added to the 2 per cent., the price of gold above the Mint price, constituted a premium of 7 per cent. on the importation of gold into England, or, deducting 1½ per cent. for expenses in time of peace, a net profit of 5 per cent., yet the exchange was not rectified thereby. Again, in 1775, 1776, and 1777, after the recoinage, we find the exchange on Paris 5, 6, 7, and 8 per cent. against London in time of peace, when half the amount would have conveyed gold to Paris, and one-fourth have paid the debts of Paris at Amsterdam.

"In the years 1781, 1782, and 1783, being years of war, the exchange was constantly from 7 to 9 per cent. in favour of Paris; and, during this period, gold was the common circulation of this country; and the Bank was compelled to provide it for the public at the Mint price. It has been already shown how little effect the precious metals produced towards equalising the exchange with Hamburgh during the years 1797 and 1798; and another instance may be adduced in the years 1804 and 1805, when the Paris exchange varied from 7 to 9 per cent. in favour of London.

"In every case here cited, the fluctuations of the exchanges greatly exceeded the expense of conveying gold from one country to the other, and to a much greater degree in most of them than in the present instance; the circumstances of the times were, it will readily be admitted, more favourable to intercourse on those occasions than they now are, and the state of metallic circulation afforded facilities not now experienced here. Yet, under all these disadvantages, the principle assumed by the Committee was not operative, and cannot therefore be admitted as a solid foundation for the superstructure of excess and depreciation attempted to be raised upon it."

If the facts had been as here stated by Mr Bosanquet, I should have found it difficult to reconcile them with my theory. That theory takes for granted, that whenever enormous profits can be made in any particular trade, a sufficient number of capitalists will be induced to engage in it, who will, by their competition, reduce the profits to the general rate of mercantile gains. It assumes that in the trade of exchange does this principle more especially operate, it not being confined to English merchants alone; but being perfectly understood, and profitably followed, by the exchange and bullion merchants of Holland, France, and Hamburgh; and competition in this trade being well known to be carried to its greatest height. Does Mr Bosanquet suppose that a theory which rests on so firm a basis of experience as this can be shaken by one or two solitary facts not perfectly known to us? Even should no explanation of them be attempted, they might safely be left to produce their natural effects on the public mind.

§ 5. But before the reasoning of the Committee can be proved defective by Mr Bosanquet's facts, we must examine the source from whence those supposed facts are derived.

"Mr Bosanquet tells us that there is annexed to Mr Mushet's pamphlet a table, showing, 1st, The rate of exchange with Hamburgh and Paris for 50 years past, and how much it has been, in each instance, above or below par.

2d, "The price of gold in London, and a comparison of this price with the English standard or Mint price.

3d, "The amount of bank notes in circulation, and the rate of their assumed depreciation, by a comparison with the price of gold."

Now, the accuracy of these tables must be admitted or proved before the conclusions, which result from the inspection of them, can command assent; but so far from this being the case, their accuracy is disowned by Mr Mushet himself, who, in the second edition of his pamphlet, acknowledged the false principle upon which his first tables were calculated, and has given us a new and amended set.

The following notice accompanied the second edition of Mr Mushet's pamphlet:—"In the first edition of this work I stated the par of exchange with Hamburgh at 33 schillings and 8 grotes, and at that considered it as a fixed par; from the best information which I have been able to obtain upon 'Change since, 34.11¼ are considered as the par, and in the present edition I have stated it as such. *I have also corrected the mistake of considering the par to be fixed;* because gold being the standard of the money of England, and silver in Hamburg, there can be no fixed par between those two countries; it will be subject to all the variations which take place in the relative value of gold and silver. For example, if 34 schillings 11 grotes and ¼ of Hamburgh currency be equal in value to a pound sterling, or $\frac{20}{21}$ of a guinea, when silver is 5s. 2d. per oz., they can no longer be so when silver falls to 5s. 1d. or 5s. per oz., because a pound sterling in gold being then worth more silver, is also worth more Hamburgh currency.

"To find the real par, therefore, we must ascertain what was the relative value of gold and silver when the par was fixed at 34.11¼, and what is the relative value at the time we wish to calculate it.

"For example, if the price of standard gold was 3*l.* 17s. 10½d. per oz., and silver 5s. 2d., an ounce of gold would then be worth 15.07 ounces of silver, being the Mint proportions; 20 of our standard shillings would then contain as much pure silver as 34 schillings 11 grotes and $\frac{1}{4}$; but if the ounce of gold was 3*l.* 17s. 10$\frac{1}{2}$d., and silver 5s. (which it was on the 2d January 1798) the ounce of gold would then be worth 15.57 ounces of silver. If 1*l.* sterling at par, therefore, be worth 15.07 ounces of silver, then at 15.57 it would be at 3 per cent. premium; and 3 per cent. premium on 34.11$\frac{1}{4}$ is 1 schilling 1 grote and $\frac{9}{10}$, so that the par, when gold is to silver as 15.57 to 1, will be 36 schillings 1 grote and $\frac{1}{10}$.

"The above calculation will be more easily made by stating as follows:—

As 15.07 : 34.11$\frac{1}{4}$: : 15.57 : 36$\frac{1}{10}$."

As it is universally admitted that gold is the standard measure of value in this country, and that silver performs the same office at Hamburgh, it is evident that no tables can be correct which assume a fixed invariable par. The true par must vary with every variation in the relative value of the two metals.

There are some objections, however, which I have yet to offer against the perfect accuracy of Mr Mushet's present tables.

In the first place, he has taken the par of silver against silver too low; he has calculated on the information which he had received, tnat 20 standard shillings in silver contained as much of that pure metal as thirty-four schillings and 11$\frac{1}{4}$ grotes; but it appears by Dr Kelly's table (Bullion Rep. page 207), that by actual assay, as well as by computation, 20 shillings are of equal value with 35 schillings and 1 grote. This difference amounts to little more than $\frac{3}{8}$ per cent.; and I have only noticed it because I think it highly desirable that we should be able, at all times, to ascertain the true par.

Secondly, Mr Mushet has calculated the degree in which the exchange was above or below par by a reference to the prices which he has quoted from Lloyd's list. Now, invariably have those prices been for bills at 2$\frac{1}{2}$ usances, and as the par of exchange is computed from a compaiison of the actual value of the coins of the two countries, payable at the same time in both, and not in one of them at the end of $2\frac{1}{2}$ months, an allowance for interest must be made for this period, which will amount to about 1 per cent.*

A deduction of $1\frac{3}{8}$ per cent. must therefore be made from the column for the favourable exchange to England in Mr Mushet's tables.

There are also, in all calculations on the true par of exchange, other sources of error, some of which will be presently noticed; so that it is not possible to ascertain with perfect accuracy, unless all those facts were before us, the actual difference which at any time existed between a remittance by bullion, and by the purchase of a bill.

§ 6. To Mr Mushet's amended tables, thus corrected, I am willing to submit the truth of the principle now disputed. It will then appear, that at no period since 1760 has the exchange with Hamburgh been more in favour of England than 7 per cent., with one exception only; and the reader will not be surprised that there should have been such an exception, when he learns that it was in the memorable year of 1797, just after the suspension of cash payments at the Bank. At this period the currency of this country was reduced particularly low; the amount of bank notes in circulation being less than it had been for ten years preceding. That, under such circumstances the exchange should have become favourable to England, and, consequently, that there should have been large importations of bullion, is entirely conformable with the principle of the Bullion Committee, and confirms the efficacy of the remedy which they have proposed. A great circulation of paper and a too abundant currency, are stated by them to be the causes of the present nominally low exchange, and they confidently predict, that a reduction

* By Mr ——'s evidence to the Bullion Committee (Appendix, page 74), it appears that the course of exchange from Hamburgh to London in ordinary times differs 1 Flemish schilling from the course of London to Hamburgh, to compensate the $2\frac{1}{2}$ usances and commission allowed on bills both ways; when the difficulties of communication existed to the greatest extent, the difference of exchange was full 2s. Flemish.

of its quantity will, as in the year 1797, raise the exchange, and by that means render the importation of bullion profitable. That this favourable exchange did, in the year 1797, produce an immense importation of gold can, by indirect evidence, be amply proved. The amount of foreign gold coined in his Majesty's Mint was,

In the year 1795	in value	L.255,721	11	8
1796	. .	72,179	14	11
1797	. .	2,486,410	6	0
1798	. .	2,718,425	9	0
1799	. .	271,846	12	8

But, it will be asked, how do those who contend that the exchanges of a country cannot, for any length of time, be either highly favourable, or highly unfavourable, account for the exchange with Hamburgh being permanently in favour of England for two or three years?

This was the case, Mr Bosanquet observes, during the years 1797 and 1798, and he affirms that the precious metals produced little effect in equalising the exchange. It appears by Mr Mushet's amended tables (always corrected by the $1\frac{3}{8}$ per cent.) that, during those years, the exchange was favourable to England, and fluctuated from 5.6 to 4.3 per cent. But the principle I understand to be this, that no country can, for any length of time, have the exchange highly favourable or highly unfavourable, because it supposes either such an increase on the one hand in her stock of money and bullion, or on the other such a diminution in that stock, as would destroy that equilibrium in the value of the currencies of countries which they naturally have a tendency to find.

§ 7. The assertion is true when applied to the exchanges, in general, of any country, but is false if the rate of her exchange with one country only be considered. It is possible that her exchange with one particular country may be permanently unfavourable, in consequence of a continued demand for bullion; but this by no means proves that her stock of coin and bullion is decreasing, unless her exchange should be also unfavourable with other countries. She may be importing from the north the bullion which she is exporting to the south,—she may be collecting it from countries where it is relatively abundant, for countries where it is relatively scarce, or where, from some particular causes, it is in particular demand; but it by no means follows, as an undeniable consequence, that her own stock of money shall be reduced below its natural level. Spain, for example, who is the great importer of bullion from America, can never have an unfavourable exchange with her colonies; and as she must distribute the bullion she receives amongst the different nations of the world, she can seldom have a favourable exchange with the countries with which she trades.*

§ 8. Applying, then, these principles to the state of our exchange with Hamburgh in 1797 and 1798, we shall observe, that it was not in consequence of what is usually termed a balance of trade that the exchange was permanently favourable to England; it was not because Hamburgh had contracted a debt to us for the balance of commodities which she had imported, that she was necessitated to pay us in gold and silver bullion, but because she could advantageously export bullion in the same way as any other commodity, in consequence of an unusual demand for that article in England. This demand proceeded from two causes: First, from the unusually low amount of our currency; secondly, from the exportation of silver to Asia by the East India Company.

In consequence of the first of these causes, and of the immense amount of guineas which at that period had been withdrawn from circulation for the purpose of hoarding, by timid people, we have already seen that the foreign gold coined into guineas during those years, amounted to no less a sum than 5,200,000*l*. Here, then, was a demand for gold unprecedented in the history of the Mint, and of itself abundantly sufficient to account

* Mr. Huskisson has commented with great ability upon the few transactions—few comparatively—which take place in bullion, and has observed, that those transactions are principally confined to the distribution of the produces of the mines to the different countries where gold and silver are in use.

both for the high exchange, and the length of time which it continued. It is a practical illustration of the truth of a most satisfactory theory.

To this, however, must be added, the demand for silver bullion in consequence of the exportation of the East India Company. It appears, by the account delivered to the Bullion Committee (No. 9), that the whole amount of foreign silver coin, exported by the Company on their own account, as well as on account of private persons, amounted

In the year 1795	to	151,795	ounces.
1796	to	290,777	
1797	to	962,880	
1798	to	3,565,691	
1799	to	7,287,327	

From this time the exportation of silver to the East Indies was considerably reduced, and has now almost wholly ceased. Thus, then, it appears that a high exchange was followed by an unusually great importation of bullion, and that, when that demand ceased, the exchange regained its natural level. On a further inspection of the table, it will appear, that in proportion as the amount of bank notes increased, the exchange became depressed, and was in 1801 more than 11 per cent. against England; and at the same time the price of gold bullion rose to 4*l.* 6s.—more than 10 per cent. above the Mint price.*

* Lord King satisfactorily accounted for the long duration of an exchange favourable to this country with Hamburgh, from the circumstance of the demands of the India Company for silver bullion for their settlements in the East. Mr Blake comments in his late publication, upon what he calls "the erroneous opinions" entertained by Lord King on this subject, and observes, "that the exportation of bullion is affected like that of any other commodity, when there is such a difference in its real prices, at any two places, as will afford a profit on its transit; an occurrence that will frequently take place with an exchange at par." An occurrence, I should say, which can never take place with an exchange at par. Who would send bullion from Hamburgh to

It must be confessed, that from September 1766 to September 1767, the exchange continued permanently in favour of England from 7.4 to 6.8 per cent.; and from that period to September 1768, it continued generally favourable above 3 per cent.; but what circumstances in the situation of Europe might then have made it profitable for England to become the agent in collection bullion from Hamburgh for some other country, it is not now material to inquire. Of this I am fully assured, that, if all the circumstances were fairly before us, it might be satisfactorily explained.

But whether explained or not explained, it proves nothing in favour of Mr Bosanquet's theory (for theory Mr Bosanquet has just as much as the Committee): it only proves that the precious metals might continue to be imported from one quarter while they were exported to another; which the theory of the Committee not only allows, but requires. To prove anything in favour of Mr Bosanquet's theory, it must be proved that the precious metals came in permanently in greater proportion than they went out; not from one place only, but from all places taken together.

§ 9. The following considerations go a certain way in accounting for the phenomena which have misled Mr Bosanquet: the tables of Mr Mushet are calculated on a comparison of the relative value of silver with bar gold. Now, bar gold is generally 2s. or 3s. per ounce worse in price than gold in coin; and, therefore, if the gold imported be intended for re-exportation, the true par will differ from 2 to 3 per cent., according as the

London at an expense of 4 or 5 per cent., whilst the exchange was at par, when by means of a bill he could obtain the same amount of bullion in London free from all charges?

I am happy that an opinion similar to that which I have expressed is also entertained by Mr Bosanquet, page 12:—"In the event of an unfavourable balance of payments, the depression of the exchange must necessarily attain this limit (the expenses of conveying and insuring the precious metals from one country to the other) before the balance can be adjusted by the exportation of gold."

[The reference is to Lord King's Thoughts on the Restriction of Payments in Specie, 1803, p. 42, &c.]

calculation is made by reference to coined or to bar gold.*

When money is wanted for our own circulation, I do not object to the calculation of the true par of exchange being made, on a comparison of the relative value of the silver of the foreign country with the value of standard gold bars in this; but in that case there must be added to the amount of expenses attending the transportation of the silver, the interest which the purchaser of gold will lose during the detention of the gold in the Mint whilst coining into money. The natural destination of a great part of all the bar gold is to some of the Mints of Europe, as it is in the state of coin only that gold can be made productive of interest to the owner. In comparing, therefore, the value of the currency of one country with the value of bullion in another, we must not leave out of our consideration the trifling superior value which coin bears above bullion in the importing country. Thus, if a merchant in Hamburgh were indebted 1*l.* sterling to a merchant in England, and should export to England as much silver as would purchase the quantity of gold contained in 1*l.*, he would not be able to discharge his debt till the gold were manufactured into coin. In addition, then, to his other expenses, the interest which he would have to pay to his creditor till the coin was returned to him, would enter into his calculation at the time that he was making a comparison of the advantages which would attend either the purchase of a bill, or the remittance of bullion.

* Mr Mushet's calculations take for granted, that the relative value of gold and silver was the same in both countries, and that the gold and silver were of the same description, viz. in bars. But it is chiefly by the value of gold in coin that a foreigner determines whether he shall export gold to this country, or make a remittance by bill; and the price of gold in coin in England must necessarily enter into his calculation. On a reference to the Appendix of the Bullion Report, No. 6, it will appear that the transactions in gold with the Continent are mostly confined to gold in coin. For fifteen months, ending in March 1810, the whole amount of sales of bar gold, by private dealers, transacted through the Bullion Office at the Bank, did not exceed in value 60,867*l.*, whilst the sales of gold in coin during the same period amounted to 683,067*l.*

This loss of interest the Bullion Committee have estimated at 1 per cent.

If these principles are correct, there must be deducted from the favourable Hamburgh exchanges of Mr Mushet's tables 1 per cent. more than we have already stated, when the bullion is wanted for our own coin, and from 2 to 3 per cent. when it is required for re-exportation. It is also necessary to observe, that the relative value of gold to silver is constantly varying in all countries, though always tending in all to an equality of value; and that the test of our currency being depreciated, is more certainly proved by the high market price of bullion than by the low exchanges.*

SECTION II.

Exchange with Paris.

§ 10. Having thus examined the objections made by Mr Bosanquet to the conclusions of the Committee, as far as the exchanges with Hamburgh are concerned, I shall now proceed to consider the circumstances which appear to him to be at variance with the principle I am defending, in the account of the exchanges between this country and Paris.

In the consideration of the par of exchange with Hamburgh, the principle on which it is calculated is easy and simple; not so that with Paris. The difficulty proceeds from this: that France as well as England has two metals, gold and silver, in circulation, both of which are legal tender in all payments.

In my former publication I endeavoured to explain the principles which appeared to me to fix the standard

* I have read in a small French tract, "Sur l'Institution des Principales Banques de l'Europe," that on one occasion the Bank of Hamburgh was obliged to suspend its payments, in consequence of having made too great advances on gold bullion. I have in vain endeavoured to find out in what year this occurred. It is evident that a circumstance of this sort must have had some influence on the exchange,—and it is not impossible that it might have happened in the years 1766, 1767.

measure of value in a country where silver and gold are both in circulation, and both a legal tender.

Lord Liverpool supposed, that when gold became the standard measure of value in this country, it arose from some capricious preference of the people to gold; but it can, I think, be clearly proved that it was caused entirely from the circumstance of the market value of silver relatively to gold having become greater than the Mint proportions. This principle is not only most fully admitted, but also most ably illustrated by his lordship.

The Mint will coin an ounce of gold into 3*l*. 17s. 10½d. of gold money, and they will also coin 15.07 ounces of silver into the same amount of silver money. What is it, then, that determines the Bank or any individual to carry an ounce of gold in preference to 15.07 ounces of silver to the Mint to be coined, as they are both by law equally useful to discharge a debt to the amount of 3*l*. 17s. 10½d.? No other consideration but their interest. If 15.07 ounces of silver can be purchased for less than an ounce of gold, silver will be coined; and if an ounce of gold can be procured for less than 15.07 ounces of silver, gold will be taken to the Mint for that purpose.

In the first case silver will become the measure of value; in the second, gold.

Now, as the relative market value of these metals is subject to constant variation, gold or silver may alternately become the standard measure of value. Since the recoinage of silver, in the reign of King William, an ounce of gold has almost uniformly been of less value than 15.07 ounces of silver, and consequently gold has, since that period, been the standard of value in this country. In the year 1798, the coinage of silver was altogether prohibited by law. Whilst that law remains in force gold must necessarily be the standard measure, whatever may be the variations in the relative value of the two metals.*

* The Bullion Committee, as well as Mr Huskisson, consider gold as the standard measure of value, in consequence of the 39th of the King, which declares that silver shall not be a legal tender for sums exceeding 25*l*., except by weight, at the rate of 5s. 2d. per ounce. But this law would not have prevented the

Whichever metal is the standard measure of value, it will also regulate the par of exchange with foreign countries, because it will be in that metal, or in paper currency representing that metal, that bills will be paid.

In France there are also two metals in circulation, and both legal tender to any amount. The relative value of gold to silver in the coins of France, previously to the Revolution, was as 15 to 1 (Bullion Report, No. 59), and is now 15½ to 1; but we are informed by a letter of Mr Grefulhe to the Bullion Committee (No. 56), that in 1785, an alteration had been made in the number of louis which were coined from a marc of gold, that number having been increased from 30 to 32. Previously to 1785, therefore, gold must have been valued in the French Mint somewhere about 14 to 1. For the same reasons that the standard of value was subject to change from gold to silver, and from silver to gold, in England, it would also be subject to do so in France. When the relative value of gold to silver was under 14 to 1, gold would have become the standard measure of value in France, and, consequently, the rate of exchange with England would have been estimated by a comparison of the gold coins of the two countries. When about 14, and under 15.07 to 1, gold would have been the standard in England, and silver in France, and the exchange rated accordingly. The par would then have been fixed by a comparison of the gold of England with the silver of France. And when the relative value was above 15.07 to 1, silver would have been the standard in both countries. The exchange would then have been rated in silver. But after 1785, when the Mint valuation of the metals was altered in France, and became nearly the same as that of England, the par of exchange would have been reckoned either in gold or in silver in both countries.

coinage of silver when under its Mint price, and, therefore, under its Mint relative value to gold. In 1798, for example, when the price of silver was 5s. per ounce, and the relative market value of silver to gold as 1 to 15.57, and when therefore silver could be profitably coined, the new silver fresh from the Mint would have been a legal tender to any amount.

§ 11. I have already observed that, to compare the amount of deviation of the exchange from par with the expenses of transmitting the precious metals from one country to the other, is not sufficient to prove that such trade would be profitable, we must also consider what the price of bullion is in the country to which it is transmitted, or the amount of expense which would be incurred in procuring the bullion to be coined into money. In this country no seignorage is charged. If an ounce of gold or silver is carried to the Mint, an ounce of coined money is returned. The only inconvenience, therefore, that an importer of bullion can experience in receiving bullion from abroad, instead of the money of England, is the delay during its detention at the Mint, and which the Bullion Committee have valued at 1 per cent. One per cent. appears, therefore, to be the natural value of English coin above bullion, provided the coin be not debased, and the currency be not excessive. But in France the seignorage, according to Dr Smith, amounted to no less than 8 per cent., besides the loss of interest during its detention at the Mint. And we have his authority, too, that no sensible inconvenience resulted from it.* An ounce of gold or silver coin was in France, therefore, of more value by 8 per cent. than an ounce of gold or silver bullion. It results from these facts that no bullion could have been imported into France, unless there was not only a profit equal to the expenses attending its importation, but a further profit of 8 per cent., the par of exchange being calculated not on the value which the coin actually passed for in currency, but on its intrinsic value as bullion.†

* Since writing the above, I have seen an extract from a Moniteur of the year 1803, by which it appears that the seignorage in France was

In 1726	on gold	$7\frac{9}{16}$	per cent. on silver	$7\frac{4}{11}$
1729	.	$5\frac{3}{16}$	. . .	$5\frac{7}{16}$
1755	.	$4\frac{1}{16}$	. . .	$3\frac{10}{11}$
1771	.	$1\frac{4}{7}$	. . .	$2\frac{7}{9}$
1785	.	$2\frac{9}{17}$	. . .	—

And was fixed in 1803 at $\frac{1}{3}$ per cent. for gold, and $1\frac{1}{2}$ for silver.

† It is only whilst the currency of France was kept at its proper

§ 12. To make this appear more evident, let us suppose that the exchange with London was, as Mr Bosanquet informs us, 8 per cent. in favour of France, in the year 1767, and that at the same time it was 6 per cent. in favour of London with Hamburgh, and that the expenses of sending gold from Hamburgh to Paris were no more than 1½ per cent. Will it not be cheaper, he asks, by 12½ per cent. to pay the debt at Paris, by sending the gold from Hamburgh,* than by remitting a bill? I answer, No; because, when the gold arrives at Paris, it must either be coined into money, or sold as bullion. If it be coined into money, 8 per cent. must be paid to the Mint; if it be sold as bullion, it will sell at 8 per cent. under the Mint price.† The profit, then, if all the other calculations be correct, will be reduced

level that the price of gold could continue 8 per cent. under the Mint price, in the same manner as the price of gold would and did continue under the Mint price of England. The currency of England was rather above its level when gold was 3*l*. 17s. 6d., as 4d. an ounce is not sufficient compensation for the delay of the Mint. It follows, therefore, that the principle here contended for can only have its full force whilst the currency is not excessive.

* As silver is the currency of Hamburgh, it would be silver, and not gold, which an English creditor would be entitled to send from Hamburgh to Paris.

† "In France, a duty of 8 per cent. is deducted for the coinage which not only defrays the expense of it, but affords a small revenue to the Government. In England, as the coinage cost nothing, the current coin can never be much more valuable than the quantity of bullion which it actually contains. In France, the workmanship, as you pay for it, adds to the value, in the same manner as to that of wrought plate. A sum of French money, therefore, containing a certain weight of pure silver, is more valuable than a sum of English money containing an equal weight of pure silver, and must require more bullion, or other commodities, to purchase it. Though the current coin of the two countries, therefore, were equally near the standards of their respective Mints, a sum of English money could not well purchase a sum of French money, containing an equal number of ounces of pure silver, nor, consequently, a bill upon France for such a sum. If, for such a bill, no more additional money was paid than what was sufficient to compensate the expense of French coinage, the real exchange might be at par between the two countries, their debts and credits might mutually compensate one another, while the computed exchange was considerably in favour of France.

from 12½ to 4½ per cent. But they are not correct, being subject to further deductions from the causes already stated.

Keeping these principles in view, it will, I believe, appear, that the exchange with Paris was in favour of England during a great portion of the four years, from 1764 to 1768, and at all the other periods mentioned by Mr Bosanquet.

I cannot help here observing, that it must excite astonishment, that a British merchant should seriously believe it possible, that, in time of peace, a net profit, after paying all expenses, of from 10½ to 12½ per cent. should have been made by the exportation of gold from Hamburgh to Paris during four years:—a profit, which, from the quick returns, would have enabled any person engaging in such undertakings to have cleared more than 100 per cent. per annum on the capital employed; and that too in a trade, the slightest fluctuations of which are watched by a class of men proverbial for their shrewdness, and in which competition is carried to the greatest extent. For any man to compare the account of the Hamburgh exchange, and of the Parisian, and not to see that the accounts were incorrect, that the facts could not be as so stated, is very like a man who is all for fact and nothing for theory. Such men can hardly ever sift their facts. They are credulous, and necessarily so, because they have no standard of reference. Those two sets of supposed facts, those in the Hamburgh exchange on the one hand, and those in the Parisian on the other, are absolutely inconsistent, and disprove one another. That facts such as these should be brought forward to invalidate a theory, the reasonableness of which is allowed, is a melancholy proof of the power of prejudice over very enlightened minds.

If less than this was paid, the real exchange might be in favour of England, while the computed was in favour of France."—*Wealth of Nations*, Chap. iii. Book iv.

SECTION III.

Supposed Fact of a Premium on English Currency in America —Favourable Exchange with Sweden.

§ 13. The next point on which I wish to make a few observations, is that first mentioned by Mr Grefulhe, and now brought forward by Mr Bosanquet. I allude to the premium which it is asserted was given in America, in hard dollars, for the depreciated currency of England. I have examined this fact with the greatest attention, and to me it appears evident; first, that the price which was called a premium of 9 per cent. given for a bill upon England, *was really a discount* of 3¼ per cent.; and, secondly, that at that price it was a cheaper remittance than if the dollars with which the bill was bought had been exported.

The par of exchange with America is reckoned in dollars; the par is called 4s. 6d. sterling for a dollar, consequently 444.4 dollars ought to contain as much pure silver as 100*l*. sterling. But this is not the fact. An American dollar, according to the Mint regulation of America, ought to weigh 17 dwt. 8 grains, and is 8½ dwts. worse than English standard silver; consequently, the value of an American dollar in our standard silver is 4s. 3¾d. According to this value, 463.7 dollars is the true par for 100*l*. of our English silver currency; but we are comparing the dollars of America with the pound sterling of England, which is gold; therefore, the true par for 100*l*. sterling at the relative value of dollars and gold in May 1809, the period alluded to, was 500 dollars. Now, for a bill of 100*l*. on London, bought with dollars in America at the highest exchange that year, viz. 109, no more was paid than 484 dollars; it was therefore purchased at 3¼ per cent. under the real par.*

* The weight of the American dollar in circulation is not more, according to Mr Williams's evidence, than 17 dwt. 6 gr., which would make the true par somewhat lower than 4s. 3½d.; and, according to Ede's book of Coins, the American dollar is 11 dwts. worse than standard, and contains no more pure silver than 4s. 2¼d. of English standard silver coin.

It should be recollected that the embargo laws were at that time most strictly enforced; that captains of packets were obliged, before they were permitted to proceed on their voyage, to swear that they had no specie on board; and, on one occasion, one of these captains was obliged to reland the specie which he had smuggled on board his vessel. At the same time, the rate of insurance was immoderately high, and a premium of 8 per cent. was paid on a few ships which broke the embargo, the underwriters being guaranteed, too, from the loss which would have attended their seizure by the American Government. Now, 8 per cent. insurance, besides commission, freight, and other expenses, together with 3¼ per cent., the actual discount of the bill bought, would, perhaps, not be much under the discount which then existed on our paper currency; so that our depreciated paper was not bought at a premium for hard dollars, but was bought at a discount, and at its actual value.

§ 14. But we are told the exchange with Sweden is favourable to England, and that the currency of Sweden is regulated in a manner precisely similar to ours, the Bank not issuing specie whenever the exchange becomes unfavourable. There is no doubt a perfect agreement in the two cases, and for that reason they are followed by similar effects, and the depreciation of both currencies requires the same remedy. This remedy is a diminution in the amount of the circulating medium, either by the exportation of the coins, or by a reduction of bank paper. If the exchange with Sweden is, as stated, 24 per cent. in favour of London, it proves only that the excess of paper currency not convertible into specie is, in Sweden, proportionably greater than in England.*

* Before, however, it can be admitted that the exchange with Sweden is 24 per cent. in favour of London, we must be informed whether both gold and silver be legal tender in Sweden, and, if so, at what relative value those metals are rated in the Swedish Mint. I suspect that a part of this favourable exchange may be accounted for by the rise in the relative value of gold to silver.

SECTION IV.

A Statement concerning the Par of Exchange, by the Bullion Committee, examined.

§ 15. Having now considered every fact, or supposed fact, advanced by Mr Bosanquet, on the subject of the exchange, with a view to prove that the principle which the Committee have avowed,—namely, that the variations in the exchange with foreign countries can never exceed for any length of time the expense of transporting and insuring the precious metals; having proved the conclusion to which the writer would lead us to be unsupported by his facts, of which not one is, as I think, at variance with the principle of the Committee, I must beg leave to point out an error in the Report itself, an error on which Mr Bosanquet founds his opinion, that all remedy may safely be delayed.

"Thus, then," says Mr Bosanquet, "it appears that, on a full admission of all the principles adopted by the Committee, and of their application to the present case, the foreign exchanges were at the time when the Report was presented, and for three months prior thereto, about 2 per cent. below the natural limit of depression."

"It will probably be thought that the question, as a practical question of national importance, is altogether at rest;—that there is no necessity, at least, for the adoption of hasty remedies, even though the correctness of the general reasoning of the Committee should, on full inquiry, be conceded."

When the exchange is admitted to be exceedingly depressed, we are told that to oblige the Bank to pay in specie would be attended with the most dangerous consequences; that we must wait till the exchange becomes more favourable; and when it is supposed to have risen within 2 per cent. of its natural limit, then we are again desired to pause, because it is no longer a question of national importance. By this mode of reasoning, a motive may be found for refusing *ad infinitum* to renew the payments of the Bank. I confidently hope that no such fallacious reasoning will be listened to;

that we shall at last open our eyes to the dangers that beset us; that we shall examine coolly, and decide manfully.

The principle upon which Mr. Mushet's amended tables are constructed, has been most fully admitted, and most correctly and concisely stated in the Report (page 10).

"If one country uses gold for its principal measure of value and another uses silver, the par between those countries cannot be estimated for any particular period, without taking into account the relative value of gold and silver at that particular period."

The Committee have, moreover, in their endeavours to find out the real par between this country and Hamburgh, kept this principle constantly in view, as will appear from the questions put to Mr —— (Report, page 73). Mr —— also fully admitted the principle; and yet, when he was requested to "state in what manner he applied those general ideas to the statement of the par of exchange, as between England and Hamburgh," he answered, "taking gold at the coinage price of 3*l*. 17s. 10½d., and taking it at Hamburgh at what we call its par, which is 96 stivers banco for a ducat, and further reducing 55 ounces of standard gold as being equal to 459 ducats, it produces a par of exchange of 34s. 3½g. Flemish for a pound sterling: a ducat contains at the rate of 23½ carats fine."

Now, here is not one word said about the relative value of gold to silver in the market; and the only information which is obtained from this answer is, that 34s. 3½g. Flemish, in gold coin, is equal to a pound sterling of gold; and this calculation agrees within ½ grote with that of Dr Kelly (Rep. No. 59). If the purchaser of a bill in London for 34s. 3g. could obtain at Hamburgh 34s. 3g. in gold currency, that might truly be called the par, but he can only obtain 34s. 3g. in silver, which is not worth, by 8 per cent., as much as 34s. 3g. in gold coin. The question proposed by the Committee was, in effect, What amount of Hamburgh currency contains the same quantity of pure silver as can be purchased by a pound sterling in gold?

At the period when the Report was made, the answer would have been 37s. 3g. Flemish; 37s. 3g. therefore was then the true par of exchange. If the Committee had calculated according to this par, instead of 34s. 3g., they would not have reported that the exchange with Hamburgh was not more unfavourable to England than 9 per cent., but nearly 17 per cent.; and Mr Bosanquet would not have had an opportunity for observing, that, admitting the reasoning of the Committee, the evil was not of sufficient magnitude to make any immediate interference necessary.

CHAPTER III.

MR BOSANQUET'S ALLEGED FACTS, IN SUPPOSED REFUTATION OF THE CONCLUSION THAT A RISE IN THE MARKET PRICE OF BULLION ABOVE THE MINT PRICE PROVES A DEPRECIATION OF THE CURRENCY, CONSIDERED.

SECTION I.

That the Negation of the above Conclusion implies the Impossibility of melting or exporting English Coin—an Impossibility contended for by nobody.

§ 16. The next proposition of the Committee, the justness of which Mr Bosanquet disputes, he has thus stated:—" That the price of gold bullion can never exceed the Mint price, unless the currency in which it is paid is depreciated below the value of gold." But this is not exactly the principle of the Committee. Their principle, when fairly stated, is, not that gold as a commodity may not rise above its value as coin, but that it cannot continue so, because the convertibility of coin into bullion would soon equalize their value. The words of the Committee are these,—" Your Committee are of opinion that, in the sound and natural state of the British currency, the foundation of which is gold, no increased demand for gold from other parts of the world, however great, or from whatever causes arising, can have the effect of producing here, *for a considerable period of time*, a material rise in the market price of gold." Nothing appears to me to be wanting to make this a self-evident proposition but the admission, that the law, which forbids the conversion of gold coin into gold bullion, cannot be successfully executed.

§ 17. I should have expected, therefore, that any one who denied its truth would have contended that the law was fully efficient for the purposes for which it was enacted; and that he would have brought forward authorities to justify this view which he had taken of it. But authorities for such an opinion would have been difficult to have been found. From the days of Locke till the present time I have nowhere seen the fact disputed. It is by all writers indiscriminately allowed, that no penalties can prevent the coin from being melted when its value as bullion becomes superior to its value as coin.

Locke calls the law which forbids the melting and exporting coin, " a law to hedge in the cuckoo." Smith observes, " that no precautions of Government can prevent it." On this subject, too, we have the authority of practical men.

The Bank Directors, in the year 1795, when the price of gold rose to 4*l*. 3s. or 4*l*. 4s. per ounce, after acquainting Mr Pitt with that fact, observe, " our guineas being to be purchased at 3*l*. 17s. 10½d. per ounce, clearly demonstrates the grounds of our fears; it being only necessary to state those facts to the Chancellor of the Exchequer." Now, what were those fears, but that there would be a run upon them for gold coin, for the purpose of melting it into bullion? Mr Newland, too, when asked (by the Committee of the Lords, 1797,) " If there were now to be a new coinage, do you think a great deal would be melted down and privately exported?" answered, " That depends entirely upon the price of bullion." In the same Committee Mr Newland was also asked, " Is it more difficult to prevent false coining, or to prevent the melting down or exporting, when it is for their advantage to export it?"—Answer, " I am at a loss to guess how you can prevent either."

These are but a few of the opinions which might be brought forward in support of the fact of the coin being melted into bullion whenever the price of bullion rises above the price of coin. I shall conclude, however, with the opinion of Mr Bosanquet himself. Speaking of the Committee, he observes, " They say nothing about the price of bullion, which is expected, doubtless, to return when the Bank shall have sufficiently controlled the exchange; although Mr Locke and many other writers have clearly demonstrated that the coins of any country can only be retained within it when the general balance of trade and payments is not unfavourable." Now, under the circumstances supposed of a low exchange, what should take our coins from us but their superior value as bullion? Who would export coins if bullion could be bought at its Mint price? It is their superior value as bullion, therefore, that is the cause of their being melted and exported.

§ 18. But the Committee have not been satisfied with simply stating a position which is almost self-evident; they have appealed to facts, and distinctly assert, that for a period of twenty-four years, since the recoinage, gold bullion in standard bars had not been at a higher price than 3*l.* 17s. 10½d. per ounce, with the exception of one year, beginning in May 1783, and ending in May 1784, when the price was 3*l.* 18s. per ounce. We are indeed informed by a letter from the Bank Directors to Mr Pitt, in October 1795, and it is on that authority reported by the Committee, that gold bullion was then as high as 4*l.* 3s. or 4*l.* 4s. per ounce; and it was stated by Mr Newland to the Lords' Committee in 1797, that the Bank had been frequently obliged to buy gold higher than the Mint price; and upon one occasion gave as much, for a small quantity which their agent procured in Portugal, as 4*l.* 8s.*

* It appears that it was in 1795, and most probably in October, that the Bank gave 4*l.* 8s. for gold, as stated by Mr Newland. On being asked concerning the time by the Lords' Committee, he answered, "I believe it was about two years since the Bank gave about 4*l.* 8s. per ounce for gold; it was but a small quantity, it was soon stopt on account of its price. The Bank at that time thought it expedient to obtain gold from Portugal, which their agent could not do at a less price than 4*l.* 8s." Mr Newland was speaking on the 28th March 1797.

It is a case by no means improbable that the Bank may frequently have bought foreign gold above the Mint price, at the same time that they could have obtained gold in bars, not exportable, at a comparatively cheaper price. They might flatter themselves that, by not purchasing English gold, they

These are the only facts on which Mr Bosanquet relies for overturning the principle in question. Prices not known to the public; not recorded in any list; given, too, by a corporation not remarkable for the good management of their concerns, are to be deemed the fair market price; and such exceptions as these are to overturn opinions grounded on a just theory, sanctioned by practical men, and confirmed by experience.

Is there any evidence that these prices continued even for a week? If we consult the price list, we shall find, that in July of that year, 1795, the price of gold is quoted 3*l.* 17s. 6d.; in December it is again quoted 3*l.* 17s. 6d., and in the intervening four months no price is marked. Does Mr Bosanquet think it possible that such a price as 4*l.* 4s. for gold could have continued, whilst it was to be obtained, by melting the coin, at 3*l.* 17s. 10½d.? Has he so good an opinion of the self-denial and virtues of all classes of the community? If he has, why are they not now to be trusted? What is the plea urged for not paying in specie? That at the present exchange, and present price of gold, it would be advantageous to export and melt the coin, so that there would be danger that every guinea would leave the country. But when you tell us that bullion has no connexion with coin, "that there is no point of contact between English and foreign gold," there can be no danger of any one's being particularly desirous to possess coin, as, for the mere purposes of circulation, bank notes are equally, if not more convenient.

would lessen the temptation to melt the guineas: at the same time their diminished stock required them to replenish their coffers. This opinion is very much confirmed by an examination of the account in the Appendix of the Bullion Report, No. 19, where it appears, that from 1797 to 1810, the amount in value of gold coined at his Majesty's Mint was 8,960,113*l.*, of which only 2,296,056*l.* was coined from English gold, the remainder was coined from foreign gold. It appears, too, that since 1804, 1,402,542*l.* has been coined from foreign gold, and not one guinea from British gold. During the whole of this period the price of foreign gold in the market exceeded the price of English gold. Is it not probable, therefore, that the Bank, who are the only importers of gold into the Mint, have been guided by some such policy as I have supposed?

§ 19. "*If,*" says Mr Bosanquet, "the demand for foreign gold was at any time very great, and the melting and exportation of guineas, however abundant, by any means effectually prevented, foreign gold might rise to double its price in English gold, and yet the intrinsic value of guineas remain undiminished."

I might apply to this *if* of Mr Bosanquet the observation which he has made on the same word, when used by the Committee, *your if is a great peace-maker.* But the above is not our case; the law cannot be effectually enforced. The remark, therefore, is of no use in the question before us.

If the law, however, could be effectually enforced, it would be attended with the most cruel injustice. Why should not the holder of an ounce of gold in coin have the same advantages from the increase in the value of his property, as the holder of an ounce of uncoined gold? From the mere circumstance of its having had a stamp put on it, is he to be made to suffer all the inconveniences from the *fall* in the value of his gold, in consequence of the opening of new mines, or from any other circumstances, and derive none of the benefits which may result from a *rise* in its value? This injustice to individuals would not be compensated by the slightest advantages to the community; as the exportation of the coin, were it freely permitted, would always cease when the value of our currency had risen to its true bullion value, and that is precisely the value at which the currencies of all countries are permanently fixed.

Such, in spite of the law, was the value of our currency till the Bank restriction bill, and for some time after. There it would inevitably fix itself again, if that most impolitic act were repealed. Increase the value of your currency to its proper level, and you are sure to retain it. No policy can be worse than forcibly detaining a million, for example, to perform those offices to which 800,000*l.* are fully adequate.

SECTION II.

Consequences which would follow on the Supposition that the Currencies of other Countries (exclusive of England) were diminished or increased one half.

§ 20. Let us suppose that the circulation of all countries were carried on by the precious metals only, and that the proportion which England possessed were one million; let us further suppose, that, at once, half of the currencies of all countries, excepting that of England, were suddenly annihilated, would it be possible for England to continue to retain the million which she before possessed? Would not her currency become relatively excessive compared with that of other countries? If a quarter of wheat, for example, had been both in France and England of the same value as an ounce of coined gold, would not half an ounce now purchase it in France, whilst in England it continued of the same value as one ounce? * Could we by any laws, under such circumstances, prevent wheat or some other commodity (for all would be equally affected) from being imported into England, and gold coin from being exported? [1] If we could, and the exportation of bullion were free, gold might rise 100 per cent.; and for the same reason, if 35 Flemish schillings in Hamburgh had before been of equal value with a pound sterling, 17½ schillings would now attain that value. If the currency of England only had been doubled, the effects would have been precisely the same.

* That commodities would rise or fall in price, in proportion to the increase or diminution of money, I assume as a fact which is incontrovertible. Mr Bosanquet, in his admission of the effects on prices from the discovery of a mine, shows that he has no such doubts on this subject as the governor of the Bank, who, when asked by the Committee, "Do you conceive that a very considerable reduction of the amount of the circulating medium would not tend in any degree to increase its relative value compared with commodities, and that a considerable increase of it would have no tendency whatever to augment the price of commodities in exchange for such circulating medium?" answered, "It is a subject on which such a variety of opinions are entertained, I do not feel myself competent to give a decided answer."

[1] [Cf. *On Protection to Agriculture*, § 5.]

Suppose, again, the case reversed, and that all other currencies remained as before, while half of that of England was retrenched. If the coinage of money at the Mint was on the present footing, would not the prices of commodities be so reduced here that their cheapness would invite foreign purchasers, and would not this continue till the relative proportions in the different currencies were restored?

If such would be the effects of a diminution of money below its natural level, and that such would be the consequences the most celebrated writers on political economy are agreed, how can it be justly contended that the increase or diminution of money has nothing to do either with the foreign exchanges, or with the price of bullion?

§ 21. Now, a paper circulation, not convertible into specie, differs in its effects in no respect from a metallic currency, with the law against exportation strictly executed.

Supposing, then, the first case to occur whilst our circulation consisted wholly of paper, would not the exchanges fall, and the price of bullion rise in the manner which I have been representing; and would not our currency be depreciated, because it was no longer of the same value in the markets of the world as the bullion which it professed to represent? The fact of depreciation could not be denied, however the Bank Directors might assure the public that they never discounted but good bills for *bona fide* transactions; however they might assert that they never forced a note into circulation; that the quantity of money was no more than it had always been, and was only adequate to the wants of commerce, which had increased and not diminished;* that the price of gold, which was here at twice its Mint value, was equally high, or higher abroad, as might be proved

* The Bank could not on their own principles, then, urge that most erroneous opinion, that the rate of interest would be affected in the money market if their issues were excessive, and would therefore cause their notes to return to them, because, in the case here supposed, the actual amount of the money of the world being greatly diminished, they must contend that the rate

by sending an ounce of bullion to Hamburgh, and having the produce remitted by bill payable in London in bank notes; and that the increase or diminution of their notes could not possibly either affect the exchange or the price of bullion. All this, except the last, might be true, and yet would any man refuse his assent to the fact of the currency being depreciated? Could the symptoms which I have been enumerating proceed from any other cause but a relative excess in our currency? Could our currency be restored to its bullion value by any other means than by a reduction in its quantity, which should raise it to the value of the currencies of other countries; or by the increase of the precious metals, which lower the value of theirs to the level of ours?

Why will not the Bank try the experiment by a reduction in the amount of their notes of two or three millions for the short period of three months? If no effects were produced on the price of bullion and the foreign exchange then might their friends boast that the principles of the Bullion Committee were the wild dreams of speculative theorists.

SECTION III.

The trifling Rise in the Price of Gold on the Continent owing solely to a Variation in the Relation of Silver to Gold.

§ 22. But the price of gold, we are told, has risen on the Continent even more than it has here, because, when it was 4*l.* 12s. in this country, 4*l.* 17s. might be procured for it at Hamburgh, a difference of 5½ per cent. This is so often repeated, and is so wholly fallacious, that it may be proper to give it particular consideration.

When an ounce of gold was to be bought in this country at 3*l.* 17s. 10½d., and the relative value of gold

of interest would generally rise, and they might therefore increase their issues. If, after the able exposition of Dr Smith, any further argument were necessary to prove that the rate of interest is governed wholly by the relation of the amount of capital with the means of employing it, and is entirely independent of the abundance or scarcity of the circulating medium, this illustration would, I think, afford it.

was to silver as 15.07 to 1, it would have sold on the Continent for nearly the same as here, or 3*l.* 17s. 10½d. in silver coin. In Hamburgh, for example, we should have received in payment of an ounce of gold 136 Flemish schillings and 7 grotes, that quantity of silver containing an equal quantity of pure metal as 3*l.* 17s. 10½d. in our standard silver coin.

Gold has since that period risen in this country 18 per cent., and is now 4*l.* 12s. per ounce, and it is said that the 4*l.* 12s. with which it is paid for is not depreciated. Now, as gold has risen 5½ more abroad than it has here, it must be there 23½ per cent. higher than when it was sold for 136s. 7g., and we therefore should be led to expect that we should now obtain for it at Hamburgh 167 Flemish schillings; but what is the fact? this ounce of gold, which we are told we sell at Hamburgh for 4*l.* 17s., actually produces no more than 140 schillings 8 grotes, an advance only of 3 per cent.; and for this the seller is indebted to the rise in the relative value of gold to silver, which, from 15.07 to 1, is now about 16 to 1. It is true that, when the ounce of gold was sold at Hamburgh at 3*l.* 17s. 10½d., or for its equivalent 136 schillings 7 grotes, the currency of England was not depreciated; that sum, therefore, could only purchase a bill payable in London in bank notes for 3*l.* 17s. 10½d.; but the currency of England being now depreciated, and being estimated on the Hamburgh exchange at 28 or 29 Flemish schillings instead of 37, the true value of a pound sterling, 140 schillings 8 grotes, or 3 per cent. more than 136s. 7g., will now purchase a bill payable in London in bank notes for 4*l.* 17s.; so that gold has not risen more than 3 per cent. in Hamburgh, but the currency of England, on a comparison with the currency of Hamburgh, has fallen 23½ per cent.

§ 23. In further proof of the truth of my assertion, that it is not gold which has risen 16 or 18 per cent. in the general market of the world, but that it is the paper currency, in which the price of gold is estimated in England, which alone has fallen, I will subjoin an account of the lowest prices of gold in Hamburgh, Holland, and England, in the year 1804, and the highest prices in each of those countries in the year 1810, by which we shall be enabled to ascertain the actual rise in the price of gold measured in the currencies of each. This account was furnished to the Bullion Committee by Mr Grefulhe, and is numbered 56.

	Lowest Price.	Highest Price.	
Hamburgh	1804—$97\frac{3}{8}$	1810—101	being a rise of $3\frac{3}{4}$ per cent.
Holland	1804—$392\frac{1}{4}$	1810—$406\frac{7}{16}$	$3\frac{5}{8}$
England	1804—4*l.*	1810—4*l.* 13s.	16

Now, in Hamburgh and in Holland, where the currency is silver, gold may not rise 3 per cent. only, but 30 per cent., without its being any proof of the depreciation of the currency; it proves only an improvement in the relative value of gold to silver. But in England, where the price of gold is estimated in gold coin, or in bank notes representing that coin, a rise of 1 per cent. cannot take place without its proving a corresponding *depression** of the coin or paper. This observation is equally applicable to the fact mentioned by Mr. Bosanquet, and of which he himself seems aware, of gold having varied in Hamburgh no less than 8 per cent. within a period of two years.

§ 24. As there is an acknowledged difference between the price of standard gold bars and the price of gold coin reduced to the English standard, arising out of the latter being a more marketable commodity on the Continent,† I cannot admit the inferences which Mr Bosanquet draws from the comparison of Mr Grefulhe's paper (No. 58) with the paper, No. 60, in the Report. It would be first necessary to ascertain whether the prices of gold, as quoted in these papers (and they do not quite agree), were for gold in coin, or for gold of any other description; and whether the prices of gold in this country at different periods were always for gold of the same quality.

Mr Bosanquet observes that, "From the calculation furnished by Mr. Grefulhe to the Committee, it appears

* This expression has been noticed by Mr Bosanquet as extremely theoretical, but I consider it so exceedingly correct that I have taken the liberty of using it after the Committee.

† See § 18, p. 90, note.

that, in the spring of 1810, an ounce of gold of English standard weight was worth at Hamburgh 4*l.* 17s. sterling, —the price being 101, and the exchange 29s.; at this time the extreme price of bullion in London was 4*l.* 12s. or 5½ per cent. below the price of Hamburgh." The reader must recollect that it is 4*l.* 17s. in bank notes that is here meant, as I have already explained. But I cannot admit the perfect accuracy of this statement. The exporter of an ounce of gold, purchased here at 4*l.* 12s., would at least have had to wait three months before he could have received the 4*l.* 17s., because, after the gold is sold at Hamburgh, the remittance is made by a bill at 2½ usances, so that, allowing for interest for this period, he would actually have obtained a profit of 4¼ per cent. only; but, as the expense of sending gold to Hamburgh is stated in evidence to be 7 per cent., a bill would at this time have been a cheaper remittance by 2¾ per cent.

Now, allowing that Mr Bosanquet is perfectly accurate in his statement, that the price of gold was in this country at 4*l.* 12s. during the months of June, July, August, and September 1809, as well as in the spring of 1810, and that in all these instances such price was given for gold of the same quality, his conclusion that in those months in the year 1809 a profit of 5½ per cent. could be made by the exportation of gold, over and above the expenses, is not warranted by the fact. "If, at 101 and 29," observes Mr Bosanquet, "there was a profit on the export of gold from hence to Hamburgh of 5½ per cent., it follows that at 104½ (the prices in Hamburgh June, July, August, and September 1809), and 28s., there was a profit of 12½ per cent.; or, deducting the expenses of conveyance, that gold, if bought here at 4*l.* 12s. per ounce, was a cheaper remittance by 5½ per cent. than a bill at the current exchange." As I have already shown that when the exchange was 29, and the price of gold in Hamburgh 101, gold was a dearer remittance than by bill by 2¾ per cent., it follows that at 28s. and 104½, it was only cheaper by 4¼ per cent.

These facts prove that in June, July, August and September 1809, whilst the exchange was at Hamburgh

28s. and gold 104½, the real exchange was in favour of Hamburgh; whilst, in the spring of 1810, it was so much less favourable that it would not cover the expenses attending the importation of gold.

As for the rise of gold in Hamburgh with an invariable exchange, it is what would have been naturally expected if there had been a corresponding rise in the price of gold here. In proportion as the English currency becomes depreciated as compared with gold, will it become worth fewer of the schillings of Hamburgh, unless a rise in the value of gold at Hamburgh should counteract the depreciation, by making a gold pound sterling more valuable.

The exchanges, again, would partake in all the variations in the value of a depreciated pound sterling, whilst the price of gold continued invariable at Hamburgh.

"It appears," says Mr Bosanquet, "by the return from the Bullion-office at the Bank, No. 7 and 8 in the Appendix to the Report, that the total amount of gold bullion imported and deposited in the Bullion-office in 1809 amounted in value to only L.520,225

That during the same period, the quantity of gold delivered out of the Bullion-office amounted in value to L.805,568

of which only 592*l.* was not exportable.

"The amount of the importation is therefore such as, when compared with the amount of exports and imports, and that of the circulating medium, to justify the assumption of comparative scarcity; and the excess of delivery beyond the importation is sufficient evidence of unusual demand."

The fact itself here insisted on would be of little importance in the question which we are now discussing; but it appears to me that Mr Bosanquet is not warranted in his conclusions by the statements in the accounts to which he refers.

The excess of delivery beyond the importation is not any evidence of unusual demand, as it is accounted for by the following note to No. 7, from which the larger sum is extracted.

"*Note.*—The above is the amount of gold which

has passed the Bullion-office in the time above named, as sales and purchases by private dealers, but *which may have passed more than once* the Bullion-office, having no information generally from whence the seller procures his gold."

The importations stated in No. 8 are actually deposited by importers from abroad, and can only be received once. Besides this objection, these accounts were not fair subjects of comparison, No. 7 being made up to the 18th April 1810, No. 8 to 30th March 1810.

"The point of view in which these facts are important," continues Mr Bosanquet, "is that which places the amount of gold imported or delivered in line of comparison with the amount of paper currency, supposed to be depreciated on the evidence of the increased price of bullion. The advance of 12s. per ounce on the total quantity of gold delivered in one year—about 200,000 ounces—amounts to 120,000*l*. or 130,000*l*., and this is assumed as an unequivocal symptom of a depreciation of 12 or 13 per cent. on 30 or 40 millions of paper, the probable amount of our paper currency." "We may soon expect to be told that the value of bank notes has increased, because the paper on which they are made is somewhat dearer than heretofore."

The value of a bank note is ascertained, not by the number of transactions which may take place in the purchase or sale of gold, but by the actual comparative value of the note with the value of the coin for which it professes to be a substitute.

As it is allowed that a Government bank might force a circulation of paper, *although our Bank cannot*, how would Mr Bosanquet calculate the depreciation of such forced notes but by a comparison of their value with the value of bullion? Would he think it necessary to inquire whether 100 ounces only had been the amount transacted in the year, or whether it had been a million? If gold be not a test by which to estimate depreciation, what is? Whilst it is a criminal offence to buy guineas at a premium it does not seem probable that we can possess the only test which would satisfy these gentlemen, namely, two prices for commodities, a price in guineas, and another in bank notes. They might, even in that case, contend, that it was the scarcity of gold abroad which had raised the value of the guinea.

SECTION IV.

Failure ascribed to Mr Locke's Theory relative to the Recoinage in 1696.

§ 25. It is correctly stated by Mr Bosanquet, that Mr Locke's theory was similar to that now held. He did most certainly maintain that an ounce of silver in coin could not be less valuable than an ounce of silver bullion of the same standard. And the Committee now maintain that in the sound state of the British currency an ounce of gold bullion cannot, for any length of time, be of more value than 3*l.* 17s. 10½d., or an ounce of gold coin: but neither of these opinions have been yet found incorrect. The effects expected from the re-coinage in King William's reign failed of being realized, not because Mr. Locke's theory was followed, but because it was not followed. It did not fail because he could not be convinced that "the value of silver bullion was become greater than the standard or Mint price" (that being impossible if estimated in silver coin), but because his suggestions were not adopted.

§ 26. It was proposed by Mr Locke that silver coin should be the only fixed legal standard of currency, and that guineas should pass current in all payments at their bullion value. Under such a system, a guinea would have partaken of all the variations in the relative value of gold and silver; it might at one time have been worth 20s., and at another 25s.; but, contrary to Mr Locke's principle, the value of the guinea was first fixed at 22s., and afterwards at 21s. 6d., whilst its value as bullion was considerably below it.* At the same time

* It may be said, that, although guineas were by law prohibited from passing at more than 21s. 6d., they were not declared a legal tender till 1717; and, therefore, that no creditor was obliged to accept of them in discharge of a debt at that rate. But if Government received them in the payment of taxes at

the silver coin, for the very reason that gold was rated too high, passed in currency at a value less than its bullion value. It was to be expected, therefore, that the gold coin would be retained, and that the silver coin would disappear from circulation. If the value of the guinea in currency had been lowered to its true market value in silver, the exportation of the silver coin would immediately have ceased, and, in fact, this was the remedy which was at last adopted. The matter being referred to Sir I. Newton in 1717, then master of the Mint, he reported, " the principal cause of the exportation of the silver coin was, that a guinea, which then passed for 21s. 6d., was generally worth no more than 20s. 8d., according to the relative value of gold to silver at the market, though its value occasionally varied." " He then suggested, that 6d. should be taken off from the value of the guinea in order to diminish the temptation to export and melt down the silver coin, acknowledging, however, that 10d. or 12d. ought to be taken from the guinea, in order that gold might bear the same proportion with silver money in England which it ought to do by the course of trade and exchange in Europe." * The same effects would have followed without the intervention of Government, if the relative value of gold and silver in the market had so varied as to have made them agree with the Mint proportions.

§ 27. Lord Liverpool, in speaking of the re-coinage in 1696, is of a very different opinion from Mr Bosanquet;—so far from considering that measure as having " subjected the nation to disappointment and inconvenience, under which we still labour, and to an unprofitable expense of nearly 3 millions sterling," he observes, " that great as this charge was, the losses which the Government as well as the people of this kingdom continued daily to suffer till the re-coinage was completed, justified almost any expense which might be incurred for their relief." [1]

such value, the effects would be nearly the same as if they had by act of Parliament been made a legal tender.

* Lord Liverpool's letter to the King. [*A Treatise on the Coins of the Realm, &c.*, p. 71, &c.]

[1] [*A Treatise on the Coins of the Realm, &c.*, p. 76.]

Mr Bosanquet is not quite correct in saying, page 34, that the price of silver has never been under the Mint price since the re-coinage in the reign of King William. On a reference to Mr Mushet's tables, it appears that it was as low as 5s. 1d. in 1793 and 1794, and in 1798 it fell to 5s., which was the occasion of the law for prohibiting the coinage of silver which I have already noticed.*

* Since this was sent to the press I have seen the second edition of Mr Bosanquet's work, in which this inaccuracy is corrected.

CHAPTER IV.

MR BOSANQUET'S OBJECTIONS TO THE STATEMENT, THAT THE BALANCE OF PAYMENTS HAS BEEN IN FAVOUR OF GREAT BRITAIN, EXAMINED.

§ 28. Having considered all those points deemed so important by Mr Bosanquet in contradiction of the opinion of the Committee, "that it is by a comparison of the market and Mint value of bullion, that the fact of the depreciation of the currency can be estimated;" and having, I trust, made it evident that there is no other test singly, by which we are enabled to judge of the sound or unsound state of our paper currency, I shall proceed to the consideration of the next disputed position of the Bullion Committee; namely, "That so far as any inference is to be drawn from Custom-house returns of exports and imports, the state of the exchanges ought to be peculiarly favourable."

Mr Bosanquet has been at the trouble of consulting numerous documents to prove that the Committee have not only committed an error to the amount of 7,500,000*l.* in their estimate of the balance of exports, but other errors to a still greater amount; and that, in fact, so far from their opinion being well founded, that the state of the exchange ought to have been favourable to this country during the past year, the actual amount of the balance of payments to the Continent had been unusually great.

As I am desirous only of defending the principles of the Committee, and as these facts are by no means essential to those principles, I shall not enter into any examination of the correctness either of the statements of the Committee, or of those of Mr Bosanquet, but will at once concede to him the facts, difficult as he would find it to prove all of them, for which he contends.

§ 29. That the balance of payments has been against this country cannot, I conceive, admit of dispute. The state of the real exchange sufficiently proves it, as that infallibly indicates from which country bullion is passing. It would, however, have been of some satisfaction to those who are desirous of clearly understanding this difficult subject, if Mr Bosanquet had acquainted us with the means which we possessed of paying the very large unfavourable balance for which he contends. Does he imagine that it has actually been discharged with our own hoard of gold? Do we usually keep unemployed such a large amount of bullion that we can afford to pay such balances year after year?

As we have no mines of our own, if we do not actually possess it, we must purchase it from foreign countries; but bank notes will be useless for such purpose. If the price of gold in bank notes be 4*l.* per ounce, or 10*l.* per ounce, we shall not obtain the slightest addition to our quantity of bullion, as it can only be procured by the exportation of goods. If we obtain it from America, for example, it is with goods we must purchase it. In that case, on a view of the whole trade of the country, we have discharged a debt in Europe by the exportation of goods to some other part of the world, and the balance of payments, however large it may be, must ultimately be paid by the produce of the labour of the people of this country. Bills of exchange never discharge a debt from one country to another; they enable a creditor of England to receive, at the place where he is resident, a sum of money from a debtor to England; they effect a transfer of a debt, but do not discharge it. That a demand for gold (if it could be allowed that our creditor would accept nothing but gold) might occasion a rise in its value, no one denies. If, therefore, goods had become exceedingly cheap, it would have been the natural effect of such a cause. But how is any rise in its price in bank notes to procure it, even if we suppose it hoarded in England?

The seller is not to be deluded with an increase of nominal value; it will be to him of little importance whether he sells his gold at 3*l.* 17s. 10½d., or at 4*l.* 12s. per ounce, provided either of those sums will procure him the commodities for which he intends ultimately to exchange his gold. If, then, bank notes to the amount of 3*l.* 17s. 10½d. be rendered of equal value in procuring the commodities which he seeks to purchase, with 4*l.* 12s., as much gold will be procured at one price as at the other. Now, can it be denied, that by reducing the amount of bank notes their value will be increased? If so, how can the reduction of bank notes prevent us from obtaining the same amount of gold, both at home and abroad, to discharge our foreign debt, as we now obtain by a nominal and fictitious price?

§ 30. "At a moment," says Mr Bosanquet, "when we were *compelled* to receive corn, even from our enemy, without the slightest stipulation in favour of our own manufacturer, and to pay neutrals for bringing it, Mr Ricardo tells us, that the export of bullion and merchandise, in payment of the corn we may import, resolves itself entirely into a question of interest, and that, if we give coin in exchange for goods, it must be from choice, not necessity. Whilst providing against famine, he tells us, that we should not import more goods than we export, unless we had a redundancy of currency."

Mr Bosanquet speaks as if the nation collectively, as one body, imported corn and exported gold, and that it was compelled by hunger so to do, not reflecting that the importation of corn, even under the case supposed, is the act of individuals, and governed by the same motives as all other branches of trade. What is the degree of *compulsion* which is employed to make us receive corn from our enemy? I suppose no other than the want of that commodity which makes it an advantageous article of import; but if it be a voluntary, as it most certainly is, and not a compulsory bargain between the two nations, I do still maintain that gold would not, even if famine raged amongst us, be given to France in exchange for corn, unless the exportation of gold was attended with advantage to the exporter, unless he could sell corn in England for more gold than he was obliged to give for the purchase of it.

Would Mr Bosanquet, would any merchant he knows, import corn for gold on any other terms? If no importer would, how could the corn be introduced into the country, unless gold or some other commodity were cheaper here? As far as those two commodities are concerned, do not these transactions as certainly indicate that gold is dearer in France, as that corn is dearer in England?

Seeing nothing in Mr Bosanquet's statement to induce me to change my opinion, I must continue to think that it is interest, and interest alone, which determines the exportation of gold, in the same manner as it regulates the exportation of all other commodities. Mr Bosanquet would have done well, before he had deemed this opinion so extravagant, to have used something like argument to prove it so; and he would not have hurt his cause, if, even in the year 1810, he had explained his reason for supporting a principle advanced by Mr Thornton in 1802, the correctness of which was questioned in 1809.

Bullion will not be exported unless we have previously imported it for such purpose, or unless from some circumstances in our internal circulation it has been rendered cheap and less useful to us. If Milan decrees, embargoes, non-intercourse acts, &c., affect the exportation of commodities, they also affect their importation, as no country can long continue to buy unless it can also sell; and least of all, England, who by the abundance of her paper has driven from her circulation every vestige of the precious metals.

"If the currency be depreciated below the value of gold," Mr Bosanquet tells us, "it is so positively, not relatively, and all exchanges must equally feel the influence of the depreciation." (Page 20.) Most true; and therefore if Mr Bosanquet could have shown that with *any one country in the world* whose currency is not debased nor depreciated, the exchange had been favourable to England, more than the expenses of transporting bullion, he would have successfully controverted the opinion of the Committee.

§ 31. Some able writers on this subject have lately taken, I think, a mistaken view of the exportation of money, and of the effects produced on the price of bullion by an increase of currency through paper circulation.

Mr Blake [1] observes, "All writers upon the subject of political economy that I have met with seem to be persuaded that, when the rate of exchange has deviated from par beyond the expenses of the transit of bullion, bullion will immediately pass; and the error has arisen from not sufficiently distinguishing the effects of a *real* and a *nominal* exchange;" and many pages are employed in proving, that on every addition to the paper circulation, even when a great part of the currency consists of the precious metals, the price of bullion will be raised in the same proportion as other commodities; and as the foreign exchange will be nominally depressed in the same degree, no advantage will arise from the exportation of bullion. The same opinion is maintained by Mr Huskisson, page 27.

"If the circulation of a country were supplied partly by gold and partly by paper, and the amount of that circulation were doubled by an augmentation of that paper, the effect upon prices at home would be the same as in the former case" (a rise in the price of commodities). "But gold not becoming, by this augmentation of currency, more abundant in such a country than in other parts of the world, as a *commodity*, its relative value to other commodities would remain unaltered; as a commodity, also, its price would rise in the same proportion as that of other commodities, although, in the state of coin, of which the *denomination* is fixed by law, it could only pass current according to that *denomination*.

"When paper is thus augmented in any country, the exportation of the gold coin, therefore, will take place; not because gold, as a *commodity*, is become more abundant and less valuable with reference to other commodities in such a country; but from the circumstance of its value as currency remaining the same, while

[1] [Francis Blake, *Observations on the Principles which Regulate the Course of Exchange, and on the present Depreciated State of the Currency*.]

its price in that currency is increased in common with the prices of all other commodities."

I should perfectly agree with these writers, that the effects on the value of gold, as an exportable commodity, would be as they describe, provided the circulation consisted wholly of paper; but no rise would take place in the price of bullion in consequence of an addition of paper currency, whilst the currency was either wholly metallic, or consisted partly of gold and partly of paper.

If an addition be made to a currency consisting partly of gold and partly of paper, by an increase of paper currency, the value of the whole currency would be diminished, or, in other words, the prices of commodities would rise, estimated either in gold coin or in paper currency. The same commodity would purchase, after the increase of paper, a greater number of ounces of gold coin, because it would exchange for a greater quantity of money. But these gentlemen do not dispute the fact of the convertibility of coin into bullion, in spite of the law to prevent it. Does it not follow, therefore, that the value of gold in coin, and the value of gold in bullion, would speedily approach a perfect equality? If, then, a commodity would sell, in consequence of the issue of paper, for more gold coin, it would also sell for more gold bullion. It cannot, therefore, be correct to say, that the relative value of gold bullion and commodities would be the same after, as before, the increase of paper.

The diminution in the value of gold, as compared with commodities, in consequence of the issues of paper in a country where gold forms part of the circulation, is, in the first instance, confined to that country only. If such country were insulated, and had no commerce whatever with any other country, this diminution in the value of gold would continue till the demand for gold for its manufactures had withdrawn the whole of its coin from circulation, and not till then would there be any visible depreciation in the value of paper as compared with gold, whatever the amount of paper might be which was in circulation.

As soon as the gold had been wholly withdrawn, the demand for manufactures still continuing, gold would rise above the value of paper, and would soon obtain that relative value to other commodities which subsisted before any addition had been made to the circulation by the issues of paper. The mines would then supply the quantity of gold required, and the paper currency would continue to be permanently depreciated. During this interval, the gold mines of such country, if it possessed any, could not be worked, because of the low value of gold, which would have reduced the profits on capital employed in the mines below the level of the profits of other mercantile concerns. As soon as this equality of profit were established, the supply of gold would be as regular as before. These would be the consequences of a great issue of paper in a country having no intercourse with any other.

But if the country supposed, as is the case with England, had intercourse with all other countries, any excess of her currency would be counteracted by an exportation of specie, and if that excess did not exceed the amount of coin in circulation, which could be easily collected by those who evade the law, no depreciation of the currency would take place.

Suppose England to have 1000 ounces of gold in the state of bullion, and 1000 ounces in the state of coin, whilst her exchange with foreign countries was at par; that is to say, whilst the value of gold abroad was precisely the same as here, and therefore could be neither advantageously exported nor imported.

Suppose, too, that the Bank were at such time to issue notes to an amount which should represent 1000 ounces more of gold, and that they were not exchangeable for specie. If her bullion retained the same value after as before the issue of paper (which is the point contended for), how could a single guinea be exported? Who would be at the trouble and risk of sending guineas to the Continent to be sold there for their value as bullion, while the value of bullion continued here as high as before, and consequently as high as the price abroad? Would not the coin be melted and sold as bullion at home, till the value of bullion had so much diminished in its relative value to the bullion of other countries, and therefore to the relative value of commodities here, as to pay the expenses of transportation ; or, in other words, till the exchange had fallen to the price at which it would repay such expenses ? At that price the whole 1000 ounces would go at once, or if any part were retained in circulation, it would not be of less value than an equal weight of gold bullion. I am all along considering the law as having no effect in preventing exportation, and if it be contended that the law could be strictly executed, that argument would be equally applicable if the addition to the currency had been made in gold coin, and not in paper currency.

It appears, therefore, evident, first, that by the addition of paper to a currency consisting partly of gold and partly of paper, gold bullion will not necessarily rise in the same degree as other commodities ; and, secondly, that such addition will cause depression not in the nominal but in the real exchange, and therefore that gold will be exported.

But to return to Mr Bosanquet. He observes, " that the three propositions," viz. those on which I have been commenting, " appear to have been brought forward by the Committee as well as by the authors on whose theories the Report is founded, to induce the admission of the depreciation of the paper currency of this country as the necessary consequence of the impossibility of accounting for the depression of the exchanges and the increased price of bullion in any other way. They may be termed negative arguments."

Now, as far as I, who am one of the authors arraigned, am concerned, Mr Bosanquet is incorrect : the third of these propositions was not on any occasion brought forward by me. The fact of the balance of payments being for or against this country could be of little consequence, in my estimation, to the proof of the theory which I maintain. Whether a part of our exports or a part of our imports consisted of gold cannot in the least affect this question ; it is abundantly certain that our currency is neither by ourselves nor by foreigners estimated at its bullion value. And why should our currency be degraded below such value more than those of America, France, Hamburgh, Holland, &c.? The answer is, because neither of those countries have a paper currency not convertible into specie at the will of the holder.

CHAPTER V.

MR BOSANQUET'S ARGUMENT TO PROVE THAT THE BANK OF ENGLAND HAS NOT THE POWER OF FORCING THE CIRCULATION OF BANK NOTES, CONSIDERED.

§ 32. The fourth proposition is what now presents itself for discussion:

"That the Bank, during the restriction, possesses exclusively the power of limiting the circulation of bank notes."

It is difficult to determine whether Mr Bosanquet thinks that even a forced paper circulation could have the effect of lowering the exchange; so confidently is it asserted by him that there is no connexion between the exchanges and the amount of bank notes. If the Bank were to become truly a Government Bank, in the sense in which Mr Bosanquet somewhere uses that term; if they were to advance all the money requisite for the service of the year; if from 20 millions they were to raise the amount of their notes to 50 millions, would not such a bank be justly said to force a circulation of paper? and would not the effect of such a forced circulation of paper be, that their notes would be depreciated, that the price of bullion would rise, and the foreign exchanges fall? Would not these effects take place although Government were to guarantee the notes of the Bank, and the final payment of them should by no one be doubted? Would not the abundance of the circulation alone produce depreciation? Or, is it to be maintained that no abundance of paper money, provided its final redemption be certain, can cause depreciation? A proposition so extravagant will hardly, I think, be supported, and it must therefore be admitted that depreciation may arise from the abundance of notes alone, however great might be the funds of those who were the issuers of them. As these symptoms, then, which accompany a forced paper currency are, at this moment, too glaring to be denied, as they cannot be accounted for in any other way either by theory or by an appeal to experience, are we not justified in our suspicions that the Bank of England, as at present constituted, is not so devoid of the power of forcing a circulation as their friends would have us believe? It is not intended by the words, forced circulation, to accuse the Bank of having departed from those cautions which have usually accompanied the issue of their paper; it is meant only that the restriction bill enables them to keep in circulation an amount of notes (allowance made for the coin that would then be in circulation) greater than they could maintain but for that measure. It is this surplus sum which I consider as producing precisely the same effects as if it were forced on the public by a Government Bank. The plea that no more is issued than the wants of commerce require is of no weight; because the sum required for such purpose cannot be defined. Commerce is insatiable in its demands, and the same portion of it may employ 10 millions or 100 millions of circulating medium; the quantity depends wholly on its value. If the mines had been ten times more productive, ten times more money would the same commerce employ. This Mr Bosanquet admits, but denies the analogy between the issues of the Bank and the produce of a new gold mine.

§ 33. On this subject Mr Bosanquet makes the following observations:

"Mr Ricardo has assimilated the Bank of England during the restriction, so far as relates to the effects of its issues, to a gold mine, the produce of which being thrown into circulation, in addition to the circulating medium already sufficient, is an excess; and has the acknowledged effect of depreciating the value of the existing medium, or, in other words, of raising the price of commodities for which it is usually exchanged. But

Mr Ricardo has not stated what is essential to the comparison, *why* it is that the discovery of a gold mine would produce this effect. It would produce it, because the proprietors would issue it, for whatever services, without any engagement, to give an equal value for it again to the holders, or any wish, or any means, of calling back and annihilating that which they have issued. By degrees, as the issues increase they exceed the wants of circulation; gold produces no benefit to the holder as gold; he cannot eat it, nor clothe himself with it; to render it useful, he must exchange it either for such things as are immediately useful, or for such as produce revenue. The demand, and consequently the prices, of commodities and real properties measured in gold, increases, and will continue to increase as long as the mine continues to produce. And this effect will equally follow whether, under the circumstances I have supposed, the issue be gold from a mine or paper from a Government Bank. All this I distinctly admit; but in all this statement, there is not one point of analogy to the issues of the Bank of England.

"But the principle on which the Bank issues its notes is that of loan. Every note is issued at the requisition of some party, who becomes indebted to the Bank for its amount, and gives security to return this note, or another of equal value, at a fixed and not remote period; paying an interest proportioned to the time allowed."

§ 34. Now, supposing the gold mine to be actually the property of the Bank, even to be situated on their own premises, and that they procured the gold which it produced to be coined into guineas, and in lieu of issuing their notes when they discounted bills or lent money to Government, that they issued nothing but guineas; could there be any other limit to their issues but the want of the further productiveness in their mine? In what would the circumstances differ if the mine were the property of the king, of a company of merchants, or of a single individual? In that case Mr Bosanquet admits that the value of money would fall, and I suppose he would also admit that it would fall in exact proportion to its increase.

What would be done with the gold by the owner of the mine? It must be either employed at interest by himself, or it would finally find its way into the hands of those who would so employ it. This is its natural destination; it may pass through the hands of 100 or 1000 persons, but it could be employed in no other manner at last. Now, if the mine should double the quantity of money, it would depress its value in the same proportion, and there would be double the demand for it. A merchant who before required the loan of 10,000*l.* would now want 20,000*l.*; and it could be of little importance to him whether he continued to borrow 10,000*l.* of the Bank, and 10,000*l.* of those with whom the money finally rested, or whether he borrowed the whole 20,000*l.* of the Bank. The analogy seems to me to be complete, and not to admit of dispute. The issues of paper not convertible are guided by the same principle, and will be attended with the same effects as if the Bank were the proprietor of the mine, and issued nothing but gold. However much gold may be increased, borrowers will increase to the same amount, in consequence of its depreciation; and the same rule is equally true with respect to paper. If money be but depreciated sufficiently, there is no amount which may not be absorbed, and it would not make the slightest difference whether the Bank with their notes actually purchased the commodities themselves, or whether they discounted the bills of those who would so employ them.

If it were granted to Mr Bosanquet that a given sum, and no more, could be absorbed in the circulation, the effects he states would follow: but I deny that there would be a surplus seeking in vain for advantageous employment, and which, not being able to find it, would necessarily either return to the Bank in payment of a bill already discounted, or would prevent an application to them for an advance of money to that amount.

If money, however abundantly issued, could retain its value, such might be the effects; but as, when once it is brought into circulation, depreciation commences, the employment for the additional sum would retain it in the currency.

Let us recur to the effect which would result from the establishment of a bank of undoubted credit in a country where the circulation was wholly metallic.

Such a bank would discount bills or make advances to Government as our Bank does; and if the principle now contended for by Mr Bosanquet be correct, their notes would necessarily return on them as soon as issued; because the metallic currency being before sufficient for the commerce of the country, no additional quantity could be employed.—But this is contrary both to theory and experience. The issues of the Bank would, as they now do, not only depreciate the currency, but the value of bullion at the same time, as I have endeavoured to explain in § 31, pp. 109, 110; this, again, would be the temptation to exportation, and the diminution of the currency would make it regain its value. The Bank would issue more notes, and the same effects would follow; but in no case would there be such an excess as would induce any holder of notes to return them to the Bank in payment of loans, if the law against the exportation of money could be effectually executed. Money would be demanded because it could be profitably exported, and not because it could not be absorbed in the circulation. But let us suppose a case in which money could not be profitably exported—Let us suppose all the countries of Europe to carry on their circulation by means of the precious metals, and that each were at the same moment to establish a Bank on the same principles as the Bank of England—Could they, or could they not, each add to the metallic circulation a certain portion of paper? and could or could they not permanently maintain that paper in circulation? If they could, the question is at an end; an addition might then be made to a circulation already sufficient, without occasioning the notes to return to the Bank in payment of bills due. If it is said they could not, then I appeal to experience, and ask for some explanation of the manner in which bank notes were originally called into existence, and how they are permanently kept in circulation.

I should find it laborious to follow up in all its bearings the analogy between the first establishment of a Bank, the discovery of a mine, and the present situation of our Bank; but of this I am fully certain, that if the principle advanced by the Bank Directors be correct, not a bank note could ever have been permanently kept in circulation, nor would the discovery of the mines of America have added one guinea to the circulation of England. The additional gold would, according to this system, have found a circulation already adequate, and in which no more could be admitted.

§ 35. The refusal to discount any bills but those for *bonâ fide* transactions would be as little effectual in limiting the circulation; because, though the Directors should have the means of distinguishing such bills, which can by no means be allowed, a greater portion of paper currency might be called into circulation, not than the wants of commerce could employ, but greater than what could remain in the channel of currency without depreciation. It is well known that the same thousand pounds may settle 20 *bonâ fide* transactions in one day. It may pay for a ship; the seller of a ship may pay with it his rope-maker;—he again may pay the Russian merchants for hemp, &c., &c. Now, as each of these was a *bonâ fide* transaction, a bill might have been drawn by each, and the Bank, by their rule, might discount them all; so that 20,000*l.* might be called into circulation to perform those payments for which 1000*l.* was equal. I am aware that the opinion of Dr Smith, as quoted by Mr Bosanquet, appears to favour his opinion; but that able writer has, in various passages of his work, and within a few pages of that from whence Mr Bosanquet has quoted, declared that "The whole paper money of every kind which can easily circulate in any country can never exceed the value of the gold and silver of which it supplies the place, or which (the commerce being supposed the same) would circulate there if there were no paper money."

To this test we must not[1] submit our currency. If at its present amount it consisted of gold and silver, no laws, however severe, could retain it in circulation; a part would be melted and exported till it was reduced to

[1] [*Sic.* It seems probable, however, that "not" was a clerical error for now.]

its just level. At that level it would be as impossible to force the exportation of it. In such case we should no longer hear of the balance of payments being against us, nor of the necessity of exporting gold in return for corn. That such would be the consequences cannot be doubted by those who are familiar with the writings of Dr Smith. But if it should be otherwise, if the Continent should adopt the almost impossible, absurd policy of wishing to buy more of that of which they already had too much, what evil consequences would ensue to us, even if our currency were reduced to the same level at which it stood before the discovery of America? Would not this be a national gain? inasmuch as the circulation of the same commerce being carried on with a smaller amount of gold, the balance might be profitably employed in procuring a return of more useful and more productive commodities. And if the circulation of paper were reduced in the same proportion would not the profits now gained by the Bank be enjoyed by those who can show a much better title to them?

It is fortunate for the public that there should exist the disinclination to discount at the Bank which Mr Bosanquet mentions,—as without some such check, it is impossible to say to what amount bank notes might by this time have been multiplied. Indeed, to all those who have given the subject any consideration, it is matter of surprise that our circulation has been confined within such moderate bounds, after knowing the principles which the Bank Directors have avowed as their guide in regulating their issues.

CHAPTER VI.

OBSERVATIONS ON THE PRINCIPLES OF SEIGNORAGE.

§ 36. Dr Smith, though favourable to a small seignorage on the coin, was fully aware of the evils which might attend a large one.

The limits, beyond which a seignorage cannot be advantageously extended, are the actual expenses incurred by the manufacturing of bullion into coin. If a seignorage exceeds these expenses, an advantage will accrue to false coiners by imitating the coins, although they should actually make them of their legal weight and standard; but even in this case, as the addition of money to the circulation beyond the regular demands of commerce will diminish the value of that money, the trade of false coiners must cease when the value of the coin does not exceed the value of bullion more than the actual expenses of fabrication. If the public could be secured from such illegal additions to the circulation medium, there could be no seignorage so high which a Government might not advantageously exact; as the coined money would, in the same degree, exceed the value of bullion. If the seignorage amounted to 10 per cent., bullion would necessarily be 10 per cent. under the Mint price; and if it were 50 per cent., that also would the value of coin exceed the value of bullion. It appears, then, that although a given weight of bullion can never exceed in value a given weight of coin, a given weight of coin may exceed in value a given weight of bullion by the whole expense of seignorage, however great that seignorage may be, provided that there was effectual security against the increase of money through the imitation of the coins by illegal means. And it appears also, that if no such security could be given, the trade of the false coiner would cease as soon as he had added so much to the amount of the coin as to diminish its value on a comparison with bullion, to the actual expenses incurred. That these principles are correct may be proved from the consideration of the circumstances which give value to a bank note. A bank note is of no more intrinsic value than the piece of paper on which it is made. It may be considered as a piece of money on which the seignorage is enormous, amounting to all its value; yet if the public is sufficiently protected against the too great increase of such notes, either by the indiscretion of the issuers, or by the practices of false coiners or forgers, they must, in the ordinary operations of trade, retain their value.

Whilst such money is kept within certain limits, any value may be given to it as currency; 3*l.* 17s. 10½d. may be worth an ounce of gold bullion, the value at which it was originally issued, or it may be reduced to the value of half an ounce; and if the Bank which issued had the exclusive privilege of procuring money to be coined at the Mint, 3*l.* 17s. 10½d. of their notes might be rendered of equal value to 1, 2, 3, or any number of ounces of gold bullion.

The value of such money must depend wholly upon its quantity; and in the case supposed, the Bank would not only have the power of limiting the amount of paper money, but of metallic money also.

§ 37. I have before endeavoured to show, that, previously to the establishment of banks, the precious metals employed as money were necessarily distributed amongst the different countries of the world in the proportion that their trade and payments required; that, whatever the value of the bullion so employed for the purposes of currency might be, the equal demands and necessities of all countries would prevent the quantity allotted to each from being either increased or diminished, unless the proportions in the trade of countries should undergo some alteration which should make a different division necessary; that England or any other country might substitute paper instead of bullion for the uses of money, but that the value of such paper must be regulated by the amount of coin of its bullion value which would have circulated had there been no paper.

Under this point of view the paper currency of any particular country represents a certain weight of bullion which, her commerce and payments continuing the same, could neither be increased nor diminished; 3*l*. 17s. 10½d. of coin or paper currency might represent an ounce of gold bullion, or 4*l*. 13s. might, in consequence of some internal regulation, do the same; but the actual amount of bullion so represented would, under the same circumstances of commerce and payments, be eternally the same.

Suppose that England's share amounted to a million of ounces; if, by a law which could be effectually executed, a million and a half of ounces in coin could be forced or retained in circulation by preventing its being melted or exported; or if, by means of a restriction bill, the Bank should be enabled to maintain an amount of paper which should represent a million and a half of ounces of coined gold in circulation, such million and a half would be of no more value in currency than a million of ounces; and consequently an ounce and a half of coined gold, or bank notes which represented that amount, would purchase no more of any commodity than an ounce of gold bullion. If, on the other hand, Government were to charge a seignorage of 50 per cent., or if the issues of the Bank were to be exceedingly limited, whilst they had also the exclusive right of coining, so that the whole amount of their notes did not exceed what should represent, at the Mint price, half a million of ounces of gold, that half million would in currency pass for the same value as the million of ounces in one case, and the million and a half in the other did before.

§ 38. From these principles it results, that there can exist no depreciation of money but from excess. However debased a coinage may become, it will preserve its Mint value, that is to say, it will pass in circulation for the intrinsic value of the bullion which it ought to contain, provided it be not in too great abundance. It is a mistaken theory, therefore, to suppose that guineas of 5 dwts. and 8 grains cannot circulate with guineas of 5 dwts. or less. As they might be in such limited quantity that both the one and the other might actually pass in currency for a value equal to 5 dwts. 10 grains, there would be no temptation to withdraw either from circulation; there would be a real profit in retaining them. In practice, indeed, it would seldom occur that the heavier pieces would escape the melting pot, but it would arise wholly from the augmentation of such currency, either by the liberal issues of the Bank, or by the supply of false money which the arts of the false coiner would throw into circulation.

Our silver currency now passes at a value in currency above its bullion value, because, notwithstanding the profit obtained by the counterfeiter, it has not yet been supplied in sufficient abundance to affect its value.

It is on this principle, too, that the fact must be accounted for, that the price of bullion previously to the recoinage in 1696 did not rise so high as might have been expected from the then debased state of the currency; the quantity had not been increased in the same proportion as the quality had been debased.

It also follows from these principles, that in a country where gold is the measure of value, the price of gold bullion (where the law offers no restraint against exportation) can never exceed its Mint price; and that it can never fall more below it than the expenses of coinage; and that these variations depend wholly on the supply of coin or paper currency being proportioned to the trade of the country; or, in other words, that nothing can raise the value of bullion even so high as the Mint price but an excess of circulation. If, indeed, any power in the State have the privilege of increasing the paper currency at pleasure, and be at the same time protected from the payment of its notes, there is no other limit to the rise of the price of gold than the will of the issuers.

CHAPTER VII.

MR BOSANQUET'S OBJECTIONS TO THE PROPOSITION, THAT THE CIRCULATION OF THE BANK OF ENGLAND REGULATES THAT OF THE COUNTRY BANKS, CONSIDERED.

§ 39. The next proposition which Mr Bosanquet attempts to disprove is that in which the Committee give it as their opinion, "That the circulation of country bank notes depends upon, and is proportionate to, the issues from the Bank."

There are many practical authorities for the truth of this principle also. It appears to be singularly unfortunate, that few of the principles of the Bullion Committee which Mr Bosanquet has selected have not the authority of practical men, to whose opinions on these subjects so much deference is paid. That the exchange can never vary for any length of time beyond the limits defined by the Committee has been, and is, the opinion of the ablest practical men.

That the price of bullion cannot long continue with a sound system of currency, above the Mint price, has received full confirmation from the same quarter, and the proposition now under discussion is not without the same sanction. Mr Huskisson has already availed himself of the authority of the Governor of the Bank for its truth, who declared in his evidence to the Committee, page 127, "The country banks, by not regulating their issues on the principle of the Bank of England, might send forth a superabundance of their notes; but this excess, in my opinion, would no sooner exist in any material degree, than it would be corrected by its own operation, for the holders of such paper would immediately return it to the issuers, when they found that in consequence of the over issue its value was reduced, or likely to be reduced, below par ; thus, though the balance might be slightly and transiently disturbed, no considerable or permanent over-issue could possibly take place, as from the nature of things the amount of bank notes in circulation must always find its level in the public wants." Mr Gilchrist of the Bank of Scotland, stated to the Committee, that "If the Bank of England were to restrict their issues, of course the Scotch banks would find it necessary to diminish theirs." "The issues of the Bank of England," he observed, "operate upon the issues of the banks of Scotland in this manner. If the banks of Scotland issue more than they ought to do in proportion to the issues of the Bank of England, they would be called upon to draw bills upon London at a lower rate of exchange." (Page 114, App.) Mr Thompson, a country banker, and a member of the Committee, was asked, "By what criterion do the country banks now regulate their issues of paper ?"—Ans. "By the plenty or scarcity of bank notes." "Then their issues bear a proportion to the issues of the Bank ?"—Ans. "In my opinion they do."

§ 40. "The Committee," Mr Bosanquet observes, "has not defined the sense in which they use the term excess of currency ; I, therefore," he continues, "suppose it to be used in the Report in the sense in which it is used by Dr Smith, as denoting a quantity greater than the circulation of the country can easily absorb or employ." And in another place, "As the fact is not *apparent,* at least (I mean that there is more paper than the country can easily absorb and employ) the *onus probandi* seems to lie on the Committee."

This is not the sense in which I consider the Committee to use the word *excess.* In that sense there can be no excess whilst the Bank does not pay in specie, because the commerce of the country can easily employ and absorb any sum which the Bank may send into circulation. It is from so understanding the word excess that Mr Bosanquet thinks the circulation cannot be excessive, because the commerce of the country could

L

not easily employ it. In proportion as the pound sterling becomes depreciated will the want of the nominal amount of pounds increase, and no part of the larger sum will be excessive, more than the smaller sum was before. By excess, then, the Committee must mean the difference in amount of circulation between the sum actually employed, and that sum which would be employed if the pound sterling were to regain its bullion value. This is a distinction of more consequence than at first sight appears, and Mr Bosanquet was well aware that it was in this sense that it was used by me. He has been so obliging as to express my meaning in a passage where it appeared obscure; he has done it most ably, and completely understood the sense in which I used the words *an excessive circulation.* He observes upon the passage, page 86, "If this interpretation be adopted, it will be nearly useless to search for, and inquire after, excess of paper as a fact; we must be content to admit proof of its existence from its effects, and our attention must be directed to ascertain depreciation, or an increased price of commodities, solely arising out of, and occasioned by, the increased amount of the circulating medium." I do most unequivocally admit, that whilst the high price of bullion and the low exchanges continue, and whilst our gold is undebased, it would to me be no proof of our currency not being depreciated if there were only 5 millions of bank notes in circulation. When we speak, therefore, of an excess of bank notes, we mean that portion of the amount of the issues of the Bank, which can now circulate, but could not, if the currency were of its bullion value. When we speak of an excess of country currency, we mean a portion of the amount of the country bank notes, which cannot be absorbed in the circulation, because they are exchangeable for, and are depreciated below, the value of bank notes.

This distinction appears to me to be an answer to Mr Bosanquet's objection, where he says, "but does it follow that the country bank paper, if issued to excess, will not be checked, because there is already more bank paper in circulation than the country can absorb and employ? If it be admitted, and how can it be denied? that the price of commodities must everywhere rise or fall in proportion to the increase or diminution of the money which circulates them; must not an increase of London money increase the prices of commodities in London only, unless a part of that money can be employed in the country circulation? and, on the contrary, must not the same rise take place in the country prices only if the country currency be increased, and if it be not convertible into London currency; or cannot circulate in London? If the case put by Mr Bosanquet be supposed possible, that the London currency only should be increased, and that London bank notes were not current in the country, then we should have an exchange with the country in the same manner as we have with Hamburgh or France, and that exchange would show that London paper was, on a comparison with country paper, depreciated.

§ 41. If each of the country banks were protected by a restriction act from paying their notes in any other medium than their own paper, and if these notes were each confined to the circulation of their particular districts, they would each be depreciated on a comparison with bullion, in proportion as their amount exceeded the amount of money of bullion value which would have circulated in those districts if they had not been protected by such an act. The notes of one bank might be depreciated 5 per cent., of another 10, another 20, and so on. The restriction bill being confined to the Bank of England alone, and all other notes being convertible into their notes, country notes can never be issued in a greater proportion than those of the London Bank. Mr Bosanquet thinks, "I was bound to show that some physical impossibility obstructs the increase of bank notes at the expense of country notes, and *vice versa*, before I assume that an increase of bank notes must produce an increase of country notes."

From what I have already said, I think it will appear that, unless London notes are employed in the circulation of places where they were not before admitted, there is, if not a physical, at least an *absolute* impossibility, that an increase of Bank of England notes should not either be followed by an increase of country bank notes, or by a depreciation in the value of the London notes as compared with the country notes.

But how is this effected? How do the issues of the Bank produce an increase in the country circulation? Mr Gilchrist has informed us. Reverse the case which he has supposed, and it would stand thus:—If the Bank of England increase their issues, the country banks might increase theirs: the prices of commodities being raised in London, whilst those of the country continued as before, money would be wanted in the country to purchase in the cheaper market; bills would be demanded for that purpose upon the country, which would therefore sell at a premium, or, in other words, bank notes would be depreciated below the value of the country currency. Such demand would cease as soon as the country currency were either brought up to the level of the London currency, or the London currency reduced to the level of the country currency.

I should not have thought that a principle so clear could have been questioned: the value of our gold currency formerly regulated the value of a pound sterling all over England. If gold became abundant from the discovery of new mines, and more money were therefore employed in the circulation of London, a proportionate increase must necessarily have taken place in the country to preserve the equality of prices. Bank notes perform now the same office; and if they be increased, the country currency must either partake in the use of the additional quantity, or the country banks must make a proportional increase to their issues. It is not difficult, under such circumstances, to determine what will be the choice of the country banks.

The Committee having stated, that "If an excess of paper be issued in a country district, while the London circulation does not exceed its due proportion, there will be a local rise in prices in that country district, but prices in London will remain as before; that those who have the country paper will prefer buying in London, where things are cheaper, and will therefore return that country paper upon the banker who issued it, and will demand of him Bank of England notes, or bills upon London; and that thus the excess of country paper being returned upon the issuers for Bank of England paper, the quantity of the latter necessarily and effectually limits the quantity of the former."

Mr Bosanquet asks, "Does this follow as a consequence? Admitting the accuracy of the reasoning, under the supposition that the country notes were actually paid in bank notes, does it apply under the admission that they are paid by bills on London, since, as we have already shown, the payment of these has very little reference to bank notes?" Most certainly it does. Suppose the excess of country paper to be 1000*l.*, and in consequence 1000*l.* in Bank of England notes is demanded of the issuer, and sent up to London for the purchase of goods, will not 1000*l.* be added to the London circulation, whilst that of the country is diminished 1000*l.* Now, suppose that instead of a Bank of England note of 1000*l.* a bill on London is given to the holder of the country note, this will as sufficiently answer his purpose of making a purchase in London; but as a bill is only an order to A in London to pay to B in London, the London currency will remain as before, but the country currency will be reduced 1000*l.*

Now, the only difference in the two cases is this, that in the former 1000*l.* was added to the London circulation, in the latter it continued at the same amount. But will not the country banker, having by the payment of the 1000*l.* Bank of England note diminished that deposit, which he thinks it necessary for the safety of his establishment to have by him, give directions to his correspondent, either by the sale of an exchequer bill, or in any other way that might be agreed upon, to send him Bank of England notes to the amount of 1000*l.*?

"If things are cheaper in Liverpool than in London, I shall prefer buying there; and if I have too many bank notes, I shall send them to Liverpool in payment,"—provided they can circulate there. If they can, Liverpool will partake with London in the increase of circulation; but it is not improbable that a Liverpool banker will find an opportunity of persuading the people of Liverpool that his note will answer their purposes as well as the Bank of England note; * he will, therefore, possess himself of it for one of his own, and will send it to London, thus will the circulation of Liverpool be increased by the issues of the Bank of England; and thus Mr Bosanquet is mistaken, when he observes that "they may restrict, but can never augment, one shilling in the circulation of the Liverpool banks." The Committee having "assumed as an axiom, that country bank paper is a superstructure raised on the foundation of the paper of the Bank of England," Mr Bosanquet asks where they have learned this? "They learned from Mr Stuckey," he continues, "a considerable and experienced banker in Somersetshire, that his houses regulate their issues by the assets they have in London to pay them, consisting of stock, exchequer bills, and other convertible securities, without much reference to the quantity of Bank of England notes or specie which they have, although they always keep a quantity of both to pay occasional demands. What is there in this evidence to sanction the opinion, that bank notes either generate or limit country notes?"

It may, I think, be shown, that the increased issues of the Bank would induce Mr Stuckey, or any other country banker, to increase the amount of his issues, although he kept precisely the securities which he has enumerated. There would be such a demand for country notes, in consequence of the alteration of prices in London, that a country banker would be enabled to obtain bills upon London in return for his notes. With the produce of the bills he might possess himself of a larger sum of stock, exchequer bills, &c., the foundation being thus increased, the superstructure might be further raised.

The Committee could not have supposed that the

* The Committee asked Mr Stuckey, "Is it not your interest as a banker to check the circulation of Bank of England notes; and with that view do you not remit to London such Bank of England notes as you may receive beyond the amount which you may think it prudent to keep as a deposit in your coffers?" *Ans.* Unquestionably.

Scotch Bank in the year 1763, when they reduced their circulation by giving bills at 40 days upon London, actually deposited bank notes, in the first instance, in the hands of their London correspondents. They might, if such were the case, have redeemed their notes at once with bank notes in Scotland. No; the Scotch Bank were situated as Mr Stuckey describes; they had securities of some sort in London, which they authorised their correspondents to turn into money in time to pay their bills. There was a transfer of money from A to B in London, and the Scotch note was withdrawn.

CHAPTER VIII.

MR BOSANQUET'S OPINION—THAT YEARS OF SCARCITY AND TAXES HAVE BEEN THE SOLE CAUSE OF THE RISE OF PRICES, EXCESSIVE CIRCULATION NO CAUSE—CONSIDERED.

§ 42. Mr Bosanquet, after having shown, as he imagines, the insufficiency of the arguments of the Committee, to prove that the Bank circulation is excessive, brings forward positive arguments to prove that it is not. The ground of these arguments is, the cause of an advance of prices which arises from years of scarcity and increased taxation. He has quoted a passage from Dr Smith in support of this opinion, which I regard as in favour of the opinion which I hold on that subject.

"A prince," says Dr Smith, "who should enact that a certain proportion of his taxes should be paid in a paper money of any kind, might thereby give a certain value to this paper money, even though the time of its final discharge and redemption should depend altogether on the will of the prince. If the Bank which issued this paper were careful to keep the quantity of it always somewhat below what could easily be employed in this manner, the demand for it might be such as even to make it bear a premium, or sell for somewhat more in the market than the quantity of gold and silver for which it was issued."

Now, asks Mr. Bosanquet, as the annual amount of taxes far exceeds the amount of bank notes, how can paper according to this principle be depreciated? But where does Dr Smith talk of the annual amount of taxes? It might as fairly be contended that the comparison of the amount of paper should be made with the amount of two or three years' taxes. I understand Dr Smith to mean, that if the quantity of paper does not exceed that amount, which can be wholly and solely employed in the payment of taxes, it will not be depreciated; he never could have maintained so extravagant a proposition as that which Mr Bosanquet ascribes to him. To try our paper circulation by this rule of Dr Smith, it should be proved that the daily payment of taxes is equal in amount to the whole of the bank notes in circulation. According to Mr Bosanquet's interpretation of this passage, as the amount of the total payments into the exchequer is 76,805,440*l.*, bank notes cannot become excessive or depreciated till they exceed that amount. Who, on reading the passage, can believe that such was the fair meaning of Dr Smith's words?

When Mr Bosanquet talked of a premium having been given for bank notes, I conceived he meant a premium in gold or in silver; I can have no other idea of a premium: but it seems Mr Bosanquet meant that a premium was given for them in paper more depreciated than themselves; in exchequer bills or banker's checks. Now, both of these securities being payable in bank notes at some future period, may, on some occasions, be less valuable than the notes which are wanted for immediate use, and which will sufficiently account for the preference. An assignat at a discount of 50 per cent. might have borne such a premium as Mr Bosanquet supposes.

One of the proofs with which Mr Bosanquet has favoured his readers of the very small increase that has taken place in the actual amount of bank notes, compared with the business which it has to perform, is, that the increase in the amount of currency since the year 1793 is 3 millions, and the increased amount of payments to Government alone above 60 millions.

In this calculation the addition to the country currency is wholly omitted. I shall endeavour presently to show, that it does not by any means necessarily follow that this enormous increase in the amount of taxes should have made any increase of circulation necessary, unless during the same time there had been an increase of commerce and trade.

At present it will be sufficient for me to remark, that had Mr. Bosanquet made a comparative statement from the year 1793 to 1797, he would have possibly seen reason to doubt the accuracy of his *theory* on this subject. During those four years there must have been a considerable addition to the taxes; and, therefore, on Mr Bosanquet's principles, there should also have been an addition to the circulating medium, which does not appear to be the fact. It is not probable that any very great addition was made to the amount of the coin in circulation; on the contrary, from the very great coinage in 1797 and 1798, the metallic currency must, in 1797, have been at an unusually low level. And it appears from the account delivered in to the Lords' Committee, that the amount of bank notes in circulation

In the year 1793 amounted to	.	L.11,451,180
... 1796 it varied from	.	10,713,460
	to	9,204,500

and in 1797 the general average, even after the restriction, did not exceed the amount of 1793.

The amount of bank notes in circulation in 1803 was nearly 18 millions. In 1808 it was not more; and yet no one will deny that in those five years our taxes and expenses must have been greatly augmented. Thus, then, it appears that considerable additions may be made to the taxes of a country without a corresponding increase in its circulating medium.

The Committee is charged by Mr Bosanquet with not having sufficiently considered the effect of taxation on the prices of commodities; and it is implied in that accusation, that they have exclusively attributed the rise in the prices of commodities to the depreciation of the currency. The Committee would indeed have been highly deserving of censure, if they had held out hopes to the people of this country that the reformation of the currency could possibly reduce the prices of commodities to that level at which they were previously to the restriction bill. The effect produced on prices by the depreciation has been most accurately defined, and amounts to the difference between the market and the Mint price of gold. An ounce of gold coin cannot be of less value, the Committee say, than an ounce of gold bullion of the same standard; a purchaser of corn, therefore, is entitled to as much of that commodity for an ounce of gold coin, or 3*l*. 17s. 10½d., as can be obtained for an ounce of gold bullion. Now, as 4*l*. 12s. of paper currency is of no more value than an ounce of gold bullion, prices are actually raised to the purchaser 18 per cent., in consequence of his purchase being made with paper instead of coin of its bullion value. Eighteen per cent. is, therefore, equal to the rise in the price of commodities, occasioned by the depreciation of paper. All above such rise may be either traced to the effects of taxation, to the increased scarcity of the commodity, or to any other cause which may appear satisfactory to those who take pleasure in such inquiries.

The theory which Mr Bosanquet has advanced with respect to taxation, and the effects which it produces on the amount of circulating medium, is exceedingly curious, and is a proof that even practical men are sometimes tempted to wander from the sober paths of practice and experience, to indulge in speculations the most wild, and dreams the most chimerical.

§ 43. Mr Bosanquet observes, there are two causes of the augmentation of prices in Great Britain since the date of the restriction bill. 1st, "The altered state of the corn trade, and the scarcity arising out of it, in 1800 and 1801." 2dly, "The increase of taxes since the commencement of the war, in 1793."

That the scarcity of corn, and the expenses which have attended its importation, must have produced some rise in the prices of commodities, I do most readily admit. But is it a self-evident proposition—is it, as Mr Bosanquet lays it down, an axiom in political economy, that the effect of taxation is to raise the prices of commodities in the full amount of the taxes levied? Does it by any means follow, because taxes, since the year 1793, have increased to the enormous amount of 48 millions, that all that sum must have gone to the increase of the prices of commodities, and that, therefore, this fact alone will account for a rise of 50 per cent. on the prices of 1793? Does it follow that every person, excepting the stockholder, has the power of indemnifying himself for the taxes which he pays?

§ 44. Does it make no difference, for example, whether the tax be laid on consumable commodities, or whether it be such a tax as an income tax, assessed taxes, and twenty others that may be named? Do they all tend to raise the prices of commodities? And is every contributor but the stockholder enabled to rid himself of the burthen? If this argument were correct, it would appear that the whole weight of taxation falls exclusively on the stockholders; that the whole annual augmentation since 1793, amounting now to 53 millions, must have come from their pockets. Their taxes must at this rate have exceeded their income, because they exceeded the interest of the national debt. This I do not consider very correct doctrine; and, if true, it would not make stockholders very much enamoured with that species of property. Wars would, on such a principle, never impoverish, and the sources of taxation could never be exhausted.

To me, however, it appears convincingly certain that neither the income tax, the assessed taxes, nor many others, do in the least affect the prices of commodities.

Unfortunate, indeed, would be the situation of the consumer if he had to pay additional prices for those commodities which were necessary to his comfort, after his means of purchasing them had been by the tax considerably abridged.

The income tax, were it fairly imposed, would leave every member of the community in the same relative situation in which it found him. Each man's expenses must be diminished to the amount of his tax; and if the seller would wish to relieve himself from the burden of the tax by raising the price of his commodity, the buyer, for the same reason, would wish to buy cheaper. These contending interests would so exactly counteract each other, that prices would undergo no alteration. The same observations are applicable to the assessed taxes, and to all other taxes which are not levied on commodities. But, if the tax should in its operation be unequal,—if it should fall particularly heavy on one class of trade, the profits of that trade would be diminished below the general level of mercantile profits, and those engaged in it would either desert it for one more profitable, or they would raise the price of the commodities in which they dealt, so as to bring it to produce the same rate of profits as other trades.

Taxes on commodities would certainly raise the price of the commodity taxed to the full amount of the tax. The price for such commodities may be considered as divided into two portions; one portion, its original and natural price and the other a tax for the liberty of consuming it. If this tax, again, were laid on a commodity, the consumption of which, by each individual, was in exact proportion to his income, no other commodity would rise but the one taxed; but if it were not in such proportion, those who paid more than their just portion would demand an increased price for the commodity in which they dealt, and, by obtaining it, the society would be put in the same relative situation in which they were before placed.

If, instead of the tax being laid on the commodity each individual were to pay no more for the commodity than the original price, and were to pay the amount of the tax at once to Government for a license to consume it, it would act precisely as the assessed taxes do; there would be only a partial rise in the prices of some commodities to compensate the inequality which, in spite of the best wishes of the legislature, must accompany every tax.

If this view of the effect of taxation be correct, it will follow that Mr Bosanquet's estimate, that 48 millions has been actually added to the prices of commodities in consequence of taxation since the year 1793, and that such addition will sufficiently account for the rise in the prices of commodities, without having recourse to the depreciation of the circulating medium as the cause, is a false theory, neither supported by reason nor probability.

From these statements Mr Bosanquet has deduced another consequence, viz. that—

As the value of commodities has been raised 48 millions since 1793, and the circulation only increased 3 millions, such increase cannot be called excessive.*

§ 45. Although, in the preceding statement, I have conceded to Mr Bosanquet that, in consequence of some of our taxes, the prices of commodities will be increased, it does not appear necessarily to follow that more money will be requisite to circulate them.

That amount of money which is received by Government in the shape of taxes, is taken from a fund which would otherwise have been expended on consumable commodities.

In proportion as the taxes are great must the expenses of the people diminish. If my income amounts to 1000*l.*, and Government requires 100*l.* in taxes from me, I shall have but 900*l.* to expend on such necessaries and comforts as are requisite for the use of my family. If Government take 200*l.*, I shall have but 800*l.* for such purposes. Now, as the amount of money actually expended by Government and by me cannot exceed 1000*l.*, no additional circulating medium would, I think, be required, although the taxes were 50 per cent. of each man's income. If the tax were laid upon bread, and, in consequence, the wages of labour were raised, the tax would eventually fall on all those who consumed the produce of the labour of man. It would make no real difference to these consumers if they had at once paid the amount of such tax into the exchequer, or if it had gone through the circuitous channel which it would then take.

Nor would any additional sum be required. Government would be in daily receipt of a portion of the taxes, whether it was paid to the exciseman or to the tax-gatherer, and their expenses in the one case would be

* If we add to these 3 millions the increase in the country circulation, and bear in mind the economy in the use of circulating medium, so ably and so clearly explained by Mr Bosanquet, it would appear to me that, granting all the facts for which Mr Bosanquet contends, the circulating medium has increased in an undue proportion.

precisely the same as in the other. Whatever the Government expended would cause a diminished expenditure in the people to the same amount: the same amount of commodities would be circulated, and the same money would be adequate to their circulation.

This is on the supposition that the people were sufficiently prudent or sufficiently rich to pay all the taxes from their annual income, and were not tempted or compelled to diminish their capital to satisfy the calls of Government. If capital were, however, diminished, the aggregate amount of productions would also diminish; and if the money which was before necessary for their circulation were to continue of the same amount, it would bear a larger proportion to the goods, and it might therefore be expected that commodities would rise; but we must not forget that the amount of money in a country is regulated by its value, and as its value would in this case be diminished, it would become relatively excessive to the money of other countries, and the excess would therefore be exported.

When we talk of a scarcity of corn, and a consequent increase of price, it is naturally concluded, because its value is doubled, that double the value of money will be necessary to circulate it, but this is by no means obvious or necessary. If double the money be necessary, there should be an equal quantity of corn at double the usual price,—but it is because there is a diminished quantity of corn that its price is doubled.

If the commerce of a country increases, that is to say, if by its savings it is enabled to add to its capital, such country will require an additional amount of circulating medium; but, under all circumstances, the currency ought to retain its bullion value; that is the only sure test by which we may know that it is not excessive.

CHAPTER IX.

MR BOSANQUET'S OPINION, THAT EVIL WOULD RESULT FROM THE RESUMPTION OF CASH PAYMENTS, CONSIDERED.

§ 46. To conclude, Mr Bosanquet is persuaded that much evil will ensue from the resumption of cash payments, and he cannot anticipate any improvement in the course of exchange, or any fall in the price of bullion from a reduction of the circulation, unless our imports are diminished and our exports increased.

To me, however, it appears perfectly clear, that a reduction of bank notes would lower the price of bullion and improve the exchange, without in the least disturbing the regularity of our present exports and imports. It would neither enable us to export or import gold in any way different to what is now actually taking place. Our transactions with foreigners would be precisely the same, we should possess only a more valuable money of the same name; and instead of being credited by Hamburgh for a depreciated pound sterling, which will only purchase 104 grains of gold, at the rate of 28 Flemish schillings, we should, by restoring our pound sterling to its true bullion value, viz. 123 grains, have a credit at the rate of 34 schillings. The difference, however, of 6 schillings, which would thus appear in our favour, would be an advantage in name and appearance solely. No mistake would be greater than to suppose there was in it any real advantage.

If, by a reduction of bank notes, they were so raised in value as to be above the value of gold bullion, we should then interfere with the real course of exchange; we should disturb the present equilibrium of imports and exports; and we should cause an importation of bullion, or, in the language of merchants, a favourable balance of trade.

If Mr Bosanquet's view of our affairs were indeed correct, gloomy would be our prospects. Obliged to support a great foreign expenditure, "to import articles with which we cannot dispense," and in return for which nothing but gold will be accepted, we might almost calculate the period at which the contest must terminate from a want of this most essential commodity. For a balance of payments so enormous as he calculates gold could not be found in this country for one twelvemonth; and if our goods can nowhere purchase it, how hopeless must be our condition!

For my part, however, I have no such apprehensions. I am persuaded that our foreign expenditure is neither paid with gold nor with bill of exchange,—that it must eventually be discharged with the produce of the labour and industry of our people.

It is only to a blind perseverance in our present system of circulation that I look with alarm,—a system which is gradually undermining our resources, and the inconveniences and evils of which, in the language of the Committee, "if not checked, must at no great distance of time work a practical conviction upon the minds of all those who may still doubt their existence; but even if their progressive increase were less probable, the integrity and honour of Parliament are concerned not to authorise longer than is required by imperious necessity the continuance in this great commercial country of a system of circulation in which that natural check or control is absent, which maintains the value of money, and, by the permanency of that common standard of value, secures the substantial justice and faith of monied contracts and obligations between man and man."

May we be permitted to hope, that what an enlightened Committee has so happily begun is a pledge of what will be accomplished by the wisdom of Parliament?

APPENDIX

After the preceding sheets were sent to the press, I read the supplementary observations of Mr Bosanquet, annexed to the second edition of his pamphlet. I shall have but few remarks to make on them.

1st, From what I have already said, it may be seen that I deny the accuracy of all Mr Bosanquet's calculations concerning the exchange with Hamburgh. Those calculations are made on the assumption of a fixed invariable par, whilst the true par, on which they should have been made, is subject to all the variations to which the relative value of gold and silver is exposed. These two metals having varied no less since the year 1801 than from 6½ per cent., under the Mint proportions, to 9 per cent. above those proportions; calculations made on such a principle may involve errors to no less an amount than 15½ per cent. 2dly, The argument attempted to be founded on the fact of the increase or diminution in the amount of bank notes not having invariably been accompanied by a fall or rise in the exchange, or by a rise or fall in the price of bullion, is of no avail against a theory which admits that the demand for circulating medium is subject to continual fluctuations, proceeding from an increase or decrease in the amount of capital and commerce, from a greater or less facility which at one period may be afforded to payments by a varying degree of confidence and credit, and, in short, which supposes that the same commerce and payments may require very different amounts of circulating medium. An amount of bank notes, which at one time may be excessive, in the sense in which I use that term, and which may therefore be depreciated, may, at another, be barely sufficient for the payments which it may have to perform, barring the effect of a temporary increase in its value above that of the bullion which it represents. It will therefore be useless to admit or to deny the correctness of the grounds on which Mr Bosanquet's calculation of the amount of country paper in circulation is founded. Those facts do not, in my opinion, bear upon the subject in dispute. Whether the paper currency be 25 or 100 millions, I consider it equally certain that it is excessive, because I am not aware of any causes but excess, or a want of confidence in the issuers of the paper (which I am sure does not now exist), which could produce such effects as we have for a *considerable time** witnessed.

Mr Bosanquet has thrown the inferences which he wishes to be drawn from the facts he has newly brought forward into the shape of four problems; the solution of which, upon the principles of the Committee, he presumes to be impossible. I hope I have already shown that his facts fall abundantly short of proving the points which he makes to rest upon them, and I think the difficulty will not be great in giving him even a solution of his problems in perfect conformity with the principles of the Committee.

The first problem is, "The fall of the exchange, from an average of 6 per cent. in favour from 1790 to 1795, to 3 per cent. below par in 1795 and 1796, with an equal circulation of 11 millions of Bank paper, convertible into specie on demand, and the advance of the exchange to 11 per cent. above par, on average in 1797 and 1798, the circulation being increased to 13 millions, and not so convertible."

The reader will perceive that this problem has already received its solution in the body of the work. The exchanges are not correctly stated, and no one denies that the exchanges may rise and fall from many causes.

It has been proved that the demand for gold for the Mint, and for silver for the East Indies, in the years 1797 and 1798, had its natural effect on the exchange, and was not counteracted by an extravagant issue of paper currency. The gold was required to fill up the exhausted coffers of the Bank; it was therefore not sent into circulation; and the addition of 2 millions in bank notes served only to supply the vacuum which the hoarding of money had occasioned; so that there was no real increase to the circulation of those years.

The second problem is, "The fall of the exchange to 6 per cent. below par, and gold 9 per cent. above the Mint price in 1800 and 1801, the Bank circulation rather above 15 millions, and the advance to 3 per cent. above par, on average of six years, from 1803 to 1808, and gold nearly at the Mint price, with an augmented circulation of 17 to 18 millions."

Besides the effects from a varying degree of commerce and credit, it should be recollected that whilst our circulation consisted partly of gold and partly of paper, the effect of an increased issue of paper, both on the exchanges and the price of bullion, was corrected, after a sufficient interval, by the exportation of the coin. That resource has been for some time lost to us.

The third problem, viz. "The fall of the exchange, from 5 per cent. above par, in July 1808, to 10 per cent. below par, in June

* Mr Bosanquet has remarked as incorrect my having used the words "length of time" in reference to a discount on bank notes, because Mr Mushet's tables did not indicate a very unfavourable exchange for more than a year before I wrote, in December 1809. We should once have thought a year a *considerable time*, when speaking of a discount on bank notes; but as I have constantly maintained that the high price of bullion was the test on which I most relied for the proof of depreciation, and as the price of gold has not been under the Mint price for about ten years, the correctness of my conclusion cannot, I think, on my principles, be questioned.

1809, the Bank circulation being the same in both instances;" is of easy solution. I cannot find the document from which Mr Bosanquet has stated that the amount of bank notes was the same in July 1808 as in June 1809; but, admitting its correctness, are they fair subjects of comparison? One period is immediately after the payment of the dividends, the other immediately before. In January and July 1809 there was no less an increase in the amount of bank notes, after the payment of the dividends, than 2,450,000*l.*, and in the January following, 1,878,000*l.*

I am not disposed to contend that the issues of one day, or of one month, can produce any effect on the foreign exchanges; it may possibly require a period of more permanent duration; an interval is absolutely necessary before such effects would follow. This is never considered by those who oppose the principles of the Committee. They conclude that those principles are defective because their operation is not immediately perceived. But what are the facts respecting the circulation of bank notes in the years 1808 and 1809? There are only three returns of their amount in the year 1808 made to the Bullion Committee. Let us compare them with the returns for the same periods in 1809, and I think my readers will agree with me, that these facts will rather confirm than appear to be at variance with the principles of the Committee.

	Amount of bank notes In 1808.		Amount of bank notes In 1809.
1 May . .	17,491,900	1 May .	18,646,880
1 August .	17,644,670	1 August .	19,811,330
1 November.	17,467,170	1 November	19,949,290

As for the fourth problem, viz. " The gradually increasing price of commodities, during the American war, when the circulation was gold, and during the six years from 1803 to 1808, when the exchange was in favour," where has it been disputed that there are not other causes besides the depreciation of money which may account for a rise in the prices of commodities? The point for which I contend is, that when such rise is accompanied by a permanent rise in the price of that bullion which is the standard of currency, then to the amount of that rise is the currency depreciated. During the American war the rise in the prices of commodities was not attended with any rise in the price of bullion, and was therefore not occasioned by a depreciation of the currency.

We are now, for the first time, left to doubt whether the principles of the Committee, against which Mr Bosanquet in the body of his work had so strongly contended, are really at variance with his own. We are now told, not that the theory is erroneous, but " that the facts must be established before they can be reasoned upon;" " and that the importance of those facts would in no degree be lessened even by an unreserved admission of the accuracy of the principles assumed." Does this declaration accord with Mr Bosanquet's conclusions? Certain principles are brought forward by the Bullion Committee, and which, if true, prove the fact of the depreciation of the currency. Your principles are plausible, and reason appears to sanction them, says Mr Bosanquet; but here are facts to prove that they are inconsistent with past experience; and he further observes from Paley, "that when a theorem is proposed to a mathematician the first thing he does with it is to try it on a simple case; if it produce a false result, he is sure there must be some error in the demonstration." "The public must proceed in this way with the Report, and submit its theories to the test of fact." Can, then, Mr Bosanquet be consistent in contending "that the importance of what, in his preceding pages, he had offered to the public would be in no degree lessened even by an unreserved admission of the accuracy of the principles assumed?"

If the theory of the Committee is allowed to be accurate on the one hand, and Mr Bosanquet's facts are accurate on the other, what follows? Either that Mr Bosanquet agrees with the Committee, or that his facts are totally inapplicable to the question. One other conclusion there is, but one which I have no intention to ascribe to Mr Bosanquet,—that there may be a theory on the one side, and facts on the other; both true, and yet inconsistent.

As for Dr Paley's test of trying the Committee's theory by a simple case, Mr Bosanquet might have tried it by a thousand, and would have found it accurately to correspond. Had he employed his leisure and ingenuity in tracing its application to the thousands of cases with which it accords, instead of hunting for two or three cases *seemingly* contradictory, and adopting them with fond credulity, he would have probably arrived at more just conclusions.

Mr Bosanquet calls in question the accuracy of the following proposition of Mr Huskisson, "that if one part of the currency of a country (provided such currency be made either directly or virtually legal tender according to its denomination) be depreciated, the whole of that currency, whether paper or coin, *must* be equally depreciated."

The fact brought forward by Mr Bosanquet, that the "extraordinary depreciation of the silver coin in the reign of King William did not depreciate the gold; that, on the contrary, the guinea, worth 21 perfect shillings, passed currently for 30s.," does not prove the principle advanced by Mr Huskisson to be at variance with experience, because gold was not then the current coin; it was not, either *directly* or *virtually* legal tender; nor was it estimated at a fixed value by public authority: it passed in all payments as a piece of bullion of known weight and fineness. If by law it could not have passed for more than 21s. of the debased silver currency, it would, whilst in the state of coin, have been equally debased with the 21s. for which it would have exchanged. If guineas were now to be considered as a commodity and were not by law prohibited from being exported or melted, they might pass in all payments at 24s. or 25s., whilst the bank note continued of its present value.

Neither is the following principle of Mr Huskisson, from which Mr Bosanquet dissents, *contrary to authority*, " that if the quantity of gold, in a country whose currency consists of gold, should be increased in any given proportion, the quantity of other articles and the demand for them remaining the same, the value of any given commodity measured in the coin of that country would be increased in the same proportion." Mr Huskisson does not question, as Mr Bosanquet supposes, the truth of the principle advanced by Dr Adam Smith, " that the increase in the quantity of the precious metals, which arises in any country from an increase of wealth, has no tendency to diminish their value ; " but says, that if the quantity of the precious metals increases in any country whilst its wealth does not increase, or whilst its commodities remain the same in quantity, then will the value of the gold coin of such country diminish, or, in other words, goods will rise in price. Mr Bosanquet himself, in the argument relating to the mine, has admitted that such would be the effect. To this passage from Mr Huskisson's book, however, I have an objection to offer, because he adds, that an increase in the prices of commodities would take place (page 5) under the circumstances supposed, " although no addition should actually be made to the coin of the country." I hold it as a conclusion which will not admit of dispute, that if neither commodities, nor the demand for them, nor the money which circulates them, suffer either increase or diminution, prices must continue unaltered whatever quantity of gold or silver may exist in the state of bullion in such country.* It is hardly necessary to remark, that the case is wholly hypothetical, and is, indeed, impossible. There can be no great addition to the bullion of a country, the currency of which is of its standard value, without causing an increase in the quantity of money.

I confess I was not a little surprised by the next point brought forward by Mr Bosanquet, and I have no doubt it must have excited equal astonishment in many of his readers. Having contended throughout his work that bank notes were not depreciated as compared with gold coin, that the same rise in the price of gold might have taken place, and actually had, on some occasions, taken place, whilst our currency consisted partly of gold, and partly of paper convertible into gold, at the will of the holder ; after denying that there was any point of contact between gold for exportation and gold in coin, and that it was for want of such contact that its price had risen, we are now seriously told by Mr Bosanquet that, " applying to this subject the most approved theories, he inclines to the belief that gold, since the new system of the Bank of England payments has been fully established, has *not*, in truth, continued to be the measure of value. Bank notes," he maintains, " have, since 1797, unquestionably become the measure of commerce, and the money of account, and it is on these grounds that he considers the proposition respecting the

* It is to be understood that I am supposing no increased or diminished *confidence* operating so as to give a diminished or increased value to the coin.

price of gold, on which so much reliance is placed, as one of those which, though he admits the principle, he hesitates at the application." Whether the Bank Directors, or others who have so confidently asserted that, admitting gold to be the standard, its high price did not prove the depreciation of the currency, will be pleased with a defence on such principles, which yields all for which the Committee contend, it is not for me to inquire. That gold is no longer in practice the standard by which our currency is regulated is a truth. It is the ground of the complaint of the Committee (and of all who have written on the same side) against the present system.

The holder of money has been injured, inasmuch as there is no standard reference by which his property can be protected. He has suffered a loss of 16 per cent. since 1797, and there is no security for him that it may not shortly be 25, 30, or even 50 per cent. more. Who will consent to hold money or securities, the interest on which is payable in money, on such terms? There is no sacrifice which a man holding such property should not make, to secure to himself some provision for the future whilst such a system is avowed. Mr Bosanquet has, in these few words, said as much in favour of the repeal of the restriction bill as all the writers, all the theorists, have advanced since the discussion of this subject commenced. What, then, does Mr Bosanquet admit that we have no standard because it is no longer gold? Let us hear what he says: "If a pound note be the *denomination*, it will, of course, be asked what is the standard?

"The question is not easy of solution. But, considering the high proportion which the dealings between Government and the public bear to the general circulation, it is probable the standard may be found in those transactions; and it seems not more difficult to imagine that the standard value of a one pound note may be the interest of 33*l*. 6s. 8d.—3 per cent. stock, than that such standard has reference to a metal, of which none remains in circulation, and of which the annual supply, even as a commodity, does not amount to one-twentieth part of the foreign expenses of Government in one year."

So then we *have* a standard for a pound bank note; it is the interest of 33*l*. 6s. 8d.—3 per cent. stock. Now, in what medium is this interest paid? because *that* must be the standard. The holder of 33*l*. 6s. 8d. stock receives at the bank a one pound note. Bank notes are, therefore, according to the theory of a *practical man*, the standard by which alone the depreciation of bank notes can be estimated!

A puncheon of rum has 16 per cent. of its contents taken out and water poured in for it. What is the standard by which Mr Bosanquet attempts to detect the adulteration? A sample of the adulterated liquor taken out of the same cask.

We are next told, that "if the Bank really possess a large stock of gold, or only to the extent of 6 or 7 millions, the best use they can make of it is to call in all the notes under 5*l*., and not re-issue any of this description."

How could bankers and manufacturers be enabled to effect their small payments if the gold, thus partially issued, were at the present exchange and price of bullion to be either exported or melted ? If the Bank did not issue small notes, and they could not procure guineas for large ones, they would be obliged to cease such payments altogether. The more I have reflected on this subject, the more convinced I am that the evil admits of no other safe remedy but a reduction in the amount of bank notes.

PROPOSALS

FOR AN

ECONOMICAL AND SECURE CURRENCY

WITH

OBSERVATIONS

ON THE

PROFITS OF THE BANK OF ENGLAND

AS THEY REGARD THE PUBLIC AND THE PROPRIETORS OF BANK STOCK

SECOND EDITION

1816

INTRODUCTION

THE following important questions concerning the Bank of England will, next session, come under the discussion of Parliament :—

1st, Whether the Bank shall be obliged to pay their notes in specie at the demand of the holders ?

2dly, Whether any alteration shall be made in the terms agreed upon in 1808, between Government and the Bank, for the management of the national debt ?

And, 3dly, What compensation the public shall receive for the large amount of public deposits from which the Bank derive profit ?

In point of importance, the first of these questions greatly surpasses the rest ; but so much has already been written on the subject of currency, and on the laws by which it should be regulated, that I should not trouble the reader with any further observations on those topics, did I not think that a more economical mode of effecting our payments might be advantageously adopted ; to explain which, it will be necessary to premise briefly some of the general principles which are found to constitute the laws of currency, and to vindicate them from some of the objections which are brought against them.

The other two questions, though inferior in importance, are, at these times of pressure on our finances, when economy is so essential, well deserving of the serious consideration of Parliament. If, on examination, it should be found that the services performed by the Bank for the public are most prodigally paid, and that this wealthy corporation has been accumulating a treasure of which no example can be brought—much of it at the expense of the public, and owing to the negligence and forbearance of Government—a better arrangement, it is hoped, will now be made; which, while it secures to the Bank a just compensation for the responsibility and trouble which the management of the public business may occasion, shall also guard against any wasteful application of the public resources.

It must, I think, be allowed, that the war, which has pressed heavily on most of the classes of the community, has been attended with unlooked-for benefits to the Bank; and that in proportion to the increase of the public burdens and difficulties have been the gains of that body.

The restriction on the cash payments of the Bank, which was the effect of the war, has enabled them to raise the amount of their notes in circulation from 12 millions to 28 millions; whilst, at the same time, it has exonerated them from all necessity of keeping any large deposit of cash and bullion, a part of their assets from which they derive no profit.

The war, too, has raised the unredeemed public debt, of which the Bank have the management, from 220 to 830 millions; and, notwithstanding the reduced rate of charge, they will receive for the management of the debt alone, in the present year, 277,000*l.*, whereas, in 1792, their whole receipt on account of the debt was 99,800*l.*

It is to the war that the Bank are also indebted for the increase in the amount of public deposits. In 1792 these deposits were probably less than 4 millions. In and since 1806 we know that they have generally exceeded 11 millions.

It cannot, I think, be doubted, that all the services which the Bank perform for the public could be performed by public servants, and in public offices established for that purpose, at a reduction or saving of expense of nearly half a million per annum.

In 1786 the auditors of public accounts stated it as their opinion, that the public debt, then amounting to 224 millions, could be managed by Government for less than 187*l.* 10s. per million. On a debt of 830 millions the Bank are paid 340*l.* per million on 600 millions, and 300*l.* per million on 230 millions.

Against the mode in which the public business is managed at the Bank no complaint can be justly made; ability, regularity, and precision, are to be found in every office; and in these particulars it is not probable that any change could be made which would be deemed an improvement.

As far as the public are bound to the Bank by any existing agreement, an objection on that score will be urged against any alteration. Inadequate as, in my opinion, was at that time, and under the circumstances in which it was granted, the compensation which the public received from the Bank, for the renewal of their charter, I shall not plead for a revision of that contract, but permit the Bank to enjoy, unmolested, all the fruits of so improvident and unequal a bargain.

But the agreement entered into with the Bank in 1808, for the management of the national debt, is not, I think, of the above description, and either party is now at liberty to annul it. The agreement was for no definite period; and has no necessary connexion with the duration of the charter, which was made eight years before it. Applying to the state of things existing at the time of its formation, or such a state as might be expected to occur within a few years, it is not any longer binding. This is declared in the following passage of Mr Perceval's letter to the Bank, dated the 15th January 1808, on accepting the scale in respect to the rate for management proposed by the Bank. "Under this impression," says Mr Perceval, "I am strongly inclined to give way to the suggestion of the Bank in the minor parts of the arrangement, and will therefore accede to the scale of allowances therein proposed for the management of the public debt, *so far as it applies to present circumstances, or to such as can be expected to occur within any short period.*" Eight years having since elapsed, and the unredeemed debt having, in that time, increased 280 millions, can it be justly contended that it is not in the power of either party, now or hereafter, to annul this agreement, or to propose such alterations in it as time and circumstances may render expedient?

To Mr Grenfell[1] I am very materially indebted; I have done little more on this part of the subject, than repeat his arguments and statements. I have endeavoured to give my feeble aid to a cause which he has already so ably advocated in parliament, and in which I trust success will crown his future efforts.

1 [Ricardo refers to Mr Pascoe Grenfell, who raised the matter in the House of Commons.]

PROPOSALS

FOR AN

ECONOMICAL AND SECURE CURRENCY.

SECTION I.

In the Medium of Circulation—Cause of Uniformity is Cause of Goodness.

§ 1. All writers on the subject of money have agreed that uniformity in the value of the circulating medium is an object greatly to be desired. Every improvement, therefore, which can promote an approximation to that object, by diminishing the causes of variation, should be adopted. No plan can possibly be devised which will maintain money at an absolutely uniform value, because it will always be subject to those variations to which the commodity itself is subject, which has been fixed upon as the standard.

While the precious metals continue to be the standard of our currency, money must necessarily undergo the same variations in value as those metals. It was the comparative steadiness in the value of the precious metals, for periods of some duration, which probably was the cause of the preference given to them in all countries, as a standard by which to measure the value of other things.

A currency may be considered as perfect, of which the standard is invariable, which always conforms to that standard, and in the use of which the utmost economy is practised.[1]

Amongst the advantages of a paper over a metallic circulation, may be reckoned, as not the least, the facility with which it may be altered in quantity, as the wants of commerce and temporary circumstances may require: enabling the desirable object of keeping money at a uniform value to be, as far as it is otherwise practicable, securely and cheaply attained.

§ 2. The quantity of metal, employed as money, in effecting the payments of any particular country, using metallic money; or the quantity of metal for which paper money is the substitute, if paper money be partly or wholly used, must depend on three things: first, on its value;—secondly, on the amount or value of the payments to be made;—and, thirdly, on the degree of economy practised in effecting those payments.

§ 3. A country using gold as its standard would require, at least, fifteen times less of that metal than it would of silver, if using silver, and nine hundred times less than it would of copper, if using that metal,—fifteen to one being about the proportion which gold bears in value to silver, and nine hundred to one the proportion which it bears to copper. If the denomination of a pound were given to any specific weight of these metals, fifteen times more of such pounds would be required in the one case, and nine hundred times more in the other, whether the metals themselves were employed as money, or paper was partly, or entirely, substituted for them. And if a country uniformly employed the same metal as a standard, the quantity of money required would be in an inverse proportion to the value of that metal. Suppose the metal to be silver, and that, from the difficulty of working the mines, silver should be doubled in value, —half the quantity only would then be wanted for money; and if the whole business of circulation were

[1] [This only takes into account the position of money as a measure of value. We must, of course, possess the qualifications required to make it a convenient medium of exchange. This was not ignored by Ricardo; but it was not pertinent to the matter immediately under review in this paragraph.]

carried on by paper, of which the standard was silver,—to sustain that paper, at its bullion value, it must in like manner be reduced one half. In the same way it might be shown, that, if silver became as cheap again, compared with all other commodities, double the quantity would be required to circulate the same quantity of goods.

§ 4. When the number of transactions increase in any country from its increasing opulence and industry—bullion remaining at the same value, and the economy in the use of money also continuing unaltered—the value of money will rise on account of the increased use which will be made of it, and will continue permanently above the value of bullion, unless the quantity be increased, either by the addition of paper, or by procuring bullion to be coined into money. There will be more commodities bought and sold, but at lower prices; so that the same money will still be adequate to the increased number of transactions, by passing in each transaction at a higher value. The value of money, then, does not wholly depend upon its absolute quantity, but on its quantity relatively to the payments which it has to accomplish; and the same effects would follow from either of two causes—from increasing the uses for money one tenth—or from diminishing its quantity one tenth; for, in either case, its value would rise one tenth.

It is the rise in the value of money above the value of bullion which is always, in a sound state of the currency, the cause of its increase in quantity; for it is at these times that either an opening is made for the issue of more paper money, which is always attended with profit to the issuers; or that a profit is made by carrying bullion to the Mint to be coined.

To say that money is more valuable than bullion or the standard, is to say that bullion is selling in the market under the Mint price. It can therefore be purchased, coined, and issued as money, with a profit equal to the difference between the market and Mint prices. The Mint price of gold is 3*l.* 17s. 10½d. If, from increasing opulence, more commodities came to be bought and sold, the first effect would be that the value of money would rise. Instead of 3*l*. 17s. 10½d. of coined money being equal in value to an ounce of gold, 3*l*. 15s. might be equal to that value; and therefore a profit of 2s. 10½d. might be made on every ounce of gold that was carried to the Mint to be coined. This profit, however, could not long continue; for the quantity of money which, by these means, would be added to the circulation, would sink its value, whilst the diminishing quantity of bullion in the market would also tend to raise the value of bullion to that of coin: from one or both these causes a perfect equality in their value could not fail to be soon restored.

It appears, then, that, if the increase in the circulation were supplied by means of coin, the value both of bullion and money would, for a time at least, even after they had found their level, be higher than before; a circumstance which, though often unavoidable, is inconvenient, as it affects all former contracts. This inconvenience is wholly got rid of, by the issue of paper money; for, in that case, there will be no additional demand for bullion; consequently its value will continue unaltered; and the new paper money, as well as the old, will conform to that value.

Besides, then, all the other advantages attending the use of paper money; by the judicious management of the quantity, a degree of uniformity, which is by no other means attainable, is secured to the value of the circulating medium in which all payments are made.

§ 5. The value of money and the amount of payments remaining the same, the quantity of money required must depend on the degree of economy practised in the use of it. If no payments were made by cheques on bankers, by means of which money is merely written off one account and added to another, and that to the amount of millions daily, with few or no bank notes or coin passing; it is obvious that considerably more currency would be required, or, which is the same in its effects, the same money would pass at a greatly increased value, and would, therefore, be adequate to the additional amount of payments.

Whenever merchants, then, have a want of confidence in each other, which disinclines them to deal on credit, or to accept in payment each other's cheques, notes, or bills: more money, whether it be paper or metallic money, is in demand; and the advantage of a paper circulation, when established on correct principles, is, that this additional quantity can be presently supplied without occasioning any variation in the value of the whole currency, either as compared with bullion or with any other commodity; whereas, with a system of metallic currency, this additional quantity cannot be so readily supplied, and when it is finally supplied, the whole of the currency, as well as bullion, has acquired an increased value.

SECTION II.

Use of a Standard Commodity—Objections to it considered.

§ 6. During the late discussions on the bullion question, it was most justly contended, that a currency, to be perfect, should be absolutely invariable in value.

But it was said, too, that ours had become such a currency, by the Bank restriction bill; for by that bill we had wisely discarded gold and silver as the standard of our money; and, in fact, that a pound note did not and ought not to vary with a given quantity of gold, more than with a given quantity of any other commodity. This idea of a currency without a specific standard [1] was, I believe, first advanced by Sir James Steuart,* but no one has yet been able to offer any test by which we could ascertain the uniformity in the value of a money so

* The writings of Sir James Steuart on the subject of coin and money are full of instruction, and it appears surprising that he could have adopted the above opinion, which is so directly at variance with the general principles he endeavoured to establish.

[1] [This subject is discussed by Sir James Steuart, *An Inquiry into the Principles of Political Economy*, Book III., Chapter I., &c. He carefully distinguishes between such money and material or artificial money, indicating their difference in principle. As to this latter, *i.e.*, gold and silver in most cases, he says, " I have shown the utter impossibility of their being a scale, or an invariable measure of value," Book III., Part II., Chapter I.]

constituted. Those who supported this opinion did not see, that such a currency, instead of being invariable, was subject to the greatest variations,—that the only use of a standard is to regulate the quantity, and by the quantity the value of the currency—and that without a standard it would be exposed to all the fluctuations to which the ignorance or the interests of the issuers might subject it.

§ 7. It has indeed been said that we might judge of its value by its relation, not to one, but to the mass of commodities. If it should be conceded, which it cannot be, that the issuers of paper money would be willing to regulate the amount of their circulation by such a test, they would have no means of so doing; for when we consider that commodities are continually varying in value, as compared with each other, and that when such variation takes place, it is impossible to ascertain which commodity has increased, which diminished in value, it must be allowed that such a test would be of no use whatever.

Some commodities are rising in value, from the effects of taxation, from the scarcity of the raw material of which they are made, or from any other cause which increases the difficulty of production. Others again are falling, from improvements in machinery, from the better division of labour, and the improved skill of the workman; from the greater abundance of the raw material, and generally from greater facility of production. To determine the value of a currency by the test proposed, it would be necessary to compare it successively with the thousands of commodities which are circulating in the community, allowing to each all the effects which may have been produced upon its value by the above causes. To do this is evidently impossible.

To suppose that such a test would be of use in practice, arises from a misconception of the difference between price and value.

The price of a commodity is its exchangeable value in money only.

The value of a commodity is estimated by the quantity of other things generally for which it will exchange.

The price of a commodity may rise while its value falls, and *vice versâ.* A hat may rise from twenty to thirty shillings in price, but thirty shillings may not procure so much tea, sugar, coffee, and all other things, as twenty shillings did before, consequently a hat cannot procure so much. The hat, then, has fallen in value, though it has increased in price.

Nothing is so easy to ascertain as a variation of price, nothing so difficult as a variation of value; indeed, without an invariable measure of value, and none such exists, it is impossible to ascertain it with any certainty or precision.

A hat may exchange for less of tea, sugar, and coffee, than before, but, at the same time, it may exchange for more of hardware, shoes, stockings, &c., and the difference of the comparative value of these commodities may either arise from a stationary value of one, and a rise, though in different degrees, of the other two; or a stationary value in one, and a fall in the value of the other two; or they may have all varied at the same time.

If we say that value should be measured by the enjoyments which the exchange of the commodity can procure for its owner, we are still as much at a loss as ever to estimate value, because two persons may derive very different degrees of enjoyment from the possession of the same commodity. In the above instance, a hat would appear to have fallen in value to him whose enjoyments consisted in tea, coffee, and sugar; while it would appear to have risen in value to him who preferred shoes, stockings, and hardware.

Commodities generally, then, can never become a standard to regulate the quantity and value of money; and although some inconveniences attend the standard which we have adopted, namely, gold and silver, from the variations to which they are subject as commodities, these are trivial, indeed, compared to those which we should have to bear if we adopted the plan recommended.

When gold, silver, and almost all other commodities were raised in price, during the last twenty years, instead of ascribing any part of this rise to the fall of the paper currency, the supporters of an abstract currency had always some good reason at hand for the alteration in price. Gold and silver rose because they were scarce, and were in great demand to pay the immense armies which were then embodied. All other commodities rose because they were taxed either directly or indirectly, or because, from a succession of bad seasons, and the difficulties of importation, corn had risen considerably in value, which, according to their theory, must necessarily raise the price of commodities. According to them, the only things which were unalterable in value were bank notes, which were therefore eminently well calculated to measure the value of all other things.

If the rise had been 100 per cent., it might equally have been denied that the currency had anything to do with it, and it might equally have been ascribed to the same causes. The argument is certainly a safe one, because it cannot be disproved. When two commodities vary in relative value, it is impossible with certainty to say whether the one rises or the other falls; so that, if we adopted a currency without a standard, there is no degree of depreciation to which it might not be carried. The depreciation could not admit of proof, as it might always be affirmed that commodities had risen in value, and that money had not fallen.

SECTION III.

The Standard, its Imperfections—Variations below without Allowance of the countervailing variations above the Standard, their Effects—Correspondence with the Standard the Rule for Paper Money.

§ 8. While a standard is used, we are subject to only such a variation in the value of money as the *standard* itself is subject to; but against such variation there is no possible remedy, and late events have proved that, during periods of war, when gold and silver are used for the payment of large armies distant from home, those variations are much more considerable than has been generally allowed. This admission only proves that gold and silver are not so good a standard as they have been hitherto supposed,—that they are themselves subject to greater variations than it is desirable a standard should be subject to. They are, however, the best with which we are acquainted. If any other commodity less variable could be found, it might very properly be adopted as the future standard of our money, provided it had all the other qualities which fitted it for that purpose; but, while these metals are the standard, the currency should conform in value to them, and whenever it does not, and the market price of bullion is above the Mint price, the currency is depreciated. This proposition is unanswered, and is unanswerable.

§ 9. Much inconvenience arises from using two metals as the standard of our money; and it has long been a disputed point whether gold or silver should by law be made the principal or sole standard of money. In favour of gold it may be said, that its greater value under a smaller bulk eminently qualifies it for the standard in an opulent country; but this very quality subjects it to greater variations of value during periods of war or extensive commercial discredit, when it is often collected and hoarded, and may be urged as an argument against its use. The only objection to the use of silver as the standard is its bulk, which renders it unfit for the large payments required in a wealthy country; but this objection is entirely removed by the substituting of paper money as the general circulation medium of the country. Silver, too, is much more steady in its value, in consequence of its demand and supply being more regular; and as all foreign countries regulate the value of their money by the value of silver, there can be no doubt that, on the whole, silver is preferable to gold as a standard, and should be permanently adopted for that purpose.

§ 10. A better system of currency may, perhaps, be *imagined* than that which existed before the late laws made bank notes a legal tender; but while the law recognised a standard, while the Mint was open to any person who chose to take thither gold and silver to be coined into money, there was no other limit to the fall in the value of money than to the fall in the value of the precious metals. If gold had become as plentiful and as cheap as copper, bank notes would necessarily have partaken of the same depreciation, and all persons, the whole of whose possessions consisted of money—such as those who hold exchequer bills, who discount merchants' bills, or whose income is derived from annuities, as the holders of the public funds, mortgagees, and many others —would have borne all the evils of such a depreciation. With what justice, then, can it be maintained, that when gold and silver rise, money should be kept by force and by legislative interference at its former value, while no means are, or ever have been, used to prevent the fall of money when gold and silver fall? If the person possessed of money is subject to all the inconveniences of a fall in the value of his property, he ought also to have the benefits of the rise. If a paper currency without a standard be an improvement, let it be proved to be so, and then let the standard be disused; but do not preserve it to the disadvantage solely, never to the advantage, of a class of persons possessed of one out of the thousands of commodities which are circulating in the community, of which no other is subject to any such rule.

The issuers of paper money should regulate their issues solely by the price of bullion, and never by the quantity of their paper in circulation. The quantity can never be too great nor too little while it preserves the same value as the standard. Money, indeed, should be rather *more* valuable than bullion, to compensate for the trifling delay which takes place before it is returned in exchange for bullion at the Mint. This delay is equivalent to a small seignorage; and coined money, or bank notes, which represent coined money, should in their natural and perfect state, be just so much more valuable than bullion. The Bank of England, by not having paid a due regard to this principle, have in former times been considerable losers. They supplied the country with all the coined money for which it had occasion, and, consequently, purchased bullion with their paper that they might carry it to the Mint to be coined. If their paper had been sustained by limiting its quantity at a value somewhat greater than bullion, they would, in the cheapness of their purchases, have covered all the expenses of brokerage and refining, including the just equivalent for the delay at the Mint.

SECTION IV.

An expedient to bring the English currency as near as possible to perfection.

§ 11. In the next session of Parliament, the subject of currency is again to be discussed; and, probably, a time will then be fixed for the resumption of cash payments, which will oblige the Bank to limit the quantity of their paper till it conforms to the value of bullion.

A well regulated paper currency is so great an improvement in commerce, that I should greatly regret if prejudice should induce us to return to a system of less utility. The introduction of the precious metals for the purposes of money may with truth be considered as one of the most important steps towards the improvement of commerce and the arts of civilized life; but it is no less true, that, with the advancement of knowledge and science, we discover that it would be another improvement to banish them again from the employment to which, during a less enlightened period, they had been so advantageously applied.

If the Bank should be again called upon to pay their notes in specie, the effect would be to lessen greatly the profits of the Bank without a correspondent gain to any other part of the community. If those who use one and two, and even five pound notes, should have their option of using guineas, there can be little doubt which they would prefer; and thus, to indulge a mere caprice, a most expensive medium would be substituted for one of little value.

Besides the loss to the Bank, which must be considered as a loss to the community, general wealth being made up of individual riches, the state would be subjected to the useless expense of coinage, and, on every fall of the exchange, guineas would be melted and exported.

§ 12. To secure the public against any other variations in the value of the currency than those to which the standard itself is subject, and, at the same time, to carry on the circulation with a medium the least expensive, is to attain the most perfect state to which a currency can be brought, and we should possess all these advantages by subjecting the Bank to the delivery of uncoined gold or silver at the Mint standard and price, in exchange for their notes, instead of the delivery of guineas; by which means paper would never fall below the value of bullion without being followed by a reduction of its quantity. To prevent the rise of paper above the value of bullion, the Bank should be also obliged to give their paper in exchange for standard gold at the price of 3*l.* 17s. per ounce. Not to give too much trouble to the Bank, the quantity of gold to be demanded in exchange for paper at the Mint price of 3*l.* 17s. 10½d., or the quantity to be sold to the Bank at 3*l.* 17s., should never be less than twenty ounces. In other words, the Bank should be obliged to purchase any quantity of gold that was offered them, not less than twenty ounces, at 3*l.* 17s.* per ounce, and to sell any quantity that might be demanded at 3*l.* 17s. 10½d. While they have the power of regulating the quantity of their paper, there is no possible inconvenience that could result to them from such a regulation.

The most perfect liberty should be given, at the same time, to export or import every description of bullion. These transactions in bullion would be very few in number, if the Bank regulated their loans and issues of

* The price of 3*l.* 17s. here mentioned, is, of course, an arbitrary price. There might be good reason, perhaps, for fixing it either a little above, or a little below. In naming 3*l.* 17s., I wish only to elucidate the principle. The price ought to be so fixed as to make it the interest of the seller of gold rather to sell it to the Bank than to carry it to the Mint to be coined.

The same remark applies to the specified quantity of twenty ounces. There might be good reason for making it ten or thirty.

paper by the criterion which I have so often mentioned, namely, the price of standard bullion, without attending to the absolute quantity of paper in circulation.*

The object which I have in view would be in a great measure attained, if the Bank were obliged to deliver uncoined bullion in exchange for their notes at the Mint price and standard; though they were not under the necessity of purchasing any quantity of bullion offered them at the prices to be fixed, particularly if the Mint were to continue open to the public for the coinage of money: for that regulation is merely suggested to prevent the value of money from varying from the value of bullion more than the trifling difference between the prices at which the Bank should buy and sell, and which would be an approximation to that uniformity in its value which is acknowledged to be so desirable.

If the Bank capriciously limited the quantity of their paper, they would raise its value; and gold might appear to fall below the limits at which I propose the Bank should purchase. Gold, in that case, might be carried to the Mint, and the money returned from thence being added to the circulation, would have the effect of lowering its value, and making it again conform to the standard; but it would neither be done so safely, so economically, nor so expeditiously, as by the means which I have proposed; against which the Bank can have no objection to offer, as it is for their interest to furnish the circulation with paper, rather than oblige others to furnish it with coin.

§ 13. Under such a system, and with a currency so regulated, the Bank would never be liable to any embarrassments whatever, excepting on those extraordinary

* I have already observed that silver appears to me to be best adapted for the standard of our money. If it were made so by law, the Bank should be obliged to buy or sell silver bullion only. If gold be exclusively the standard, the Bank should be required to buy or sell gold only; but if both metals be retained as the standard, as they now by law are, the Bank should have the option which of the two metals they would give in exchange for their notes, and a price should be fixed for silver rather under the standard, at which they should not be at liberty to refuse to purchase.

occasions, when a general panic seizes the country, and when every one is desirous of possessing the precious metals as the most convenient mode of realizing or concealing his property. Against such panics, Banks have no security, *on any system*; from their very nature they are subject to them, as at no time can there be in a Bank, or in a country, so much specie or bullion as the monied individuals of such country have a right to demand. Should every man withdraw his balance from his banker on the same day, many times the quantity of bank notes now in circulation would be insufficient to answer such a demand. A panic of this kind was the cause of the crisis in 1797; and not, as has been supposed, the large advances which the Bank had then made to Government.[1] Neither the Bank nor Government were at that time to blame; it was the contagion of the unfounded fears of the timid part of the community, which occasioned the run on the Bank, and it would equally have taken place if they had not made any advances to Government, and had possessed twice their present capital. If the Bank had continued paying in cash, probably the panic would have subsided before their coin had been exhausted.

With the known opinion of the Bank Directors as to the rule for issuing paper money, they may be said to have exercised their powers without any great indiscretion. It is evident that they have followed their own principle with extreme caution. In the present state of the law, they have the power, without any control whatever, of increasing or reducing the circulation in any degree they may think proper; a power which should neither be intrusted to the State itself nor to any body in it, as there can be no security for the uniformity in the value of the currency when its augmentation or diminution depends solely on the will of the issuers. That the Bank have the power of reducing the circulation to the very narrowest limits will not be denied, even by those who agree in opinion with the Directors, that they

[1] [As to this see notes to *High Price of Bullion*, § 25. The question was discussed in the evidence given before the Secret Committee of 1797.]

have not the power of adding indefinitely to its quantity. Though I am fully assured that it is both against the interest and the wish of the Bank to exercise this power to the detriment of the public, yet when I contemplate the evil consequences which might ensue from a sudden and great reduction of the circulation, as well as from a great addition to it, I cannot but deprecate the facility with which the State has armed the Bank with so formidable a prerogative.

§ 14. The inconvenience to which country banks were subjected before the restriction on cash payments, must at times have been very great. At all periods of alarm, or of expected alarm, they must have been under the necessity of providing themselves with guineas, that they might be prepared for every exigency which might occur. Guineas on these occasions were obtained at the Bank in exchange for the larger notes, and were conveyed by some confidential agent, at expense and risk, to the country bank. After performing the offices to which they were destined, they found their way again to London, and in all probability were again lodged in the Bank, provided they had not suffered such a loss of weight as to reduce them below the legal standard.

If the plan now proposed, of paying bank notes in bullion, be adopted, it would be necessary either to extend the same privilege to country banks, or to make bank notes a legal tender, in which latter case there would be no alteration in the law respecting country banks, as they would be required, precisely as they now are, to pay their notes when demanded in Bank of England notes.

The saving which would take place from not submitting the guineas to the loss of weight from the friction which they must undergo in their repeated journeys, as well as of the expenses of conveyance, would be considerable; but by far the greatest advantage would result from the permanent supply of the country, as well as of the London circulation, as far as the smaller payments are concerned, being provided in the very cheap medium, paper, instead of the very valuable medium, gold, thereby enabling the country to derive all the profit which may be obtained by the productive employment of a capital to that amount. We should surely not be justified in rejecting so decided a benefit, unless some specific inconvenience could be pointed out as likely to follow from adopting the cheaper medium.

§ 15. Much has been ably written on the benefits resulting to a country from the liberty of trade, leaving every man to employ his talents and capital as to him may seem best, unshackled by restrictions of every kind. The reasoning by which the liberty of trade is supported is so powerful, that it is daily obtaining converts. It is with pleasure that I see the progress which this great principle is making amongst those whom we should have expected to cling the longest to old prejudices. In the petitions to Parliament against the corn bill, the advantages of an unrestricted trade were generally recognised, but by none more ably than by the clothiers of Gloucestershire, who were so convinced of the impolicy of restriction, that they expressed a willingness to relinquish every restraint which might be found to attach to their trade. These are principles which cannot be too widely extended, nor too generally adopted in practice; but if foreign nations are not sufficiently enlightened to adopt this liberal system, and should continue their prohibitions and excessive duties on the importation of our commodities and manufactures, let England set them a good example by benefiting herself; and instead of meeting their prohibitions by similar exclusions, let her get rid as soon as she can of every vestige of so absurd and hurtful a policy.

The pecuniary advantage which would be the result of such a system would soon incline other states to adopt the same course, and no long period would elapse before the general prosperity would be seen to be best promoted by each country falling naturally into the most advantageous employment of its capital, talents, and industry.

Advantageous, however, as the liberty of trade would prove, it must be admitted that there are a few, and a very few exceptions to it, where the interference of Government may be beneficially exerted. Monsieur Say, in his able work on Political Economy, after showing the advantages of a free trade, observes,* that the interference of Government is justifiable only in two cases; first, to prevent a fraud, and secondly, to certify a fact. In the examinations to which medical practitioners are obliged to submit, there is no improper interference; for it is necessary to the welfare of the people, that the fact of their having acquired a certain portion of knowledge respecting the diseases of the human frame should be ascertained and certified. The same may be said of the stamp which Government puts on plate and money; it thereby prevents fraud, and saves the necessity of having recourse on each purchase and sale to a difficult chemical process. In examining the purity of drugs sold by chemists and apothecaries, the same object is had in view. In all these cases, the purchasers are not supposed to have, or to be able to acquire, sufficient knowledge to guard them against deception; and Government interferes to do that for them which they could not do for themselves.

§ 16. But if the public require protection against the inferior money which might be imposed upon them by an undue mixture of alloy, and which is obtained by means of the Government stamp when metallic money is used; how much more necessary is such protection when paper-money forms the whole, or almost the whole, of the circulating medium of the country? Is it not inconsistent, that Government should use its power to protect the community from the loss of one shilling in a guinea, but does not interfere to protect them from the loss of the whole twenty shillings in a one-pound note? In the case of Bank of England notes, a guarantee is taken by the Government for the notes which the Bank issue; and the whole capital of the Bank, amounting to more than 11½ millions, must be lost before the holders of their notes can be sufferers from any imprudence they may commit. Why is not the same principle followed with respect to the country banks? What objection can there be against requiring of those who take upon themselves the office of furnishing the public with a circulating medium, to deposit with Government an

* Economie Politique, livre i. chap. 17.

adequate security for the due performance of their engagements? In the use of money, every one is a trader; those whose habits and pursuits are little suited to explore the mechanism of trade are obliged to make use of money, and are no way qualified to ascertain the solidity of the different banks whose paper is in circulation; accordingly, we find that men living on limited incomes, women, labourers, and mechanics of all descriptions, are often severe sufferers by the failures of country banks, which have lately become frequent beyond all former example. Though I am by no means disposed to judge uncharitably of those who have occasioned so much ruin and distress to the middle and lower classes of the people, yet, it must be allowed by the most indulgent, that the true business of banking must be very much abused before it can be necessary for any bank, possessing the most moderate funds, to fail in their engagements; and I believe it will be found, in by far the major part of these failures, that the parties can be charged with offences much more grave than those of mere imprudence and want of caution.

Against this inconvenience the public should be protected, by requiring of every country bank to deposit with Government, or with commissioners appointed for that purpose, funded property or other Government security, in some proportion to the amount of their issues.

Into the details of such a plan it is not necessary to enter very minutely. Stamps for the issue of notes might be delivered on the required deposit being made, and certain periods in the year might be fixed upon, when the whole or any part of the security should be returned, on proof being given, either by the return of the cancelled stamps, or by any other satisfactory means, that the notes for which it was given were no longer in circulation.

Against such a regulation no country bank of respectability would object; on the contrary, it would, in all probability, be most acceptable to them, as it would prevent the competition of those who are at present so little entitled to appear in the market against them.

SECTION V.

A Practice which creates a great Mass of Mercantile Inconvenience —Remedy Proposed.

§ 17. After all the improvements, however, that can be made in our system of currency, there will yet be a temporary inconvenience to which the public will be subject, as they have hitherto been, from the large quarterly payment of dividends to the public creditors,—an inconvenience which is often severely felt, and to which, I think, an easy remedy might be applied.

The national debt has become so large, and the interest which is paid quarterly upon it is so great a sum, that the mere collecting the money from the receivers general of the taxes, and the consequent reduction of the quantity in circulation, just previously to its being paid to the public creditor in *January*, *April*, *July*, and *October*, occasions, for a week or more, the most distressing want of circulating medium. The Bank, by judicious management, discounting bills probably very freely, just at the time that these monies are paid into the Exchequer, and arranging for the receipt of large sums immediately after the payment of the dividends, have, no doubt, considerably lessened the inconvenience to the mercantile part of the community. Nevertheless, it is well known to those who are acquainted with the money market that the distress for money is extreme at the periods I have mentioned. Exchequer bills, which usually sell at a premium of five shillings per 100*l*., are at such times at so great a discount that, by the purchase of them then, and the re-sale when the dividends are paid, a profit may often be made equal to the rate of 15 to 20 per cent. interest for money. At these times, too, the difference between the price of stock for ready money, and the price for a week or two to come, affords a profit, to those who can advance money, even greater than can be made by employing money in the purchase of exchequer bills. This great distress for money is frequently, after the dividends are paid, followed by as great a plenty, so that little use can for some time be made of it.

The very great perfection to which our system of economizing the use of money has arrived, by the various operations of banking, rather aggravates the peculiar evil of which I am speaking ; because, when the quantity of circulation is reduced, in consequence of the improvements which have been adopted in the means of effecting our payments, the abstraction of a million or two from that reduced circulation becomes much more serious in its effects, being so much larger a proportion of the whole circulation.

On the inconvenience to which trade and commerce are exposed by this periodical distress for money, I should think no difference of opinion can possibly exist. The same unanimity may not prevail with respect to the remedy which I shall now propose.

§ 18. Let the Bank be authorised by Government to deliver the dividend warrants to the proprietors of stock a few days *before* the receivers general are required to pay their balances into the Exchequer.

Let these warrants be payable to the bearer exactly in the same manner as they now are.

Let the day for the payment of these dividend warrants in bank notes be regulated precisely as it now is.

If the day of payment could be named on or before the delivery of the warrants, it would be more convenient.

Finally, let these warrants be receivable into the Exchequer from the receivers general, or from any other person who may have payments to make there, in the same manner as bank notes, the persons paying them allowing the discount for the number of days which will elapse before they become due.

If a plan of this sort were adopted, there could never be any particular scarcity of money before the payment of the dividends, nor any particular plenty of it after. The quantity of money in circulation would be neither increased nor diminished by the payment of the dividends. A great part of these warrants would, from the stimulus of private interest, infallibly find their way into the hands of those who had public payments to make, and from them to the Exchequer. Thus, then, would a great part of the payments to Government, and the payments from Government to the public creditor, be effected without the intervention of either bank notes or money, and the demands for money for such purposes, which are now so severely felt by the mercantile classes, would be effectually prevented.

Those who are well acquainted with the economical system now adopted in London throughout the whole banking concern, will readily understand that the plan here proposed is merely the extension of this economical system to a species of payments to which it has not yet been applied. To them it will be unnecessary to say anything further in recommendation of a plan, with the advantages of which in other concerns they are already so familiar.

SECTION VI.

The public services of the Bank excessively overpaid—Remedy proposed.

§ 19. Mr. Grenfell has lately called the attention of Parliament to a subject of importance to the financial interests of the community. At a time when taxes bear so heavily on the people, brought upon them by the unexampled difficulties and expenses of the war, a resource so obvious as that which he has pointed out will surely not be neglected.

It appears by the documents which Mr. Grenfell's motions have produced, that the Bank have, for many years, on an average, had no less a sum of the public money in their hands, on which they have obtained an interest of 5 per cent., than 11 millions; and the only compensation which the public have derived for the advantage which the Bank have so long enjoyed is a loan of 3 millions from 1806 to 1814, a period of eight years, at an interest of 3 per cent.,—and a farther loan of 3 millions, without interest, which the Bank, in 1808, agreed to afford the public till six months after the definitive treaty of peace, and which by an act of last session was continued without interest till April 1816. From 1806 to 1816, a period of ten years, the Bank have gained 5 per cent. per annum on 11,000,000*l.*, which will amount to £5,500,000

During the same time, the public have received the following compensation:—the difference between 3 per cent. and 5 per cent. interest, or 2 per cent. per annum on 3,000,000*l.* for eight years, or	£480,000	
From 1808 to 1816, the public will have had the advantage of a loan of 3,000,000*l.* without interest, which at 5 per cent. per annum would amount in eight years to	1,200,000	
		1,680,000
Balance gained by the Bank .		£3,820,000

3,820,000*l.* will have been gained by the Bank in ten years, or 382,000*l.* per annum, for acting as bankers to the public, when, perhaps, the whole expense attending this department of their business does not exceed 10,000*l.* per annum.

§ 20. In 1807, when these advantages were first noticed by a committee of the House of Commons, it was contended by many persons, in favour of the Bank, and by Mr. Thornton, one of the directors, who had been governor, that the gains of the Bank were in proportion to the amount of their notes in circulation, and that no advantage was derived from the public deposits further than as they enabled the Bank to maintain a larger amount of notes in circulation. This fallacy was completely exposed by the committee.[1]

If Mr. Thornton's argument were correct, no advantage whatever would have resulted to the Bank from the deposits of the public money—for those deposits do not enable them to maintain a larger amount of notes in circulation.

Suppose that, before the Bank had any of the public deposits, the amount of their notes in circulation were 25 millions, and that they derived a profit by such circulation. Suppose, now, that Government received 10 millions for taxes in bank notes, and deposited them permanently with the Bank. The circulation would be

[1] [See passage cited in next paragraph, § 21.]

immediately reduced to 15 millions, but the profits of the Bank would be precisely the same as before; though 15 millions only were then in circulation, the Bank would obtain a profit on 25 millions. If, now, they again raise the circulation to 25 millions by employing the 10 millions in discounting bills, purchasing exchequer bills, or advancing the payments on the loan for the year for the holders of scrip receipts, will they not have added the interest of 10 millions to their usual profits, although they should at no time have raised their circulation above the original sum of 25 millions.

That the increase in the amount of public deposits should enable the Bank to add to the amount of their notes in circulation, is neither supported by theory nor experience. If we attend to the progress of these deposits we shall observe, that at no time did they increase so much as from 1800 to 1806, during which time there was no increase in the circulation of notes of 5*l.* and upwards; but, from 1807 to 1815, when there was no increase whatever in the amount of public deposits, the amount of notes of 5*l.* and upwards had increased 5 millions.

§ 21. Nothing can be more satisfactory on the subject of the profits of the Bank, from the public deposits, than the report of the committee on public expenditure, in 1807. It is as follows:—

"In the evidence upon this part of the subject, it is admitted that the notes of the Bank are productive of profit; but it appears to be assumed that the Government balances are only so in proportion as they tend to augment the amount of notes; whereas your committee are fully persuaded that both balances and notes are and must necessarily be productive.

"The funds of the Bank, which are the sources of profit, and which constitute the measure of the sum which they have to lend (subject only to a deduction on account of cash and bullion) may be classed under three heads.

"*First,* The sum received from their proprietors as capital, together with the savings which have been added to it.

"*Secondly*, The sum received from persons keeping cash at the Bank. This sum consists of the balances of the deposit accounts, both of Government and of individuals. In 1797, this fund, including all the balances of individuals, was only 5,130,140*l*. The present Government balances alone have been stated already at between 11 and 12 millions, including bank notes deposited in the Exchequer.*

"*Thirdly*, The sum received in return for notes put into circulation. A correspondent value for every note must originally have been given, and the value thus given for notes constitutes one part of the general fund to be lent at interest. A note-holder, indeed, does not differ essentially from a person to whom a balance is due. Both are creditors of the Bank; the one holding a note, which is the evidence of the debt due to him, the other having the evidence of an entry in the ledger of the Bank. *The sum at all times running at interest will be in exact proportion to the amount of these three funds combined, deduction being made for the value of cash and bullion.*"†

Every word of this statement appears to me unanswerable, and the principle laid down by the committee would afford us an infallible clue to ascertain the net profits of the Bank, if we knew the amount of their savings,—

* By some of my readers the words "including bank notes deposited in the Exchequer" may not be understood. They are bank notes never put into circulation; neither are they included in any return made by the Bank. They are called at the Exchequer special notes, and are mere vouchers (not having even the form of bank notes) of the payment to the Bank from the Exchequer of such monies as are daily received at the latter office. They are the record, therefore, of a part of the public deposits lodged with the Bank.

† In 1797 the Bank stated their finances to be as follows:—

Bank notes in circulation, . . .	£8,640,000
Public and private deposits, . . .	5,132,140
Surplus capital, ...	3,826,890
	£17,597,030

On the other side of the account they showed in what securities these funds were invested, and, with the exception of cash and bullion, and a small sum for stamps, they were all yielding interest and profit to the Bank.

their cash and bullion, and their annual expenses, as well as the other particulars, are known to us.

§ 22. It will be seen by the above extract, that in 1807 the amount of the public deposits was between 11 and 12 millions, whereas, in 1797 the amount of public and private deposits were, together, only equal to 5,130,140*l.* In consequence of this report Mr. Perceval applied to the Bank, on the part of the public, for a participation in their additional profits from this source, either in the way of an annual payment or as a loan of money without interest; and, after some negociation, a loan of 3 millions was obtained without interest, payable six months after a definitive treaty of peace.

The same report also notices the exorbitant allowance which was made to the Bank for the management of the national debt. The public paid the Bank at that time at the rate of 450*l.* per million for management; and it was stated by the committee, that the additional allowance for management in the ten years ending in 1807, in consequence of the increase of the debt, was more than 155,000*l.*, whilst the "whole increase of the officers who actually transact the business, in the last eleven years, is only 137, whose annual expense may be from 18,449*l.* to 23,290*l.*, the addition to the other permanent charges being probably about one-half or two-thirds of that sum."

After this report, a new agreement was made with the Bank for the management of the public debt.

450*l.* per million was to be paid if the unredeemed capital exceeded 300 millions, but fell below 400 millions.

340*l.* per million if the capital exceeded 400 millions, but fell below 600 millions.

300*l.* per million on such part of the public debt as exceeded 600 millions.

Besides these allowances, the Bank are paid 800*l.* per million for receiving contributions on loans; 1000*l.* on each contract for lotteries; and 1250*l.* per million, or ⅛th per cent., for receiving contributions on the profits arising from property, professions, and trades. This agreement has been in force ever since.

As the period is now approaching when the affairs of the Bank will undergo the consideration of Parliament, and when the agreement which regards the public deposits will expire, by the payment of the 3 millions borrowed of the Bank without interest, in 1808; no time can be more proper than the present to point out the undue advantages which were given to the Bank in the terms settled between them and Mr Perceval in 1808. This, I apprehend, was the chief object of Mr Grenfell, for it is not alone to the additional advantages which the Bank have obtained since the agreement in 1808 that he wishes to call the attention of Parliament, but also to that agreement itself, under which the public are now paying, and have long paid, in one shape or another, enormous sums for very inadequate services.

Mr Grenfell probably thinks, and if he does I most heartily concur with him, that a profit of 382,000*l.* per annum, which is the sum at which the advantages of the public deposits to the Bank, for a period of ten years, may be calculated, as will be seen, page 178,[1] very far exceeds the just compensation which the public ought to pay to the Bank for doing the mere business of bankers; particularly when, in addition to this sum, 300,000*l.* per annum is now also paid for the management of the national debt, loans, &c.; when, moreover, the Bank have been enjoying, ever since the renewal of their charter, immense additional profits, from the substitution of paper money in lieu of a currency consisting partly of metallic and partly of paper money, which additional profits were not in contemplation, either of Parliament which granted, or of the Bank which obtained that charter, when the bargain was made in 1800, and of which they might be in a great measure deprived by the repeal of the bill which restricts them from paying their notes in specie. Under these circumstances it must, I think, be allowed, that in 1808 Mr Perceval by no means obtained for the public what they had a right to expect; and it is to be hoped that, with the known sentiments of the Chancellor of the Exchequer as to the right of the public to participate in the additional advantages of the Bank arising from public deposits, terms more consonant with the public interest will now be insisted on.

[1] [§ 19, *supra*, p. 178.]

It is true that the above sums, though paid by the public, are not the net profits of the Bank; from them a deduction must be made for the expenses of that part of the Bank establishment which is exclusively appropriated to the public business; but those expenses do not probably exceed 150,000*l.* per annum.

The committee on public expenditure stated in their report to the House of Commons in 1807, "that the number of clerks employed by the Bank exclusively or principally in the public business, was

In 1786,	. .	243
1796,	. .	313
1807,	. .	450

whose salaries, it is presumed, may be calculated at an average of between 120*l.* and 170*l.* for each clerk: taking them at 135*l.*, which exceeds the average of those employed in the South Sea House, the sum is . £60,750

At 150*l.*, the sum is 67,500

At 170*l.*, the sum is 76,500

Either of which two last sums would be sufficient to provide a superannuation fund.

"The very moderate salaries," the report continues, "received by the governor, deputy governor, and directors, amount to £8,000

"Incidental expenses may be estimated at about	15,000
"Building additional and repairs, at about.	10,000
"Law expenses and loss by frauds, forgeries, at about	10,000
	£43,000
"Add the largest estimate for clerks, .	76,500
Total,	£119,500"

Allowing, then, the very highest computation of the committee, the expense of managing the public business in 1807, including the *whole* of the salaries of the directors, incidental expenses, additional buildings and repairs, together with law expenses and loss by frauds and forgeries, amounted to 119,500*l.*

The committee also stated, that the increased expenses

of the Bank for managing the public business, after a period of eleven years, from 1796 to 1807, were about 35,000*l.* per annum, on an increased debt of 278 millions, being at the rate of 126*l.* per million. From 1807 to the present time the unredeemed debt managed by the Bank has increased from about 550 millions to about 830 millions, or about 280 millions,—little more than from 1796 to 1807, and therefore at the same rate of 126*l.* per million, would be attended with a similar expense of 35,000*l.*; but, "as the rate of expense diminishes as the scale of business enlarges," I shall estimate it at 30,500*l.*, which, added to 119,500*l.*, the expenses of 1807, will make the whole expense of managing the public business amount to 150,000*l.* The auditors of public accounts in 1786 estimated that 187*l.* 10s. per million was sufficient to pay the expenses of managing a debt of 224 millions. The estimate which I have just made is about 180*l.* per million, on a debt of 830 millions, which will appear an ample allowance when it is considered in what different proportions the debt itself increases, compared with the work which it occasions.

Supposing, then, the expenses to be about 150,000*l.*, the net profits obtained by the Bank by all its transactions with the public this year will be as follows:—

Charge for managing the national debt for one year, ending the 1st *February* 1816,*	£254,000
For receiving contributions on loans, at 800*l.* per million, on 36 millions, .	28,800
Ditto, lotteries, ...	2,000
Average profits on public deposits,† .	382,000
Allowance for receiving property tax, .	3,480
	£670,280
Expenses attending the management of public business, ...	150,000
Net profits of the Bank paid by the public, ...	£520,280

* This charge is calculated on the debt as it stood in February 1815: more than 75 millions have been added since.

† See page 178.

Of this vast sum, 372,000*l.* probably arises from the deposits alone, an expense which might almost wholly be saved to the nation, if Government were to take the management of that concern into their own hands, by having a common treasury, on which each department should draw, in the same manner as they now do on the Bank of England, investing the 11 millions, which appears to be the average deposits in exchequer bills, a part of which might be sold in the market, if any unforeseen circumstances should reduce the deposits below that sum.

§ 23. The resolutions, proposed by Mr Grenfell, and on which Parliament will decide the next session, after briefly recapitulating the facts contained in the documents which his motions have produced, conclude thus:—"That this House will take into early consideration the advantages derived by the Bank, as well from the management of the national debt, as from the amount of balances of public money remaining in their hands, with the view to the adoption of such an arrangement, when the engagements now subsisting shall have expired, as may be consistent with what is due to the interest of the public, and the rights, credit, and stability of the Bank of England."

Mr Mellish, the governor of the Bank, has also proposed resolutions to be submitted to Parliament next session. These resolutions admit all the facts stated by Mr Grenfell's; they mention also one or two trifling services which the Bank perform for the public, one without charge,* and another at a less charge than is

* The one without charge is the calculating the deduction from each dividend warrant for property tax.

The other is receiving contributions from those who pay their property tax into the Bank, for which the Bank receives 1,250*l.* per million, or one-eighth per cent.

If the collector had gone from house to house to receive this money, he would have had an allowance of five pence per pound, which would have cost the public 58,007*l.* instead of 3,480*l.* paid to the Bank.

Perhaps no part of the business of the Bank is more easily transacted than this which they have pointed out. Instead of being under-paid, it appears to me to be paid most liberally.

The saving to the public is really effected by the money being incurred by employing the ordinary collector of taxes. But the 8th and 9th resolutions advance an extraordinary pretension,—they appear to question whether *on the expiration of the loan of* 3,000,000*l.* *in* 1816, Government will be at liberty before 1833, the time when the charter will expire, to demand any compensation whatever from the Bank for the advantages they derive from the public deposits, or to make any new arrangement respecting the charge for management of the national debt. These resolutions are as follows:

8th. "That by the 39 and 40 Geo. 3. c. 28. s. 13, it is enacted, 'That during the continuance of the charter, the Bank shall enjoy all privileges, profits, emoluments, benefits, and advantages whatsoever, which they now possess and enjoy by virtue of any employment by or on behalf of the public.

"That previously to such renewal of their charter, the Bank was employed as the public banker, in keeping the cash of all the principal departments in the receipt of the public revenue, and in issuing and conducting the public expenditure, &c.

9th. "That whenever the engagements now subsisting between the public and the Bank shall expire, it may be proper to consider the advantages derived by the Bank from its transactions with the public, with a view to the adoption of such arrangements as may be consistent with those principles of equity and good faith, which ought to prevail in all transactions between the public and the Bank of England.'" *

brought to one focus, instead of being collected from various quarters. The Bank appear to consider the rule, by which they are to measure the moderation of their charges, to be the saving which they effect to their employer, rather than the just compensation for their own trouble and expense. What would they think of an engineer, if in his charge for the construction of a steam-engine he should be guided by the value of the labour which the engine was calculated to save, and not by the value of the labour and materials necessary to its construction.

* Since the first edition of this work was published, the first Lord of the Treasury, and the Chancellor of the Exchequer, have proposed to the Bank that they shall continue the advance of 3 millions, which would have been due in April next, for two years without interest:—and further, that the Bank shall

That the Bank should now *for the first time* intimate that their charter precludes the public from making any demand on the Bank for a participation in the advantages arising from the public deposits, after all that has passed since 1800 on that subject, does indeed appear surprising.

§ 24. The charter of the Bank was renewed in 1800 for twenty-one years, from its expiration in 1812; consequently it will not now terminate till 1833. But since 1800, so far from the Bank asserting any such claim of right to the whole advantages of the public deposits, they in 1806 lent Government 3,000,000*l.* till 1814, at 3 per cent. interest, and in 1808 they lent 3,000,000*l.* more till the termination of the war, without interest, and in the last session of Parliament the loan of 3,000,000*l.* was continued without interest till *April* 1816. These loans were expressly granted, in con-

advance the sum of 6 millions at 4 per cent. for two years certain, and shall continue the same for three years longer from such period, subject to repayment upon six months' notice, to be given at any time between the 10th October in any year and the 5th of April following, either by the Lords of the Treasury to the Bank, or by the Bank to their Lordships. This proposal was agreed to by a General Court of Proprietors of Bank Stock, held, on the 8th of February, for the purpose of considering the same.

At this general court, on asking for some explanation respecting the deposit of the public money at the end of the two years, I noticed with approbation the departure of the Bank from the claim which they had set up in the above resolutions, in which they appeared to me to assert the *right* of the Bank to the custody of the public money without paying any remuneration whatever; to which the governor of the Bank, Mr Mellish, replied, that I had totally misconceived the meaning of those resolutions, and he was sure if I read them again with attention, I should be convinced that no such construction could be put on them. I am glad the Bank disclaim having had the intention of depriving the public of the advantage which they have enjoyed since the report of the Committee on Public Expenditure; though I regret, that they have expressed themselves so obscurely, as to have given me and many others a different impression. The resolutions still appear to me to assert that the privilege of being public banker was for a valuable consideration secured to the Bank during the continuance of their charter, and that at the expiration of that engagement, and not before, it might be proper to consider of a new arrangement.

sideration of the increase in the amount of the public deposits.

The committee on public expenditure, in their report (1807), to which I have already referred, speaking of the loan of 3,000,000*l.* to the public in 1806, at 3 per cent. interest, observe, " But the transaction is most material in another view, as it evinces that the agreement made in 1800 was not considered either by those who acted on the part of the public, or by the Bank Directors themselves, as a bar against further participation, whenever the increase of their profits derived from the public, and the circumstances of public affairs, might, upon similar principles, *make such a claim reasonable and expedient.*" And what is Mr Perceval's language at the same period, when, in consequence of this report, he applied for and obtained a loan of 3,000,000*l.* till the end of the war? In his letter to the governor and deputy governor of the Bank, dated the 11th of *January* 1808, he says, " I think it necessary to observe, that the proposal to confine the duration of the advance, by way of loan, or of the annual payment into the Exchequer, to the period of the present war, and twelve months after the termination of it, is by no means to be understood as an admission on my part that, at the expiration of such period, the public will no longer be entitled to look to any advantage from the continuance of such deposits, but simply as a provision by which the Government and the Bank may be respectively enabled, under the change in the state of affairs which will then have taken place, probably affecting the amount of public balances in the hands of the latter, to consider of a new arrangement." On the 19th of *January*, Mr Perceval's proposals were submitted to the Court of Directors in a more official from,—they conclude thus: " And it is understood that *during the continuance of this advance by the Bank,* no alteration is to be proposed in the general course of business between the Bank and the Exchequer, nor any regulation introduced by which the accounts, now by law directed to be kept at the Bank, shall be withdrawn from thence." These proposals were recommended for acceptance by the Court of Directors to the

Court of Proprietors, and were, without comment, agreed to on the 21st of *January.*

Mr Vansittart, in his application to the Bank in *November* 1814, relative to continuing the loan of 3,000,000*l.*, which would have become due on the 17th of *December* following, till *April* 1816, uses these words: "But I beg to be distinctly understood as not departing from the reservation made by the late Mr Perceval, in his letter to the governor and deputy governor of the Bank, of the 11th *January*, 1808, by which he guarded against the possibility of any misconstruction which could preclude the public, after the expiration of the period of the loan then agreed upon, from asserting its title to future advantage from the continuance or increase of such deposits,—and as adhering generally to the principles maintained by Mr Perceval in the discussion which then took place."

No comment whatever appears to have been made by the Bank on these observations: a General Court of Proprietors was called, and the loan of 3 millions was continued till *April* 1816.

It surely will not come with a very good grace now from the Bank, to insist that the agreement of 1800 precludes the public from demanding any compensation for the advantages which the Bank have derived from the increase of the public deposits since that period, when, on so many occasions, the right of participation has been so expressly claimed on the part of Government, and acceded to by the Court of Directors.

In addition to these strong facts, by a reference to the basis on which the agreement for the renewal of the charter was founded, as detailed by Mr Thornton in his evidence before the committee of public expenditure in 1807,* it will still further appear that the Bank have no claim whatever to shelter themselves under their charter, in refusing to let the public participate in the profits which have accrued from the augmentation of the public deposits.

It must be recollected that Mr Thornton was, in 1800,

* Report, page 104.

the governor of the Bank,—that he was the negotiator, on the part of the Bank, with Mr. Pitt, for the renewal of the charter,—and that, in fact, the idea of renewing the charter so long before its expiration originated with him. Mr Thornton told the committee, that the only sums of public money on which the Bank derived profit, and which were referred to by him and Mr Pitt, with a view to settle the compensation which the public should receive for prolonging the exclusive privileges of the Bank, were those lodged at the Bank for the payment of the growing dividends, and for the quarterly issues to the commissioners for the redemption of the national debt.

The first of these sums Mr Thornton estimates to be on an average £2,500,000*
And it appears by an account lately produced that the second amounted to . 615,842

£3,115,842

Mr Thornton expressly states, that all other public accounts were of trifling amount, and "the probable augmentation of the balances of public money from the various departments of Government was not taken into the account,"—"that such augmentation was neither adverted to nor provided for."

If, then, it is acknowledged by the very negotiator on the part of the Bank that the probable augmentation of the public balances formed no part of the consideration in settling the pecuniary remuneration which was given to the public for continuing to the Bank their exclusive privileges, how can it now, with any justice, be contended by the Bank, that the profits derived from those augmented balances, which were "neither adverted to nor provided for," belong of right exclusively to the Bank, and that the public have no claim either to participate in them, or to withdraw the balances to any use to which they may think proper to apply them.

* By an account laid before Parliament last session it appears, that the amount of exchequer bills and bank notes deposited with the Exchequer as cash, amounted, on an average of the year ending *March* 1800, to 3,690,000*l*.

It is to be observed that Mr Thornton, in his evidence before alluded to, represented all the other public accounts, excepting the two before mentioned, as of trifling amount; but, by accounts which were last session presented to Parliament, it appears that in 1800, the year to which Mr Thornton's evidence refers, when the charter was renewed, the public balances of all descriptions deposited with the Bank amounted to 6,200,000*l.*, exceeding the aggregate amount stated by Mr Thornton by 3 millions, which he would, if he had been aware of this fact, hardly have called "a trifling amount."

If, then, the fact of this large additional deposit did not come under the consideration of Mr Thornton and Mr Pitt, at the time of renewing the charter,—if no part of the remuneration which the public then received was founded on this fact, the large amount of public deposits in 1800, so far from entitling the Bank to retain the whole profits arising from the still larger deposits at the present period, binds them in justice to be particularly liberal in any new engagement they may now make with the public, as affording a remuneration for a profit so long enjoyed, which, it is to be presumed, they would not have been allowed to enjoy, if the facts had been clearly known and considered at the time of settling the terms on which the charter was renewed.

But, whether known or not known, must have been of little consequence in Mr Thornton's estimation, whose opinion, that the profits of the Bank were not increased by the augmentation of the public balances, otherwise than as they contributed to increase the amount of bank notes in circulation, is so emphatically given.

Is it not lamentable to view a great and opulent body like the Bank of England exhibiting a wish to augment their hoards by undue gains wrested from the hands of an overburdened people? Ought it not rather to have been expected that gratitude for their charter, and the unlooked-for advantages with which it has been attended, —for the bonuses and increased dividends which they have already shared, and for the great undivided treasure which it has further enabled them to accumulate, would have induced the Bank voluntarily to relinquish to the State the whole benefit which is derived from the employment of 11 millions of the public money, instead of manifesting a wish to deprive them of the small portion of it which they have for a few years enjoyed?

When the rate of charge for the management of the national debt was under discussion, in 1807, Mr Thornton said "that, in a matter between the public and the Bank, he was sure nothing but a fair compensation for trouble, risk, and actual losses, and the great responsibility that attaches to the office, would be required."

How comes it that the language of the Directors of the present day is so much changed? Instead of expecting only a fair compensation for trouble, risk, and actual losses, they endeavour to deprive the public even of the inadequate compensation which they have hitherto received, and appeal now, for the first time, to their charter for their right to hold the public money, and to enjoy all the profit which can be derived from its use, without allowing the least remuneration to the public.

If the charter were as binding as the Bank contend for, a great public company, possessing so advantageous a monopoly, and so intimately connected with the State, might be expected to act on a more liberal policy towards its generous benefactors.

Till the last session of Parliament, the Bank were also particularly favoured in the composition which they paid for stamp duties. In 1791, they paid a composition of 12,000*l.* per annum, in lieu of all stamps either on bills or notes. In 1799, on an increase of the stamp-duty, this composition was advanced to 20,000*l.*, and an addition of 4,000*l.*, raising the whole to 24,000*l.*, was made for the duty on notes under 5*l.*, which the Bank had then begun to circulate. In 1804, an addition of not less than 50 per cent. was made to the stamp-duty imposed by the act of 1799 on notes under 5*l.*, and a considerable increase on the notes of a higher value; and, although the Bank circulation of notes under 5*l.* had increased from one and a half to four and a half millions, and the amount of notes of a higher description had also increased, yet the whole composition of the Bank was only raised from 24,000*l.* to 32,000*l.* In 1808, there was a further increase of 33 per cent. to the stamp-duty, at which time the composition was raised from 32,000*l.* to 42,000*l.* In both these instances the increase was not in proportion even to the increase of duty, and no allowance whatever was made for the increase in the amount of the Bank circulation.

In the last session of Parliament, on a further increase of the stamp-duty, the principle was for the first time established, that the Bank should pay a composition, in some proportion to the amount of their circulation. It is now fixed as follows. Upon the average circulation of the three preceding years, the Bank is to pay at the rate of 3500*l.* per million, without reference to the classes or value of the notes of which the aggregate circulation may consist.

The average of the Bank circulation for three years, ending 5th *April* 1815, was 25,102,600*l.*, and upon this average they will pay this year about 87,500*l.*

Next year the average will be taken upon the three years ending in *April* 1816, and if it differs from the last, the duty will vary accordingly.

If the same course had been followed now as in 1804 and 1808, the Bank would have had to pay, even with the additional duty, only 52,500*l.*, so that 35,000*l.* per annum has been saved to the public, by Parliament having at last recognised the principle which should have been adopted in 1799, and by the neglect of which the public have probably been losers, and the Bank consequently gainers, of a sum little less than 500,000*l.*

SECTION VII.

Bank Profits and Savings—Misapplication—Proposed Remedy.

§ 25. I have hitherto been considering the profits of the Bank as they regard the public, and have endeavoured to show that they have greatly exceeded what a just consideration for *their* rights and interests could warrant—I propose now to consider them in relation to the interests of the proprietors of Bank stock, for which purpose I shall endeavour to state a basis on which the profits of the Bank may be calculated, with a view to ascertain what the accumulated savings of the Bank now are. If we knew accurately the expenses of the Bank, and the amount of cash and bullion which they may at different times have had in their hands, we should have the means of making a calculation on this subject which should be a very near approximation to the truth.

§ 26. The profits of the Bank are derived from sources which are well known. They arise, as has been already stated, from the interest on public and private deposits,—the interest on the amount of their notes in circulation, after deducting the amount of cash and bullion,—the interest on their capital and savings,—the allowance paid them for the management of the public debt,—the profits from their dealings in bullion, and from the destruction of their notes.—All these form the gross profits of the Bank, from which must be deducted only their expenses, the stamp-duty, and the property tax, in order to ascertain their net profits.

Under the head of expenses must be included all the charges attending the management of the national debt, as well as those incurred by the proper business of the Bank. In estimating the former of these charges, I have already stated my grounds for believing that it could not exceed 150,000*l*. In the management of the public business, it was stated by the committee on public expenditure, that 450 clerks were employed in 1807, and it is probable that the number may now be increased to between 500 and 600.

It has also, I understand, been stated from the best authority in Parliament, that the Bank employed in the whole of their establishment about 1000 clerks; consequently, if 500 are employed exclusively on the public business, 500 more must be engaged in the business of the Bank. Supposing now the expenses to bear some regular proportion to the number of clerks employed, as

150,000*l.* has been calculated to be the expense attending the employment of 500 clerks in the public business, we may estimate a like expense to be incurred by the employment of the other 500, and therefore the whole expenses of the Bank to be at the present time about 300,000*l.*, including all charges whatsoever.*

But although this large sum is now expended, it must have been of gradual growth since 1797; when, probably, the whole expenses of the establishment were not more than one-half the present amount. In the first place, since 1797, the amount of bank notes in circulation has increased from about 12 millions to 28 millions, but the expenses of their circulation, instead of increasing in the same proportion only, have at least, increased as one to ten.

The amount of notes of 5*l.* and upwards has been raised from 12 to 18 millions, and if the average value of notes, of all descriptions above 5*l.*, be even so low as 15*l.*, a circulation of 12 millions would consist of 800,000 notes, and a circulation of 18 millions of 1,200,000 notes, an increase in the proportion, as one to one and one-half; but the 9 millions of notes under 5*l.*, which are now in circulation, have been wholly created since 1797, and if they consist of 5 millions of notes of 1*l.*, and 2 millions of notes of 2*l.*, a number of 7 millions of notes has been further added to the circulation, and the whole number of notes has been raised since 1797, from 800,000 to 8,200,000, or as one to ten, and at an expense ten times greater than was incurred at that time, the expense being in proportion to the number, and not to the

* It has been remarked, that a sufficient allowance is not made in my calculations for the losses of the Bank by bad debts in consequence of the bad bills which they occasionally discount. Their losses from this source, I am told, are often very large. On the other hand, I have been informed that the profits of the Bank from private deposits, for which I have taken no credit, must be considerable, as the East India Company and many other public boards keep their cash at the Bank.

A deduction from the Bank profits should have been made for their loss by Aslett, and for the expenses attending their military corps. My argument will not be affected by their surplus capital being only 12 or 11 instead of 13 millions.

amount of notes. It is probable, too, that the notes of 1*l.* and 2*l.*, which are so constantly used in the circulation, are more often renewed than notes of a higher value.

The public debt, too, under the management of the Bank, is more than doubled since 1797, and must have added considerably to the expenses of that department. These expenses have been already calculated to have risen since 1796, from 84,500*l.* to 150,000*l.* or 65,500*l.**

The public deposits, too, are at least double what they were in 1797, from all which I have a right to infer, that the expenses of the Bank in 1797, could not have exceeded 150,000*l.*, and that they have been gradually increasing since that period; perhaps at the rate of 7000*l.* or 8000*l.* per annum.

The next subject for consideration, is the amount of cash and bullion in the Bank, which at no time has been laid before the public;—that, and the amount of their discounts, were the only material facts which the Bank concealed from the public in the eventful year 1797. They stated in the account laid before Parliament, that their cash and bullion, and their bills and notes discounted, amounted together to 4,176,080*l.* on the 26th of *February*, 1797. They gave also a scale of discounts from 1782 to 1797, and a scale of the cash and bullion in the Bank for the same period. By comparing these tables with each other, and with some parts of the evidence delivered before the Parliamentary Committees, an ingenious calculator discovered the whole secret which the Bank wished to conceal. According to his table the cash and bullion in the Bank, on the 26th of *February* 1797, was reduced as low as 1,227,000*l.*, and 4 millions was about the sum which the Bank considered as fair cash; to which it never attained after *December* 1795, though previously to that year it was on some occasions more than double that amount.

For the first year or two after the suspension of cash

* The Committee on public expenditure calculated these expenses at 119,500*l.* in 1807, and stated the increase from 1796 to 1807 at about 35,000*l.*

payments, the Bank must have made great efforts to replenish their coffers with cash and bullion, as they were then by no means sure that they should not be again required to pay their notes in specie. We find, accordingly by accounts returned to Parliament by the Mint, that the amount of gold coined in 1797 and 1798, was very little less in value than 5,000,000*l.**

Whatever might have been the amount of cash and bullion, which the Bank had acquired in the first two years after the suspension of cash payments, it is probable that their stock has been decreasing since that period, as they could have no motive for keeping a large amount of such unproductive capital, when they must have been quite secure that no call could be made on them by the holders of their notes for guineas, and that before they were again required to pay in specie, they would have ample notice to prepare a due store of the precious metals. It does not appear possible, then, under all the circumstances of the case, that the Bank can have added to their stock of bullion, since the great coinages of 1797 and 1798; but it is highly probable that they have considerably reduced it.

In estimating the profits of the Bank, as far as those profits are influenced by their stock of cash and bullion, I shall be justified in considering them greater since 1797 and 1798, as since those years they would naturally keep a less part of their capital in that unproductive shape, and, consequently, more in exchequer bills, or in merchants' acceptances, securities which pay interest, and are productive of profit.—On an average of the whole eighteen years, from 1797 to 1815, the cash and bullion of the Bank cannot be estimated as amounting to more

* The Committee of Secrecy reported to Parliament, that the cash and bullion in the Bank, in *November* 1797, had increased to an amount more than five times the value of that at which they stood on the 25th of *February* 1797. They stated, too, that the bankers and traders of London, who had a right, by the Act of Parliament, to demand three-fourths of any deposit in cash, which they had made in the Bank, of 500*l.* and upwards, after the 25th of *February* 1797, had only claimed in *November* 1797, about one-sixteenth.

than 3 millions, though, probably, for the first year or two, it amounted to 4 or 5 millions.

These circumstances being premised, it will not be difficult to calculate the profits of the Bank, from 1797 to the present time, all the facts necessary to such calculation being known to us excepting the two I have just stated, viz. the amount of expenses and of cash and bullion, but which cannot differ much from that at which I have calculated them.

Proceeding, then, on this basis, it appears, as will be seen by the accounts, that the profits and surplus capital of the Bank for a series of years, after paying all dividends and bonuses, have been as follows:—

Year commencing in January.	Surplus capital.	Profits after paying dividend and bonuses.	Dividend and bonus together.
1797,	£3,826,890	£89,872	7 per cent.
1798,	3,916,762	533,621	7 ...
1799,	4,450,383	*	17 ...
1800,	3,941,228	611,981	7 ...
1801,	4,553,209	116,038	12 ...
1802,	4,669,247	460,509	9½ ...
1803,	5,129,756	765,859	7 ...
1804,	5,895,615	306,794	12 ...
1805,	6,202,409	346,335	12 ...
1806,	6,548,744	368,008	12 ...
1807,	6,916,752	581,274	10 ...
1808,	7,498,026	385,865	10 ...
1809,	7,883,891	470,760	10 ...
1810,	8,354,651	651,483	10 ...
1811,	9,006,134	722,188	10 ...
1812,	9,728,322	739,867	10 ...
1813,	10,468,189	809,786	10 ...
1814,	11,279,975	1,081,649	10 ...
1815,	12,359,624	1,066,625	
1816,	13,426,249		

If in the accounts referred to, it should be thought that I have estimated the expenses of the Bank too low, it may on the other hand be remarked that I have not

* There was this year a loss of 509,155*l*.

allowed for any profit from the deposits of individuals. Those deposits may not be very large, as the Bank do not afford the same accommodation to individuals as given by other bankers. Some profit must, however, be made from this source, as well as from the loss and destruction of notes, which it may be presumed, after a time, are not included in the amount stated to be in circulation. By the purchase of silver, and coinage of tokens, the Bank must, on the whole, have been gainers; for the value of the token has been generally lower in the market, than it has passed for in circulation at the time of its issue.

In point of fact, too, the Bank receives more than five per cent. interest for their money; for exchequer bills paying 3½d. per day, pay 5*l.* 6s. 5½d. per cent. per annum; and in discounting bills, the interest being immediately deducted, is employed as capital, and is instantly productive of profit; at the same time it must be observed that during a part of the time for which these calculations are made, exchequer bills bore an interest of only 3¼d. per day, which amounts to 4*l.* 18s. 0¼d. per cent. per annum, rather less than five per cent.

In *March* 1801, when a bonus of 5 per cent., in navy 5 per cents., was divided amongst the proprietors of Bank stock, Mr Tierney said in the House of Commons, "that when the affairs of the Bank of England were investigated by the House of Commons in 1797, the surplus profits were considered by some as a security for the engagements of the Bank to the public." To which Mr Samuel Thornton, then governor of the Bank, replied, that "he could assure the honourable member, that the security of the public would not be lessened from what it was in 1797, by the division of the sum of 582,120*l.* voted at the general court, on the 19th instant, as exclusive of that sum, the surplus profits of the Bank were more now than they were in 1797." *

On an inspection of the account in the Appendix, it will be seen, that, after paying all the dividends and

* Allardyce's Address to the proprietors of the Bank of England.

bonuses to the proprietors, the Bank had accumulated in *April* 1801 savings to the amount of 3,945,109*l.*, exceeding the savings of 1797 by 118,219*l.*, an increase not inconsistent with the declaration of Mr Thornton, and therefore tending to confirm the correctness of the basis on which these calculations are made.*

It will appear on an examination of the accounts in the Appendix for the subsequent years, that the profits of the Bank for every year since 1801 have exceeded the annual dividend paid to the proprietors, and that in 1815, the surplus for that year only must have amounted to 1,066,625*l.*, so that the Bank could have paid a dividend for that year of 19 per cent. instead of 10 per cent.

§ 27. It will appear, too, that if the Bank affairs have been only moderately well managed, they must now have an accumulated fund of no less than 13 millions, which, in defiance of the clearest language of an act of Parliament, the Directors have hitherto withheld from the proprietors.

With such an accumulated fund, the Bank could make a division of 100 per cent. bonus without infringing on their permanent capital; and if they could maintain their present profits, with a deduction only of 523,908*l.* per annum, the interest (less income tax) on the surplus capital proposed to be divided, they would still have an unappropriated income of 542,000*l.*, which would enable

* The accounts are made up from *January* to *January*. The bonus in question was paid in *April* 1801. The net profits of the Bank for the whole year 1801 were 1,526,019*l.*, consequently for

the quarter ending in April they may be stated at .		£381,504
Which, added to the surplus capital of *January*, 1801,		4,553,209
Gives the total of the surplus capital in *April* 1801, before paying the dividend and bonus, . .		£4,934,713
Deduct—		
Dividend 3½ per cent. for half a year, .	£407,484	
Bonus 5 per cent., ...	582,120	
		989,604
Leaving a surplus capital in *April* 1801 of . .		£3,945,109
And exceeding that in 1797 of		3,826,890
By		£118,219

them to increase their permanent dividend from 10 to 14½ per cent. in addition to the bonus of 100 per cent.

If they divided only a bonus of 75 per cent., they would retain a surplus capital exceeding that of 1797, and might, on the above supposition, have an unappropriated income of 673,000*l.*,—they might therefore raise their permanent dividend from 10 to 15½ per cent. in addition to the bonus of 75 per cent.

But it cannot be expected that the Bank will, during peace, have the same opportunities of making profit as during war, and the proprietors must prepare themselves for a considerable reduction in their annual income. What that reduction may be will depend on the new agreement now to be entered into with Government, on the future amount of public deposits, and on the conditions on which the restoration of metallic payments may be enforced. It is evident that if the plan which I have recommended in the fourth section of this work be adopted, the Bank profits from this last item will not be materially reduced.

Supposing, however, that the reduction of the annual income of the Bank should, from the falling off of their profits in all these departments, be as much as 500,000*l.*, the profits of the Bank would nevertheless be equal to the payment of the present permanent dividend of 10 per cent., even after a division of 100 per cent. bonus to the proprietors of Bank stock; for, if my calculations be correct, the profits of the Bank, after the payment of the annual dividend of 10 per cent. to the proprietors, were, for the year ending January 1, 1816 . . . £1,066,625

Deduct then the interest now made on 11,642,400*l.* proposed to be divided, less property tax, ...	£523,908	
Loss by a peace arrangement, . .	500,000	
		1,023,908
Leaving a surplus of, per annum, ...		£42,717

If, instead of 100 per cent., 50 per cent. bonus only were paid to the proprietors, the annual surplus profit of the Bank, after paying 10 per cent. dividend, would be

304,671*l.*, a sum equal to a permanent increase of dividend of 2½ per cent.

And if no bonus whatever were paid, but the savings were considered as part of the Bank capital, the annual surplus profit of the Bank, after paying 10 per cent. dividend, would be 566,625*l.*, very nearly equal to a permanent increase of dividend of 5 per cent.

These estimates are made on a supposition, too, that the property tax should permanently continue, which is calculated to be an annual charge of more than 200,000*l.* to the Bank, and consequently more than equal to a dividend of 1¾ per cent.

But the Directors are bound, in my opinion, under every case, to divide the surplus profits amongst the proprietors, the law imperatively enjoining such a division, and policy being no wise opposed to it.

Well was it urged by the Hon. Mr Bouverie, who moved in the last Bank court that an account of the surplus capital of the Bank be laid before the proprietors, that this law respecting the division of profits was probably enacted by the legislature, on a consideration of the powers of accumulation at compound interest, and the dangers which might arise to the constitution or the country, from any corporation becoming possessed of millions of treasure. If the profits of the Bank were to continue at the present rate, and no addition were to be made to the dividend now paid of 10 per cent., the accumulation of the surplus profits in forty years would give to the Bank a disposable fund of more than 120 millions. Wisely, then, did the legislature enact, that "All the profits, benefits, and advantage from time to time arising out of the management of the said corporation, shall (the charges of managing the business of the said governor and company *only excepted*) be applied from time to time to the uses of all the members of the said corporation for the time being, rateably and in proportion to each member's part, share, and interest, in the common capital, and principal stock, of the said governor and company of the Bank of England."

Those who vindicated the Directors at the last general court for their departure from the line of conduct prescribed by the law, recommended the increase of the capital of the Bank,—and they thought that the accumulated savings might be advantageously employed for such purpose.

It is said that the Bank Directors are favourable to such a plan.

If the measure should be a good one, the sum of capital to be added should be at once defined,—the proprietors should have accounts laid before them of the amount of their accumulated fund, and should be consulted on the expediency of such a disposition of it,—and lastly, the sanction of Parliament should be obtained.

§ 28. The Bank, however, have waited for none of these conditions,—they have been, in fact, for years adding the annual surplus profits to their capital, without defining the amount added, or to be added; they do it without laying any accounts before the proprietors—without consulting them; and not only without the sanction of Parliament, but in defiance of an express law on the subject.

But if the Bank complied with all these conditions, would the measure itself be expedient, and are the reasons given in support of it, namely the enlarged business of the Bank, and that it would tend to the security both of the Bank and the public, of sufficient weight to justify its adoption?

The business and income of the Bank depend, as before stated, on the amount of the aggregate fund which they have to employ, and this fund is derived from the three following sources: The amount of bank notes in circulation, deducting only the cash and bullion: The amount of public and private deposits: And the amount of that part of the capital of the Bank which is not lent to Government. But it is only the two former of these funds which contribute to the real profit of the Bank; for the interest received for surplus capital, being only 5 per cent., might be made with as much facility by each individual proprietor, on his share of such capital, if under his own management, as by combining the whole into one fund. If the proprietors were to add from their own individual property 10 millions to the capital of the

Bank, the income of the Bank would indeed be increased 500,000*l.* or 5 per cent. on 10 millions; but the proprietors would not be gainers by such an arrangement. If, however, 10 millions were added to the amount of notes, and could be permanently maintained in circulation,—or if the public and private deposits were to be increased 10 millions, the *income* of the Bank would not only be increased 500,000*l.* but their *real profits* also, and this advantage would arise wholly from their acting as a joint company, and could not be otherwise obtained.

There is this material difference between a bank and all other trades: A bank would never be established, if it obtained no other profits but those from the employment of its own capital; its real advantage commences only when it employs the capital of others. Other trades, on the contrary, often make enormous profits by the employment of their own capital only.

But if this argument be correct, with respect to an additional capital to be actually raised from amongst the proprietors, it is equally so to one withheld from them.

To increase the *profits* of the Bank proprietors, then, an increase of capital would be neither necessary nor desirable.

Neither would such an addition contribute towards the *security* of the Bank; for the Bank can never be called upon for more than the payment of their notes, and the public and private deposits; these constituting, at all times, the whole of their debts. After paying away their cash and bullion, their remaining securities, consisting of merchants' acceptances and Exchequer bills, must be at least equal to the value of their debts; and in no case can these securities be deficient, even without *any* surplus capital, excepting the Bank should lose all that which constitutes their growing dividend; and even then they could not be distressed, unless we suppose that at the same time payment were demanded for every note in circulation, and for the whole of their deposits, both public and private.

Is it against such a contingency that the proprietors are called upon to provide; when even under these, almost impossible circumstances, the Bank would have an untouched fund of 11,686,000*l.* which Government owe them?

Would the security of the public be increased? In one respect it would. If the Bank have no other capital but that which they lend to Government, they must lose all that capital by their trade, or more than 11½ millions, before the public can be sufferers; but if the capital of the Bank were doubled, the Bank might lose 23 millions, before any creditor of theirs could suffer loss. Are the friends to an increase of the capital of the Bank prepared to say, that it is against the consequences of the loss of the whole Bank capital that they are desirous of protecting the public?

It remains to be considered, whether the ability of the Bank to pay their notes in specie would be increased by an increase of their capital. The ability of the Bank, to pay their notes in specie, must depend upon the proportion of specie which they may keep, to meet the probable demand for payment of their notes; and in this respect their power cannot be increased, for they may now, *if they please*, have a stock of specie, not only equal to all their notes in circulation, but to the whole of the public and private deposits, and under no possible circumstances can more be demanded of them. But the profits of the Bank essentially depend on the smallness of the stock of cash and bullion; and the whole dexterity of the business consists in maintaining the largest possible circulation, with the least possible amount of their funds in the unprofitable shape of cash and bullion. The amount of notes in circulation depends in no degree on the amount of capital possessed by the issuers of notes, but on the amount required for the circulation of the country; which is regulated, as I have before attempted to show, by the value of the standard, the amount of payments, and the economy practised in effecting them.

The only effect, then, of the increase of the capital of the Bank would be to enable them to lend to Government or to merchants those funds, which would otherwise have been lent by individuals of the community. The

Bank would have more business to do—they would accumulate more merchants' acceptances and exchequer bills: they would even increase the income of the Bank; but the profits of the proprietors would be neither more nor less, if the market rate of interest for money were at 5 per cent., and the business of the Bank were carried on with the same economy. The proprietors would be positive losers, if they could individually have employed their shares of this capital in trade, or otherwise, at a greater profit.

§ 29. But not only do the Bank refuse, in direct contradiction to an act of Parliament, to make a division of their accumulated profits, but they are equally determined not to communicate to the proprietors what those profits are, notwithstanding their bye-law enjoins, "that twice in every year a general court shall be called, and held for considering *the general state and condition of this corporation,* and for the making of dividends, *out of all and singular* the produce and profit of the capital stock and fund of this corporation and the trade thereof, amongst the several owners and proprietors therein, according to their several shares and proportions."

If the law had been silent on the subject, the Bank Directors would, I think, be bound to show some specific evil which would result from publicity, before they refused to show a statement of their affairs to the proprietors.

It is in fact the only security which the proprietors have, against the abuse of the trust reposed in the Directors.

The affairs of the Bank may not always be managed by such men as are now in the direction, against whom not a shadow of suspicion any where exists.

Without accounts; without a division of profits; and without any other proof of the accumulated fund of the Bank, but the notoriety of the increase of the sources from which the Bank profits are made—and that for a period of more than ten years; what security have the proprietors against a corrupt administration of their affairs. It is not consistent with the delicacy of the situation of those who are entrusted with the management of millions to demand such unbounded confidence—so much reliance on their own personal character, without stating some grounds for such a demand. Yet the only answer which the Directors made to a motion for a statement of profits, in the last general court, was, that they should consider the passing of such a resolution as betraying a want of confidence in them, and as a censure on their proceedings.

On all sides, such an intention was disclaimed; yet, strange to say, no other reply could be obtained from the Directors.

The publication of accounts, besides being necessary as a check against the *corrupt* administration of the Directors, is also necessary to give assurance to the proprietors, that their affairs are *ably* administered. Since 1797, no statement has been made of the condition of the Bank; and, even in that year, it was made to Parliament, on a particular exigence, and not to the proprietors of bank stock. How, then, can the proprietors know whether, in the favourable circumstances in which the Bank have been placed, the Directors have availed themselves of all the opportunities which have offered, of employing the funds entrusted to their charge to the best advantage? Would it not be desirable, that from time to time the proprietors should be able to ascertain whether their just expectations had been realised, and whether their affairs had been ably as well as honourably administered? If the practice of laying all accounts before the proprietors had been always followed, perhaps the Directors of 1793, 1794, and 1795, might have been admonished for so badly managing the affairs of the Bank, as to keep permanently in their coffers a sum of cash and bullion, generally more than three-fourths, and seldom less than one-half the whole amount of their notes in circulation. They might possibly have been told, that such a waste of the resources of the Bank showed a very limited knowledge of the principles by which a paper currency should be regulated.*

* For the account of cash and bullion in the Bank in the above years I trust to the calculations to which I have already alluded, page 196. I can see no reason to doubt their general accuracy.

These irregularities in the proceedings of the Bank excited the attention of an independent proprietor, Mr Allardyce, in 1797 and 1801. In his excellent publication on Bank affairs, he has pointed out with great force and ability the illegal conduct of the Bank. His opinion was confirmed by Mr, now Sir James Mansfield, who was consulted by him, as to the course necessary to be pursued, to compel the Directors to lay an account before the proprietors of the state of the Company. Sir James Mansfield's opinion was given as follows :—

"I am of opinion, that *every* proprietor, at a general half yearly court, has a *right* to require from the Directors, and it is the *duty* of the latter to produce all such accounts, books and papers, as are necessary to enable the proprietors to judge of the state and condition of the corporation and its funds, and to determine what dividend ought to be paid. The proper method to be pursued by those who consult me in order to obtain such a production is, that a number of respectable proprietors should immediately give notice to the Governor and other Directors, that they shall require at the next general court a production of all the necessary books, accounts and papers ; and at the general court, when it shall be held, to attend and require such a production. If it shall not be obtained, I then advise them immediately, or within a few days after the holding of the general court, to make an application to the Governor to call a general court, which application must be made by nine members at least, having each 500*l.* stock. If the Governor shall refuse to call such general court, then the nine members who shall have applied to him to have a court called, may themselves call one in the manner prescribed by the charter ; and whether the Governor calls such court, or it is called by the nine members, I advise them, as soon as it is called, to apply to the Court of King's Bench for a mandamus to the Governor and Directors, to produce at such court all the necessary books, accounts and papers.

"J. MANSFIELD."

"Temple, March 9, 1801."

In consequence of this opinion, Mr Allardyce delivered a demand in writing at the next general court, held the 19th March 1801, that the accounts should be produced, and no doubt intended to follow up this proceeding in the way recommended by Sir James Mansfield,—but he soon after died; and since that time no proprietor has made any demand for accounts, till at the last general court in December. It is remarkable that, very unexpectedly to the proprietors, a bonus of 5 per cent., in navy 5 per cents., was voted in the general court of the 19th March 1801, the day on which Mr Allardyce's demand was made and refused. The first motion for accounts made by Mr Allardyce was in the general court, held 14th December 1797; and in March 1799, there was a bonus of 10 per cent. in 5 per cents. 1797. Mr Allardyce did not, I believe, make any motion in the Bank court between December 1797 and March 1801.

Since 1797, then, the proprietors have remained in utter ignorance of the affairs of the Bank. During eighteen years the Directors have been silently enjoying their lucrative trade, and may now possibly think that the same course is best adapted to the interests of the Bank, particularly as negociations are about to take place with Government, when it might be as well that the amount of their accumulated fund should not be known. But the public attention has been lately called to the affairs of the Bank; and the subject of their profits is generally canvassed and understood. Publicity would now probably be more beneficial than hurtful to the Bank; for exaggerated accounts of their profits have been published which may raise extravagant expectations, and which may be best corrected by official statements. Besides which, the Bank are secure of their charter for seventeen years to come; and the public cannot, during that time, deprive them of the most profitable part of their trade. If, indeed, the charter were about to expire, the public might question the policy of permitting a company of merchants to enjoy all the advantages which attend the supplying of a great country with paper money; and although they would naturally look with jealousy, after the experience furnished by other states, to allowing that power to be in the hands of Government, they might probably think that in a free country means might be found by which so considerable an advantage might be obtained for the State, independently of all control of ministers. Paper money may be considered as affording a seignorage equal to its whole exchangeable value,—but seignorage in all countries belongs to the State, and with the security of convertibility as proposed in the former part of this work, and the appointment of commissioners responsible to Parliament only, the State, by becoming the sole issuer of paper money in town as well as in the country, might secure a net revenue to the public of no less than 2 millions sterling. Against this danger, however, the Bank is secure till 1833, and therefore on every ground publicity is expedient.

APPENDIX

No. I.*

Table showing the Amount annually paid by the Public, from 1797 to 1815, for Management of the British, Irish, German, and Portuguese Debt.

Year commencing 5th January.			
1797	L.162,431	5	3
1798	212,592	1	5
1799	218,190	17	0
1800	238,294	3	8
1801	236,772	15	8
1802	263,105	14	6
1803	247,538	11	0
1804	267,786	19	7
1805	271,911	11	9
1806	292,127	9	10
1807	297,757	16	1
1808	210,549	2	7
1809	222,775	2	4
1810	217,825	13	5
1811	228,349	16	0
1812	223,705	12	5
1813	238,827	17	7
1814	242,263	14	7

* The particulars in the above table are taken from the annual finance book, printed by order of the House of Commons. They include not only what is paid to the Bank, but to the Exchequer and South Sea Company. The annual charge of the South Sea Company is now about 14,560*l*. In 1797 it was 14,657*l*. The Exchequer charge was as high as 6760*l*. 6s. 8d., in 1807 it fell gradually to 2485*l*. and has now, I believe, ceased.

The Bank have also been paid for management of life annuities since 1810,—and since 1812, about 1200*l*. or 1300*l*. per annum for management of a loan of 2½ millions, raised for the East India Company, which are not included in this table.

No. II.

Table showing the Amount annually received by the Bank from 1797 to 1815, for receiving Contributions on Loans.*

Year commencing Michaelmas.	L.	s.	d.
1796	L.20,506	3	4
1797	27,410	0	4
Year commencing 5th January.			
1799	L.16,115	6	8
1800	12,489	15	5
1801	39,080	17	11
1802	22,538	12	3
1803	9,669	10	0
1804			
1805	11,683	19	7
1806	18,130	16	3
1807	16,115	16	8
1808	12,650	18	7
1809	8,400	0	0
1810	11,680	0	0
1811	14,705	0	0
1812	19,031	14	0
1813	21,639	8	9
1814	42,200	0	0

No. III.

The total Amount of the Unredeemed Funded Debt of Great Britain and Ireland, including Loans to the Emperor of Germany and Prince Regent of Portugal, payable in Great Britain, was on the 1st of February 1815, according to accounts laid before Parliament,				L.727,767,421	2	5¾
Do. for East India Company,				3,929,561	0	0
				L.731,696,982	2	5¾
Debt contracted from Feb. 1 to Aug. 1, 1815,	L.87,448,402	16	0			
Redeemed from Feb. 1 to Aug. 1, 1815,	11,099,166	0	0			
				76,349,236	16	0
Total of unredeemed funded debt on Aug. 1, 1815,				L.808,046,218	18	5¾

* This table is taken from an account laid before Parliament, on the 19th of June 1815.

The charge for management on which is as follows:—

L.15,233,484	13	11	South Sea Stock and annuities, for the management of which South Sea Co. is paid . . .	L.14,560	4	11
11,686,000	0	0	due to the Bank of England, . . .	5,898	3	5
600,000,000	0	0	at 340*l*. per million, .	204,000	0	0
181,126,734	4	6¾	at 300*l*. do. . . .	54,338	0	5
L.808,046,218	18	5¾				
2,795,340	0	0	life annuities, . .	899	5	0
39,735,898	6	8	for 1,589,435*l*. 6s. 8d. anns. at 25 years' purchase, . . .	11,920	15	4
L.850,577,457	5	1¾				
				L.291,616	9	7
Deduct the first sum paid to the South Sea Company, ...				14,560	4	11
Management paid to the Bank of England on the debt as it stood Aug. 1, 1815 . . .				L.277,056	4	8

No. IV.

Average Amount of Bank of England Notes, including Bank Post Bills, in circulation in each of the following years.

Years.	Notes of five pounds and upwards, including Bank post bills.	Notes under five pounds.	Total.
1797	10,095,620	1,096,100	11,191,720
1798	11,527,250	1,807,502	13,334,752
1799	12,408,522	1,653,805	14,062,327
1800	13,598,666	2,243,266	15,841,932
1801	13,454,367	2,715,182	16,169,594
1802	13,917,977	3,136,477	17,054,454
1803	12,983,477	3,864,045	16,847,522
1804	12,621,348	4,723,672	17,345,020
1805	12,697,352	4,544,580	17,241,932
1806	12,844,170	4,291,230	17,135,400
1807	13,221,988	4,183,013	17,405,001
1808	13,402,160	4,132,420	17,534,580
1809	14,133,615	4,868,275	19,001,890
1810	16,085,522	6,644,763	22,730,285
1811	16,286,950	7,260,575	23,547,525
1812	15,862,120	7,600,000	23,462,120
1813	16,057,000	8,030,000	24,087,000
1814	18,540,780	9,300,000	27,840,780
1815	18,157,956	9,161,454	27,319,410

No. V.

[The Detailed Tables of Accounts are omitted.]

No. VI.

RESOLUTIONS PROPOSED CONCERNING THE BANK OF ENGLAND, BY MR GRENFELL.

1. That it appears, that there was paid by the public to the Bank of England, for managing the national debt, including the charge for contributions on loans and lotteries, in the year ending 5th of July 1792, the sum of 99,803*l.* 12s. 5d.; and that there was paid for the like service, in the year ending 5th April 1815, the sum of 281,568*l.* 6s. 11¼d.; being an increase of 181,764*l.* 14s. 6¼d. In addition to which, the Bank of England have charged at the rate of 1,250*l.* per million on the amount of property duty received at the Bank on profits arising from professions, trades, and offices.

2. That the total amount of bank notes and bank post bills, in circulation in the years 1795 and 1796 (the latter being the year previous to the restriction on cash payments), and in the year 1814, was as follows:—

1795, 1st Feb.	L.12,735,520;	and 1st Aug.	L.11,214,000
1796, 1st Feb.	10,784,740;	and 1st Aug.	9,856,110
1814, 1st Feb.	25,154,950;	and 1st Aug.	28,802,450

3. That at present, and during many years past, more particularly since the year 1806, considerable sums of public money, forming together an average stationary balance amounting to many millions, have been deposited with, or otherwise placed in the custody of the Bank of England, acting in this respect as the bankers of the public.

4. That it appears, from a report ordered to be printed 10th of August 1807, from "the Committee on the Public Expenditure of the United Kingdom," that the aggregate amount of balances and deposits of public money in the hands of the Bank of England, including bank notes deposited in the Exchequer, made up in four different periods of the quarter ending 5th January 1807, fluctuated betwixt the sums

Vide Report, p. 74 & 75.

of L.11,461,200 and 12,198,236 } including bank notes deposited in the chests of the Exchequer,

or

8,178,536 and 9,948,400 } excluding bank notes deposited at the Exchequer.

5. That the aggregate amount of such deposits, together with the exchequer bills and bank notes deposited in the chests of the

four tellers of the Exchequer, was, on an average, in the year 1814,

L.11,966,371; including bank notes deposited at the Exchequer, amounting to
642,264
or
11,324,107; excluding bank notes deposited at the Exchequer.

6. That it appears, that this aggregate amount of deposits, together with such portions of the amount of bank notes and bank post bills in circulation as may have been invested by the Bank in securities bearing interest, was productive, during the same period, of interest and profit to the Bank of England.

7. That the only participation hitherto enjoyed by the public, since the year 1806, in the profits thus made on such deposits by the Bank, has consisted in a loan of 3 millions, advanced to the public by the Bank, by the 46 Geo. III. cap. 41, bearing 3 per cent. interest; which loan was discharged in December 1814: And in another loan of 3 millions, advanced to the public by the Bank, by the 48 Geo. III. cap. 3, free of any charge of interest; which loan became payable in December 1814, but has, by an Act of the present session of Parliament, cap. 16, been continued to the 5th of April 1816.

8. That this house will take into early consideration the advantages derived by the Bank, as well from the management of the national debt, as from the amount of balances of public money remaining in their hands, with the view to the adoption of such an arrangement, when the engagements now subsisting shall have expired, as may be consistent with what is due to the interests of the public, and to the rights, credit and stability, of the Bank of England.

13th June 1815.

No. VII.

RESOLUTIONS PROPOSED CONCERNING THE BANK OF ENGLAND, BY MR MELLISH.

1. That by the Act of 31 Geo. III. cap. 33, there was allowed to the Bank of England, for the management of the public debt, 450*l.* per million on the capital stock transferable at the Bank, amounting in the year ending 5th July 1792, to 98,803*l.* 12s. 5d. on about 219,596,000*l.* then so transferable; and that by the Act 48 Geo. III. cap. 4, the said allowance was reduced to the rate of 340*l.* per million on all sums not exceeding 600 millions, and to 300*l.* per million on all sums exceeding that amount,

whereby the Bank was entitled, in the year ending 5th April 1815, to the sum of 241,971*l.* 4s. 2¼d. on about 726,570,700*l.* capital stock, and 798*l.* 3s. 7d. on 2,374,588*l.*, 3 per cents., transferred for life annuities, being an increase of 143,965*l.* 15s. 4¼d. for management, and an increase of about 509,322,000*l.* capital stock : Also the Bank was allowed 1000*l.* for taking in contributions, amounting to 812,500*l.* on a lottery in the year ending 5th July 1792 ; and 38,798*l.* 19s. 2d. for taking in contributions, amounting to 46,585,533*l.* 6s. 8d. on loans and lotteries in the year ending 5th April 1815.

2. That it appears, that the Bank, in pursuance of the Act 46 Geo. III. cap. 65, has, from the year 1806 to the present time, made the assessments of the duty on profits arising from property, on the proprietors of the whole of the funded debt, transferable at the Bank of England, and has deducted the said duty from each of the several dividend warrants, which in one year, ending 5th April 1815, amounted in number to 565,600 ; and that this part of the business has been done without any expense to, or charge on, the public.

That in pursuance of the above-mentioned Act, the duties so deducted have from time to time been placed to the " account of the commissioners of the treasury, on account of the said duties," together with other sums received from the public by virtue of the said Act : part of this money is applied to the payment of certificates of allowances, and the remainder is paid into the Exchequer.

That by virtue of the said Act, the Lords Commissioners of the Treasury have made annual allowances, at the rate of 1,250*l.* per million, upon the amount so placed to the account of the Commissioners of the Treasury at the Bank of England, as a compensation for receiving, paying, and accounting for the same ; which allowances, however, have not in any one year exceeded the sum of 3,480*l.*, and upon an average of eight years have amounted annually to 3,154*l.* only.

The amount of duties received for the year ending 5th April 1814, was 2,784,343*l.*, which, if it had been collected in the usual manner, at an allowance of 5d. per pound, would have cost the public 58,007*l.* ; and the cost for collecting 20,188,293*l.*, being the whole of the duty received from 1806 to 1814, on which allowances have been made, would at the same rate have amounted to 420,589*l.*

That all monies received by the Bank on account of duties on property are paid into the Exchequer immediately after the receipt thereof : when this circumstance is contrasted with the ordinary progress of monies into the Exchequer, the advantage resulting to the public may be fairly estimated at 2 per cent., which, on the amount of duties for the year ending 5th April 1814, would be 55,686*l.*, and, on the total amount from 1806 to 1814, would be 403,765*l.*

3. That the total amount of bank notes and bank post bills in circulation in the years 1795 and 1796 (the latter being the year

previous to the restriction on cash payments), and in the year 1814, was as follows :—

1795, 1st Feb.	L.12,735,520 ;	and 1st Aug.	L.11,214,000
1796, 1st Feb.	10,784,740 ;	and 1st Aug.	9,856,110
1814, 1st Feb.	25,154,950 ;	and 1st Aug.	28,802,450

4. That at present, and during many years past, both before and since the renewal of the charter of the Bank, considerable sums of the public money have been deposited with or otherwise placed in the custody of the Governor and Company of the Bank of England, who act in this respect as the banker of the public. The average balances of these deposits, both before and after the renewal of the charter, were as follows :—

Public balances on an average of one year ending the 15th January 1800, ...	L.1,724,747
Unclaimed dividends for the average of one year ending 1st January 1800, ...	837,966
	L.2,562,713
Public balances on an average of eight years, from 1807 to 1815, ...	L.4,375,405
Unclaimed dividends, do. do. . .	634,614
	L.5,010,019

5. That it appears from a report ordered to be printed 10th August 1807, from "the Committee on Public Expenditure of the United Kingdom," that the aggregate amount of balances and deposits of public money in the Bank of England, including bank notes deposited in the Exchequer, made up in four different periods of the quarter ending 5th January 1807, fluctuated between the sums of 11,461,200*l*. and 12,198,236*l*. ; or, excluding bank notes deposited at the Exchequer, the amount fluctuated between 8,178,536*l*. and 9,948,400*l*., the reason for which exclusion is not obvious, as by the Act of 48 Geo. III. cap. 3, the tellers of the Exchequer are authorised to take as securities on monies lodged, either exchequer bills or notes of the Governor and Company of the Bank of England. And it also appears, according to accounts laid before this house in the present session of Parliament, that the aggregate amount of such deposits, together with the exchequer bills and bank notes deposited in the chests of the four tellers of the Exchequer, was, on an average, in the year 1814—
L.11,966,371 ; including bank notes deposited at the Exchequer, amounting to 642,264*l*.
11,324,107 ; excluding bank notes deposited at the Exchequer.

6. That it appears, according to accounts before this house, that the average of the aggregate amount of balances of public money in the hands of the Bank of England, from February 1807 to February 1815, was 5,010,019*l*. ; and that the average of bills

and bank notes deposited in the chests of the four tellers of the Exchequer, from August 1807 to April 1815, was 5,968,793*l*., making together 10,978,812*l*., being 850,906*l*. less than the average of the said accounts for one year ending 5th January 1807, as stated in the report of the Committee on the Public Expenditure.

7. That by the 39 and 40 Geo. III. cap. 28, extending the charter of the Bank for twenty-one years, the Bank advanced to the public 3,000,000*l*. for six years without interest, and extended the loan of 11,686,800*l*. for twenty-one years at an interest of 3 per cent. per annum, as a consideration for the privileges, profits, emoluments, benefits, and advantages granted to the Bank by such extension of its charter.

That the interest of 3,000,000*l*. for six years, at 5 per cent. per annum, is	L.900,000
That the difference between 3 per cent. and 5 per cent. on 11,686,800*l*. is 233,736*l*., which in twenty-one years amounts to	4,908,456
That the above loan of 3,000,000*l*. was continued to the public from 1806, when it became payable, until 1814, at an interest of 3 per cent., making an advantage in favour of the public of 2 per cent. or 60,000*l*. per annum, which in eight years and eight months amounts to	520,000
That in 1808, the Bank advanced to the public 3,000,000*l*. without interest, which, by an Act of the present session, is to remain without interest until the 5th of April 1816; the interest on this advance, at 5 per cent., will, for eight years, amount to	1,200,000

8. That by the 39 and 40 Geo. III. cap. 28, sec. 13, it is enacted, that during the continuance of the charter, the Bank shall enjoy all privileges, profits, emoluments, benefits, and advantages whatsoever, which they now possess and enjoy by virtue of any employment by or on behalf of the public.

That, previously to such renewal of their charter, the Bank was employed as the public banker, in keeping the cash of all the principal departments in the receipt of the public revenue, and in issuing and conducting the public expenditure.

That the average amount of the public balances in the hands of the Bank, between the 1st February 1814 and the 15th January 1815, upon accounts opened at the Bank previously to the renewal of the charter on the 28th March 1800, was	L.4,337,025
Unclaimed dividends for the average of one year ending 1st January 1815, ...	779,794
	L.5,116,819

That the average public balances in the hands of the Bank during the same period, upon accounts opened at the Bank between the 28th March 1800 and the 27th February 1808, was . .	L.370,018
That the average public balances in the hands of the Bank during the same period, upon accounts opened at the Bank subsequent to the 27th February 1808, was	L.261,162

9. That whenever the engagements now subsisting between the public and the Bank shall expire, it may be proper to consider the advantages derived by the Bank from its transactions with the public with a view to the adoption of such arrangements as may be consistent with those principles of equity and good faith which ought to prevail in all transactions between the public and the Bank of England.

June 26, 1815.

AN ESSAY

ON THE

INFLUENCE OF A LOW PRICE OF CORN ON THE PROFITS OF STOCK

SHEWING THE

INEXPEDIENCY OF RESTRICTIONS ON IMPORTATIONS

WITH

REMARKS ON MR MALTHUS'S TWO LAST PUBLICATIONS:

"AN INQUIRY INTO THE NATURE AND PROGRESS OF RENT;" AND
"THE GROUNDS OF AN OPINION ON THE POLICY OF RESTRICTING THE IMPORTATION OF FOREIGN CORN"

SECOND EDITION

1815

INTRODUCTION

In treating on the subject of the profits of capital, it is necessary to consider the principles which regulate the rise and fall of rent, as rent and profits, it will be seen, have a very intimate connexion with each other. The principles which regulate rent are briefly stated in the following pages, and differ in a very slight degree from those which have been so fully and so ably developed by Mr Malthus in his late excellent publication, to which I am very much indebted. The consideration of those principles, together with those which regulate the profit of stock, has convinced me of the policy of leaving the importation of corn unrestricted by law. From the general principle set forth in all Mr Malthus's publications, I am persuaded that he holds the same opinion, as far as profit and wealth are concerned with the question; but, viewing, as he does, the danger as formidable of depending on foreign supply for a large portion of our food, he considers it wise, on the whole, to restrict importation. Not participating with him in those fears, and perhaps estimating the advantages of a cheap price of corn at a higher value, I have come to a different conclusion. Some of the objections urged in his last publication—"Grounds of an Opinion," &c., I have endeavoured to answer; they appear to me to be unconnected with the political danger he apprehends, and to be inconsistent with the general doctrines of the advantages of a free trade, which he has himself, by his writings, so ably contributed to establish.

ESSAY

ON THE

INFLUENCE OF A LOW PRICE OF CORN ON THE PROFITS OF STOCK

§ 1. Mr Malthus very correctly defines "the rent of land to be that portion of the value of the whole produce which remains to the owner after all the outgoings belonging to its cultivation, of whatever kind, have been paid, including the profits of the capital employed, estimated according to the usual and ordinary rate of the profits of agricultural stock at the time being."

Whenever, then, the usual and ordinary rate of the profits of agricultural stock, and all the outgoings belonging to the cultivation of land, are together equal to the value of the whole produce, there can be no rent.

And, when the whole produce is only equal in value to the outgoings necessary to cultivation, there can neither be rent nor profit.

In the first settling of a country rich in fertile land, and which may be had by any one who chooses to take it, the whole produce, after deducting the outgoings belonging to cultivation, will be the profits of capital, and will belong to the owner of such capital, without any deduction whatever for rent.

Thus, if the capital employed by an individual on such land were of the value of 200 quarters of wheat, of which half consisted of fixed capital, such as buildings, implements, &c., and the other half of circulating capital,—if, after replacing the fixed and circulating capital, the value of the remaining produce were 100 quarters of wheat, or of equal value with 100 quarters of wheat, the neat profit to the owner of capital would be 50 per cent., or 100 profit on 200 capital.

For a period of some duration the profits of agricultural stock might continue at the same rate because land equally fertile and equally well situated [1] might be abundant, and, therefore, might be cultivated on the same advantageous terms, in proportion as the capital of the first and subsequent settlers augmented.

Profits might even increase, because, the population increasing at a more rapid rate than capital, wages might fall; and, instead of the value of 100 quarters of wheat being necessary for the circulating capital, 90 only might be required, in which case the profits of stock would rise from 50 to 57 per cent.

Profits might also increase, because improvements might take place in agriculture, or in the implements of husbandry, which would augment the produce with the same cost of production.

If wages rose, or a worse system of agriculture were practised, profits would again fall.

These are circumstances which are more or less at all times in operation—they may retard or accelerate the natural effects of the progress of wealth, by raising or lowering profits—by increasing or diminishing the supply of food, with the employment of the same capital on the land.*

* Mr Malthus considers, that the surplus of produce obtained in consequence of diminished wages, or of improvements in agriculture, to be one of the causes to raise rent. To me it appears that it will only augment profits.

"The accumulation of capital, beyond the means of employing it on land of the greatest natural fertility, and the greatest advantage of situation, must necessarily lower profits; while the tendency of population to increase beyond the means of subsistence must, after a certain time, lower the wages of labour.

"The expense of production will thus be diminished, but the value of the produce, that is, the quality of labour, and of the

[1] [This phrase deserves to be noted, as showing that Ricardo did not, as has sometimes been alleged, ignore the importance of situation in determining both rent and also the order in which land in a new country is taken into cultivation.]

We will, however, suppose that no improvements take place in agriculture, and that capital and population advance in the proper proportion, so that the real wages of labour continue uniformly the same ;—that we may know what peculiar effects are to be ascribed to the growth of capital, the increase of population, and the extension of cultivation, to the more remote and less fertile land.

In this state of society, when the profits on agricultural stock, by the supposition, are 50 per cent., the profits on all other capital, employed either in the rude manufactures common to such a stage of society, or in foreign commerce, as the means of procuring in exchange for raw produce those commodities which may be in demand, will be also 50 per cent.*

If the profits on capital employed in trade were more than 50 per cent., capital would be withdrawn from the land to be employed in trade. If they were less, capital would be taken from trade to agriculture.

§ 2. After all the fertile land in the immediate neighbourhood of the first settlers were cultivated, if capital

other products of labour besides corn, which it can command, instead of diminishing, will be increased.

"There will be an increasing number of people demanding subsistence, and ready to offer their services in any way in which they can be useful. The exchangeable value of food will therefore be in excess above the cost of production, including in this cost the full profits of the stock employed upon the land, according to the actual rate of profits at the time being. And this excess is rent."—*An Inquiry into the Nature and Progress of Rent*, page 18.

In page 19, speaking of Poland, one of the causes of rent is again attributed to cheapness of labour. In page 22 it is said that a fall in the wages of labour, or a reduction in the number of labourers necessary to produce a given effect, in consequence of agricultural improvements, will raise rent.

* It is not meant, that strictly the rate of profits on agriculture and manufactures will be the same, but that they will bear some proportion to each other. Adam Smith has explained why profits are somewhat less on some employments of capital than on others, according to their security, cleanliness, and respectability, &c., &c.

What the proportion may be, is of no importance to my argument, as I am only desirous of proving that the profits on agricultural capital cannot materially vary, without occasioning a similar variation in the profits on capital employed on manufactures and commerce.

and population increased, more food would be required, and it could only be procured from land not so advantageously situated. Supposing, then, the land to be equally fertile, the necessity of employing more labourers, horses, &c., to carry the produce from the place where it was grown to the place where it was to be consumed, although no alteration were to take place in the wages of labour, would make it necessary that more capital should be permanently employed to obtain the same produce. Suppose this addition to be of the value of 10 quarters of wheat, the whole capital employed on the new land would be 210, to obtain the same return as on the old; and, consequently, the profits of stock would fall from 50 to 43 per cent., or 90 on 210.*

On the land first cultivated, the return would be the same as before, namely 50 per cent., or 100 quarters of wheat; but the general profits of stock being regulated by the profits made on the least profitable employment of capital on agriculture, a division of the 100 quarters would take place, 43 per cent., or 86 quarters, would constitute the profit of stock, and 7 per cent., or 14 quarters, would constitute rent. And that such a division must take place is evident, when we consider that the owner of the capital of the value of 210 quarters of wheat would obtain precisely the same profit, whether he cultivated the distant land, or paid the first settler 14 quarters for rent.

In this stage, the profits in all capital employed in trade would fall to 43 per cent.

If, in the further progress of population and wealth, the produce of more land were required to obtain the same return, it might be necessary to employ, either on account of distance, or the worse quality of land, the value of 220 quarters of wheat, the profits of stock would

* Profits of stock fall, because land equally fertile cannot be obtained, and through the whole progress of society profits are regulated by the difficulty or facility of procuring food. This is a principle of great importance, and has been almost overlooked in the writings of Political Economists. They appear to think that profits of stock can be raised by commercial causes, independently of the supply of food.

[A necessary standard wage is assumed throughout.]

then fall to 36 per cent., or 80 on 220, and the rent of the first land would rise to 28 quarters of wheat, and on the second portion of land cultivated, rent would now commence, and would amount to 14 quarters.

The profits on all trading capital would also fall to 36 per cent.

Thus, by bringing successively land of a worse quality, or less favourably situated into cultivation, rent would rise on the land previously cultivated, and precisely in the same degree would profits fall; and if the smallness of profits do not check accumulation[1] there are hardly any limits to the rise of rent, and the fall of profit.

If instead of employing capital at a distance on new land, an additional capital of the value of 210 quarters of wheat be employed on the first land cultivated, and its return were in like manner 43 per cent. or 90 on 210; the produce of 50 per cent. on the first capital would be divided in the same manner as before,—43 per cent. or 86 quarters would constitute profit, and 14 quarters rent.

If 220 quarters were employed in addition with the same result as before, the first capital would afford a rent of 28; and the second of 14 quarters, and the profits on the whole capital of 630 quarters would be equal, and would amount to 36 per cent.

Supposing that the nature of man was so altered, that he required double the quantity of food that is now necessary for his subsistence, and consequently, that the expenses of cultivation were very greatly increased. Under such circumstances, the knowledge and capital of an old society employed on fresh and fertile land in a new country would leave a much less surplus produce; consequently, the profits of stock could never be so high. But accumulation, though slower in its progress, might still go on, and rent would begin just as before, when more distant or less fertile land were cultivated.

The natural limit to population would of course be much earlier, and rent could never rise to the height to which it may now do; because, in the nature of things,

[1] [Cf. *Principles*, § 44, p. 100, § 31, p. 57. Unfortunately Ricardo did not investigate the connexion between interest and accumulation.]

land of the same poor quality would never be brought into cultivation ;—nor could the same amount of capital be employed on the better land with any adequate return of profit.*

The following table is constructed on the supposition, that the first portion of land yields 100 quarters profit on a capital of 200 quarters ; the second portion, 90 quarters on 210, according to the foregoing calculations.† It will be seen that, during the progress of a country, the whole produce raised on its land, will increase, and for a certain time that part of the produce which belongs to the profits of stock, as well as that part which belongs to rent, will increase ; but that, at a later period, every accumulation of capital will be attended with an absolute, as well as a proportionate diminution of profits,—though rents will uniformly increase. A less revenue, it will be seen, will be enjoyed by the owner of stock, when 1,350 quarters are employed on the different qualities of land, than when 1,100 were employed. In the former case the whole profits will be only 270, in the latter 275 ; and when 1,610 are employed, profits will fall to 241½.‡

* In all that I have said concerning the origin and progress of rent, I have briefly repeated, and endeavoured to elucidate the principles which Mr Malthus has so ably laid down, on the same subject, in his " Inquiry into the Nature and Progress of Rent ; " a work abounding in original ideas,—which are useful not only as they regard rent, but as connected with the question of taxation ; perhaps, the most difficult and intricate of all the subjects on which Political Economy treats.

† It is scarcely necessary to observe, that the data on which this table is constructed are assumed, and are probably very far from the truth. They were fixed on as tending to illustrate the principle, which would be the same, whether the first profits were 50 per cent. or 5,—or, whether an additional capital of 10 quarters, or of 100, were required to obtain the same produce from the cultivation of new land. In proportion as the capital employed on the land, consisted more of fixed capital, and less of circulating capital, would rent advance, and property fall less rapidly.

‡ This would be the effect of a constantly accumulating capital, in a country which refused to import foreign and cheaper corn. But after profits have very much fallen, accumulation will be checked, and capital will be exported to be employed in those countries where food is cheap and profits high. All European colonies have been established with the capital of the mother countries, and have thereby checked accumulation. That part

This is a view of the effects of accumulation which is exceedingly curious, and has, I believe, never before been noticed.

It will be seen by the table, that, in a progressive country, rent is not only absolutely increasing, but that it is also increasing in its ratio to the capital employed on the land; thus, when 410 was the whole capital employed, the landlord obtained 3½ per cent.; when 1,100, 13¼ per cent.; and when 1,880, 16½ per cent. The landlord not only obtains a greater produce, but a larger share.—(*See Table on next page.*)

§ 3. Rent,* then, is in all cases a portion of the profits previously obtained on the land. It is never a new creation of revenue, but always part of a revenue already created.

Profits of stock fall only, because land equally well adapted to produce food cannot be procured; and the degree of the fall of profits, and the rise of rents, depends wholly on the increased expense of production.

If, therefore, in the progress of countries in wealth and population, new portions of fertile land could be added to such countries, with every increase of capital, profits would never fall, nor rents rise.†

If the money price of corn, and the wages of labour, did not vary in price in the least degree, during the progress of the country in wealth and population, still profits would fall and rents would rise; because *more* labourers would be employed on the more distant or

of the population, too, which is employed in the foreign carrying trade, is fed with foreign corn. It cannot be doubted, that low profits, which are the inevitable effects of a really high price of corn, tend to draw capital abroad; this consideration ought therefore to be a powerful reason to prevent us from restricting importation.

* By rent I always mean the remuneration given to the landlord for the use of the original and inherent power of the land. If either the landlord expends capital on his own land, or the capital of a preceding tenant is left upon it at the expiration of his lease, he may obtain what is indeed called a larger rent, but a portion of this is evidently paid for the use of capital. The other portion only is paid for the use of the original power of the land.

† Excepting, as has been before observed, the real wages of labour should rise, or a worse system of agriculture be practised.

TABLE, showing the Progress of Rent and Profit under an assumed Augmentation of Capital.

Capital estimated in quarters of wheat.	Profit per cent.	Neat produce in quarters of wheat, after paying the cost of production on each capital.	Profit of 1st portion of land in quarters of wheat.	Rent of 1st portion of land in quarters of wheat.	Profit of 2d portion of land in quarters of wheat.	Rent of 2d portion of land in quarters of wheat.	Profit of 3d portion of land in quarters of wheat.	Rent of 3d portion of land in quarters of wheat.	Profit of 4th portion of land in quarters of wheat.	Rent of 4th portion of land in quarters of wheat.	Profit of 5th portion of land in quarters of wheat.	Rent of 5th portion of land in quarters of wheat.	Profit of 6th portion of land in quarters of wheat.	Rent of 6th portion of land in quarters of wheat.	Profit of 7th portion of land in quarters of wheat.	Rent of 7th portion of land in quarters of wheat.	Profit of 8th portion of land in quarters of wheat.
200	50	100	100	none.													
210	43	90	86	14	90	none.											
220	36	80	72	28	76	14	80	none.									
230	30	70	60	40	63	27	66	14	70	none.							
240	25	60	50	50	52½	37½	55	25	57½	12½	60	none.					
250	20	50	40	60	42	48	44	36	46	24	48	12	50	none.			
260	15	40	30	70	31½	58½	33	47	34½	35½	36	24	37½	12½	40	none.	
270	11	30	22	78	23	67	24	56	25.3	44.7	26.4	33.6	½	22½	27.6	12.4	29.7

	When the whole capital employed is	Whole amount of rent received by landlords in quarters of wheat.	Whole amount of profits in quarters received by owners of stock.	Profit per cent. on the whole capital.	Rent per cent. on the whole capital.	Total produce in quarters of wheat, after paying the cost of production.
1st Period	200	none.	100	50		100
2d Ditto	410	14	176	43	3½	190
3d Ditto	630	42	228	36	6¾	270
4th Ditto	860	81	259	30	9½	340
5th Ditto	1100	125	275	25	11½	400
6th Ditto	1350	180	270	20	13¼	450
7th Ditto	1610	248½	241½	15	15½	490
8th Ditto	1880	314½	205½	11	16½	520

less fertile land, in order to obtain the same supply of raw produce; and therefore the cost of production would have increased, whilst the value of the produce continued the same.

§ 4. But the price of corn, and of all other raw produce, has been invariably observed to rise as a nation became wealthy, and was obliged to have recourse to poorer lands for the production of part of its food; and very little consideration will convince us, that such is the effect which would naturally be expected to take place under such circumstances.

The exchangeable value of all commodities rises as the difficulties of their production increase. If, then, new difficulties occur in the production of corn, from more labour being necessary, whilst no more labour is required to produce gold, silver, cloth, linen, &c., the exchangeable value of corn will necessarily rise, as compared with those things. On the contrary, facilities in the production of corn, or of any other commodity of whatever kind, which shall afford the same produce with less labour, will lower its exchangeable value.* Thus we see that improvements in agriculture, or in the implements of husbandry, lower the exchangeable value of corn;† improvements in the machinery connected with the manufacture of cotton, lower the exchangeable value of cotton goods; and improvements in mining or the discovery of new and more abundant mines of the precious metals, lower the

* The low price of corn, caused by improvements in agriculture, would give a stimulus to population, by increasing profits and encouraging accumulation, which would again raise the price of corn and lower profits. But a larger population could be maintained at the same price of corn, the same profits and the same rents. Improvements in agriculture may then be said to increase profits, and to lower for a time rents.

† The causes, which render the acquisition of an additional quantity of corn more difficult are, in progressive countries, in constant operation, whilst marked improvements in agriculture, or in the implements of husbandry, are of less frequent occurrence. If these opposite causes acted with equal effect, corn would be subject only to accidental variation of price, arising from bad seasons, from greater or less real wages of labour, or from an alteration in the value of the precious metals, proceeding from their abundance or scarcity.

value of gold and silver, or, which is the same thing, raise the price of all other commodities. Wherever competition can have its full effect, and the production of the commodity be not limited by nature, as is the case with some wines, the difficulty or facility of their production will ultimately regulate their exchangeable value.* The sole effect, then, of the progress of wealth on prices, independently of all improvements, either in agriculture or manufactures, appears to be to raise the price of raw produce and of labour, leaving all other commodities at their original prices, and to lower general profits in consequence of the general rise of wages.

This fact is of more importance than at first sight appears, as it relates to the interest of the landlord, and the other parts of the community. Not only is the situation of the landlord improved (by the increasing difficulty of procuring food, in consequence of accumulation,) by obtaining an increased quantity of the produce of the land, but also by the increased exchangeable value of that quantity. If his rent be increased from 14 to 28 quarters, it would be more than doubled, because he would be able to command more than double the quantity of commodities, in exchange for the 28 quarters. As rents are agreed for, and paid in money, he would, under the circumstances supposed, receive more than double of his former money rent.

In like manner, if rent fell, the landlord would suffer two losses; he would be a loser of that portion of the raw produce which constituted his additional rent; and further, he would be a loser by the depreciation in the real or exchangeable value of the raw produce in which, or in the value of which, his remaining rent would be paid.†

* Though the price of all commodities is ultimately regulated by, and is always tending to, the cost of their production, including the general profits of stock, they are all subject, and perhaps corn more than most others, to an accidental price proceeding from temporary causes.

† It has been thought that the price of corn regulates the prices of all other things. This appears to me to be a mistake. If the price of corn is affected by the rise or fall of the value of the

As the revenue of the farmer is realized in raw produce, or in the value of raw produce, he is interested, as well as the landlord, in its high exchangeable value, but a low price of produce may be compensated to him by a great additional quantity.

§ 5. It follows, then, that the interest of the landlord is always opposed to the interest of every other class in the community.[1] His situation is never so prosperous, as when food is scarce and dear : whereas, all other persons are greatly benefited by procuring food cheap. High rent and low profits, for they invariably accompany each other, ought never to be the subject of complaint, if they are the effect of the natural course of things.

They are the most unequivocal proofs of wealth and prosperity, and of an abundant population, compared with the fertility of the soil. The general profits of stock depend wholly on the profits of the last portion of capital employed on the land ; if, therefore, landlords were to relinquish the whole of their rents, they would neither raise the general profits of stock, nor lower the price of corn to the consumer. It would have no other effect, as Mr Malthus has observed, than to enable those farmers, whose lands now pay a rent, to live like gentlemen, and they would have to expend that portion of the general revenue which now falls to the share of the landlord.

A nation is rich, not according to the abundance of its money, nor to the high money value at which its com-

precious metals themselves, then indeed will the price of commodities be also affected, but they vary, because the value of money varies, not because the value of corn is altered. Commodities, I think, cannot materially rise or fall, whilst money and commodities continue in the same proportions, or rather whilst the cost of production of both estimated in corn continues the same. In the case of taxation, a part of the price is paid for the liberty of using the commodity, and does not constitute its real price.

[1] [The interest of the landlord in this phrase means the interest of the landlord as the recipient of that which is given for the use of " the original and inherent power of the land." It has no reference to the part he takes or may take in agriculture by looking after the land or investing his capital in it. This is clear from the note (†) to § 3, *supra*.]

modities circulate, but according to the abundance of its commodities, contributing to its comforts and enjoyments. Although this is a proposition, from which few would dissent, many look with the greatest alarm at the prospect of the diminution of their money revenue, though such reduced revenue should have so improved in exchangeable value, as to procure considerably more of all the necessaries and luxuries of life.

§ 6. If, then, the principles here stated as governing rent and profit be correct, general profits on capital can only be raised by a fall in the exchangeable value of food, and which fall can only arise from three causes :—

1st. The fall of the real wages of labour, which shall enable the farmer to bring a greater excess of produce to market.

2d. Improvements in agriculture, or in the implements of husbandry, which shall also increase the excess of produce.

3dly. The discovery of new markets, from whence corn may be imported at a cheaper price than it can be grown for at home.

The first of these causes is more or less permanent, according as the price from which wages fall, is more or less near that remuneration for labour which is necessary to the actual subsistence of the labourer.

The rise or fall of wages is common to all states of society, whether it be the stationary, the advancing, or the retrograde state. In the stationary state, it is regulated wholly by the increase or falling off of the population. In the advancing state, it depends on whether the capital or the population advance, at the more rapid course. In the retrograde state, it depends on whether population or capital decrease with the greater rapidity.

As experience demonstrates that capital and population alternately take the lead, and wages in consequence are liberal or scanty, nothing can be positively laid down, respecting profits, as far as wages are concerned.

But I think it may be most satisfactorily proved, that in every society advancing in wealth and population, independently of the effect produced by liberal or scanty wages, general profits must fall, unless there be improvements in agriculture, or corn can be imported at a cheaper price.

It seems the necessary result of the principles which have been stated to regulate the progress of rent.

§ 7. This principle will, however, not be readily admitted by those who ascribe to the extension of commerce, and discovery of new markets, where our commodities can be sold dearer, and foreign commodities can be bought cheaper, the progress of profits, without any reference whatever to the state of the land, and the rate of profit obtained on the last portions of capital employed upon it. Nothing is more common than to hear it asserted, that profits on agriculture no more regulate the profits of commerce, than that the profits of commerce regulate the profits on agriculture. It is contended that they alternately take the lead; and, if the profits of commerce rise, which it is said they do, when new markets are discovered, the profits of agriculture will also rise; for it is admitted, that if they did not do so, capital would be withdrawn from the land to be employed in the more profitable trade. But if the principles respecting the progress of rent be correct, it is evident, that, with the same population and capital, whilst none of the agricultural capital is withdrawn from the cultivation of the land, agricultural profits cannot rise, nor can rent fall: either then it must be contended, which is at variance with all the principles of political economy, that the profits on commercial capital will rise considerably, whilst the profits on agricultural capital suffer no alteration, or that, under such circumstances, the profits on commerce will not rise.*

* Mr Malthus has supplied me with a happy illustration—he has correctly compared "the soil to a great number of machines, all susceptible of continued improvement by the application of capital to them, but yet of very different original qualities and powers." How, I would ask, can profits rise whilst we are obliged to make use of that machine which has the worst original qualities and powers? We cannot abandon the use of it; for it is the condition on which we obtain the food necessary for our population, and the demand for food is by the supposition not diminished; but who would consent to use it if he could make greater profits elsewhere?

It is this latter opinion which I consider as the true one. I do not deny that the first discoverer of a new and better market may, for a time, before competition operates, obtain unusual profits. He may either sell the commodities he exports at a higher price than those who are ignorant of the new market, or he may purchase the commodities imported at a cheaper price. Whilst he, or a few more exclusively follow this trade, their profits will be above the level of general profits. But it is of the general rate of profit that we are speaking, and not of the profits of a few individuals; and I cannot doubt that, in proportion as such trade shall be generally known and followed, there will be such a fall in the price of the foreign commodity in the importing country, in consequence of its increased abundance, and the greater facility with which it is procured, that its sale will afford only the common rate of profits—that so far from the high profits obtained by the few who first engaged in the new trade elevating the general rate of profits—those profits will themselves sink to the ordinary level.

The effects are precisely similar to those which follow from the use of improved machinery at home.

Whilst the use of the machine is confined to one, or a very few manufacturers, they may obtain unusual profits, because they are enabled to sell their commodities at a price much above the cost of production—but as soon as the machine becomes general to the whole trade, the price of the commodities will sink to the actual cost of production, leaving only the usual and ordinary profits.

During the period of capital moving from one employment to another, the profits on that to which capital is flowing will be relatively high, but will continue so no longer than till the requisite capital is obtained.

There are two ways in which a country may be benefited by trade—one by the increase of the general rate of profits, which, according to my opinion, can never take place but in consequence of cheap food, which is beneficial only to those who derive a revenue from the employment of their capital, either as farmers, manufacturers, merchants, or capitalists, lending their money at interest—the other by the abundance of commodities, and by a fall in their exchangeable value, in which the whole community participate. In the first case, the revenue [1] of the country is augmented—in the second, the same revenue becomes efficient in procuring a greater amount of the necessaries and luxuries of life.

It is in this latter mode only * that nations are benefited by the extension of commerce, by the division of labour in manufactures, and by the discovery of machinery,—they all augment the amount of commodities, and contribute very much to the ease and happiness of mankind; but they have no effect on the rate of profits, because they do not augment the produce compared with the cost of production on the land, and it is impossible that all other profits should rise whilst the profits on land are either stationary, or retrograde.[2]

§ 8. Profits, then, depend on the price, or rather on the value of food. Every thing which gives facility to the production of food, however scarce, or however abundant commodities may become, will raise the rate of profits, whilst on the contrary, every thing which shall augment the cost of production without augmenting the quantity of food,† will, under every circumstance, lower the general rate of profits. The facilities of obtaining food are bene-

* Excepting where the extension of commerce enables us to obtain food at really cheaper prices.

† If by foreign commerce, or the discovery of machinery, the commodities consumed by the labourer should become much cheaper, wages would fall; and this, as we have before observed, would raise the profits of the farmer, and therefore, all other profits.

[1] [As to *revenue*, cf. *Principles*, Chapter XXXII., § 151.]

[2] [This important passage, which throws a great deal of light on Ricardo's general conceptions and particularly on the relations he indicates between profits and wages, is dealt with in the Introductory Essay to this volume; see also note to § 16 of *Protection to Agriculture*.

Two things must be borne in mind in connexion with the whole argument. Firstly, the particular meaning attached to the phrase " rate of profits "; secondly, the assumption stated in a previous note that " the demand for food is by the supposition not diminished."

Compare *Principles*, Chapter XX., Value and Riches, § 97, where a like distinction to that between the two modes by which a country benefits from trade is suggested.]

ficial in two ways to the owners of capital; it at the same time raises profits and increases the amount of consumable commodities. The facilities in obtaining all other things only increase the amount of commodities.

§ 9. If, then, the power of purchasing cheap food be of such great importance, and if the importation of corn will tend to reduce its price, arguments almost unanswerable respecting the danger of dependence on foreign countries for a portion of our food—for in no other view will the question bear an argument—ought to be brought forward to induce us to restrict importation, and thereby forcibly to detain capital in an employment which it would otherwise leave for one much more advantageous.

If the legislature were at once to adopt a decisive policy with regard to the trade in corn—if it were to allow a permanently free trade, and did not, with every variation of price, alternately restrict and encourage importation, we should undoubtedly be a regularly importing country. We should be so in consequence of the superiority of our wealth and population, compared to the fertility of our soil over our neighbours. It is only when a country is comparatively wealthy, when all its fertile land is in a state of high cultivation, and that it is obliged to have recourse to its inferior lands to obtain the food necessary for its population; or when it is originally without the advantages of a fertile soil, that it can become profitable to import corn.*

It is, then, the dangers of dependence on foreign supply for any considerable quantity of our food, which can alone be opposed to the many advantages which, circumstanced as we are, would attend the importation of corn.

§ 10. These dangers do not admit of being very correctly estimated; they are in some degree matters of opinion, and cannot, like the advantages on the other side, be reduced to accurate calculation. They are generally stated to be two—1st, That in the case of war a combination of the Continental powers, or the influence of our principal enemy, might deprive us of our accus-

* This principle is most ably stated by Mr Malthus in page 42 of "An Inquiry," &c.

tomed supply—2dly, That when bad seasons occurred abroad, the exporting countries would have, and would exercise, the power of withholding the quantity usually exported to make up for their own deficient supply.*

If we became a regularly importing country, and foreigners could confidently rely on the demand of our market, much more land would be cultivated in the corn countries with a view to exportation. When we consider the value of even a few weeks' consumption of corn in England, no interruption could be given to the export trade, if the Continent supplied us with any considerable quantity of corn, without the most extensively ruinous commercial distress—distress which no sovereign, or combination of sovereigns, would be willing to inflict on their people; and, if willing, it would be a measure to which probably no people would submit. It was the endeavour of Buonaparte to prevent the exportation of the raw produce of Russia, more than any other cause, which produced the astonishing efforts of the people of that country against the most powerful force perhaps ever assembled to subjugate a nation.

§ 11. The immense capital which would be employed on the land, could not be withdrawn suddenly, and under such circumstances, without immense loss; besides which, the glut of corn in their markets, which would affect their whole supply, and lower its value beyond calculation; the failure of those returns, which are essential in all commercial adventures, would occasion a scene of wide-spreading ruin, which, if a country would patiently endure, would render it unfit to wage war with any prospect of success. We have all witnessed the distress in this country, and we have all heard of the still greater distress in Ireland, from a fall in the price of corn, at a time, too, when it is acknowledged that our own crop has been deficient; when importation has been regulated by price, and when we have not experienced any of the effects of a glut. Of what nature would that distress

* It is this latter opinion which is chiefly insisted upon by Mr Malthus, in his late publication, "The Grounds of an Opinion," &c.

have been if the price of corn had fallen to a half a quarter, or an eighth part of the present price? For the effects of plenty or scarcity, on the price of corn, are incalculably greater than in proportion to the increase or deficiency of quantity. These, then, are the inconveniences which the exporting countries would have to endure.

Ours would not be light. A great diminution in our usual supply, amounting probably to one-eighth of our whole consumption, it must be confessed, would be an evil of considerable magnitude; but we have obtained a supply equal to this, even when the growth of foreign countries was not regulated by the constant demand of our market. We all know the prodigious effects of a high price in procuring a supply. It cannot, I think, be doubted, that we should obtain a considerable quantity from those countries with which we were not at war; which, with the most economical use of our own produce, and the quantity in store,* would enable us to subsist till we had bestowed the necessary capital and labour on our own land, with a view to future production. That this would be a most afflicting change, I certainly allow; but I am fully persuaded that we should not be driven to such an alternative, and that, notwithstanding the war, we should be freely supplied with the corn, expressly grown in foreign countries for our consumption. Buonaparte, when he was most hostile to us, permitted the exportation of corn to England by licenses, when our prices were high from a bad harvest, even when all other commerce was prohibited. Such a state of things could not come upon us suddenly; a danger of this nature would be partly foreseen, and due precautions would be taken. Would it be wise, then, to legislate with the view of preventing an evil which might never occur; and, to ward off a most improbable danger, sacrifice annually a revenue of some millions?

In contemplating a trade in corn, unshackled by restrictions on importation, and a consequent supply from France, and other countries, where it can be brought

* As London is to be a depôt for foreign corn, this store might be very great.

to market at a price not much above half that at which we can ourselves produce it on some of our poorer lands, Mr Malthus does not sufficiently allow for the greater quantity of corn which would be grown abroad, if importation was to become the settled policy of this country. There cannot be the least doubt that if the corn countries could depend on the markets of England for a regular demand, if they could be perfectly secure that our laws respecting the corn trade would not be repeatedly vacillating between bounties, restrictions, and prohibitions, a much larger supply would be grown, and the danger of a greatly diminished exportation, in consequence of bad seasons, would be less likely to occur. Countries which have never yet supplied us might, if our policy was fixed, afford us a considerable quantity.

It is at such times that it would be particularly the interest of foreign countries to supply our wants, as the exchangeable value of corn does not rise in proportion only to the deficiency of supply, but two, three, four times as much, according to the amount of the deficiency.

If the consumption of England is 10 million quarters, which, in an average year, would sell for 40 millions of money; and, if the supply should be deficient one-fourth, the 7,500,000 quarters would not sell for 40 millions only, but probably for fifty millions or more. Under the circumstances, then, of bad seasons the exporting country would content itself with the smallest possible quantity necessary for their own consumption, and would take advantage of the high price in England to sell all they could spare, as not only would corn be high, as compared with money, but as compared with all other things; and if the growers of corn adopted any other rule, they would be in a worse situation, as far as regarded wealth, than if they had constantly limited the growth of corn to the wants of their own people.

If 100 millions of capital were employed on the land to obtain the quantity necessary to their own subsistence, and 20 millions more that they might export the produce, they would lose the whole return of the 20 millions in the scarce year, which they would not have done had they not been an exporting country. At whatever price exportation might be restricted by foreign countries, the chance of corn rising to that price would be diminished by the greater quantity produced in consequence of our demand.

§ 12. With respect to the supply of corn, it has been remarked, in reference to a single country, that if the crops are bad in one district they are generally productive in another; that if the weather is injurious to one soil, or to one situation, it is beneficial to a different soil and different situation; and, by this compensating power Providence has bountifully secured us from the frequent recurrence of dearths. If this remark be just as applied to one country, how much more strongly may it be applied to all the countries together which compose our world? Will not the deficiency of one country be made up by the plenty of another? and after the experience which we have had of the power of high prices to procure a supply, can we have any just reason to fear that we shall be exposed to any particular danger from depending on importation for so much corn as may be necessary for a few weeks of our consumption?

From all that I can learn, the price of corn in Holland, which country depends almost wholly on foreign supply, has been remarkably steady, even during the convulsed times which Europe has lately experienced,—a convincing proof, notwithstanding the smallness of the country, that the effects of bad seasons are not exclusively borne by importing countries.

§ 13. That great improvements have been made in agriculture, and that much capital has been expended on the land, it is not attempted to deny; but, with all those improvements, we have not overcome the natural impediments resulting from our increasing wealth and prosperity, which obliges us to cultivate at a disadvantage our poor lands if the importation of corn is restricted or prohibited. If we were left to ourselves, unfettered by legislative enactments, we should gradually withdraw our capital from the cultivation of such lands, and import the produce which is at present raised upon them.

The capital withdrawn would be employed in the manufacture of such commodities as would be exported in return for the corn.* Such a distribution of part of the capital of the country would be more advantageous or it would not be adopted. This principle is one of the best established in the science of political economy, and by no one is more readily admitted than by Mr Malthus. It is the foundation of all his arguments, in his comparison of the advantages and disadvantages attending an unrestricted trade in corn, in his "Observations on the Corn Laws."

In his last publication, however, in one part of it, he dwells with much stress on the losses of agricultural capital, which the country would sustain, by allowing an unrestricted importation. He laments the loss of that which by the course of events has become of no use to us, and by the employment of which we actually lose. We might just as fairly have been told, when the steam-engine, or Mr Arkwright's cotton machine was brought to perfection, that it would be wrong to adopt the use of them, because the value of the old clumsy machinery would be lost to us. That the farmers of the poorer lands would be losers, there can be no doubt, but the public would gain many times the amount of their losses; and, after the exchange of capital from land to manufactures had been effected, the farmers themselves, as well as every other class of the community, except the landholders, would very considerably increase their profits.

It might, however, be desirable, that the farmers, during their current leases, should be protected against the losses which they would undoubtedly suffer from the new value of money, which would result from a cheap

* If it be true, as Mr Malthus observes, that in Ireland there are no manufactures in which capital could be profitably employed capital would not be withdrawn from the land, and then there would be no loss of agricultural capital. Ireland would in such case have the same surplus corn produce, although it would be of less exchangeable value. Her revenue might be diminished; but if she would not or could not manufacture goods, and would not cultivate the ground, she would have no revenue at all.

price of corn, under their existing money engagements with their landlords.

Although the nation would sacrifice much more than the farmers would save even by a temporary high price of corn, it might be just to lay restrictive duties on importation for three or four years, and to declare that, after that period, the trade in corn should be free, and that imported corn should be subject to no other duty than such as we might find it expedient to impose on corn of our own growth.*

Mr Malthus is, no doubt, correct, when he says, " If merely the best modes of cultivation now in use, in some parts of Great Britain, were generally extended, and the whole country was brought to a level, in proportion to its natural advantages, of soil and situation, by the further accumulation and more equable distribution of capital and skill, the quantity of additional produce would be immense, and would afford the means of subsistence to a very great increase of population." †

This reflection is true, and is highly pleasing—it shows that we are yet at a great distance from the end of our resources, and that we may contemplate an increase of prosperity and wealth far exceeding that of any country which has preceded us. This may take place under

* I by no means agree with Adam Smith, or with Mr Malthus, respecting the effects of taxation on the necessaries of life. The former can find no term too severe by which to characterise them. Mr Malthus is more lenient. They both think that such taxes, incalculably more than any other, tend to diminish capital and production. I do not say that they are the best of taxes, but they do not, I think, subject us to any of the disadvantages of which Adam Smith speaks in foreign trade ; nor do they produce effects very different from other taxes. Adam Smith thought that such taxes fell exclusively on the landholder ; Mr Malthus thinks they are divided between the landholder and consumer. It appears to me that they are paid wholly by the consumer.

[See *Principles*, Chapter IX., § 56, Chapter XVI., § 82. In the present note Ricardo does not deal with the ultimate incidence of such taxes when they tend to bring about a rise in wages. Speaking here of their incidence on the consumer he treats of the immediate effect. In the *Principles*, as above, he urges that their effect on wages will react upon profits ; a position which is in conflict with that laid down by Adam Smith.]

† Page 22, " Grounds," &c.

either system, that of importation or restriction, though not with an equally accelerated pace, and is no argument why we should not, at every period of our improvement, avail ourselves of the full extent of the advantages offered to our acceptance—it is no reason why we should not make the very best disposition of our capital, so as to ensure the most abundant return. The land has, as I before said, been compared by Mr Malthus, to a great number of machines, all susceptible of continued improvement by the application of capital to them, but yet of very different original qualities and powers. Would it be wise at a great expense to use some of the worst of these machines, when at a less expense we could hire the very best from our neighbours?

§ 14. Mr Malthus thinks that a low money price of corn would not be favourable to the lower classes of society, because the real exchangeable value of labour, that is, its power of commanding the necessaries, conveniences, and luxuries of life, would not be augmented but diminished by a low money price. Some of his observations on this subject are certainly of great weight, but he does not sufficiently allow for the effects of a better distribution of the national capital on the situation of the lower classes. It would be beneficial to them, because the same capital would employ more hands; besides, that the greater profits would lead to further accumulation; and thus would a stimulus be given to population by really high wages, which could not fail for a long time to ameliorate the condition of the labouring classes.

The effects on the interests of this class, would be nearly the same as the effects of improved machinery, which, it is now no longer questioned, has a decided tendency to raise the real wages of labour.

Mr Malthus also observes, "that of the commercial and manufacturing classes, only those who are directly engaged in foreign trade will feel the benefit of the importing system."

If the view which has been taken of rent be correct,—if it rise as general profits fall, and fall as general profits rise,—and if the effect of importing corn is to lower rent, which has been admitted, and ably exemplified by Mr

Malthus himself,—all who are concerned in trade,—all capitalists whatever, whether they be farmers, manufacturers, or merchants, will have a great augmentation of profits. A fall in the price of corn, in consequence of improvements in agriculture or of importation, will lower the exchangeable value of corn only,—the price of no other commodity will be affected. If, then, the price of labour falls, which it must do when the price of corn is lowered, the real profits of all descriptions must rise; and no person will be so materially benefited as the manufacturing and commercial part of society.

If the demand for home commodities should be diminished, because of the fall of rent on the part of the landlords, it will be increased in a far greater degree by the increased opulence of the commercial classes.

§ 15. If restrictions on the importation of corn should take place, I do not apprehend that we shall lose any part of our foreign trade; on this point I agree with Mr Malthus. In the case of a free trade in corn it would be considerably augmented; but the question is not, whether we can retain the same foreign trade—but, whether, in both cases, it will be equally profitable.

Our commodities would not sell abroad for more or less in consequence of a free trade, and a cheap price of corn; but the cost of production to our manufacturers would be very different if the price of corn was eighty, or was sixty shillings per quarter; and consequently profits would be augmented by all the cost saved in the production of the exported commodities.

§ 16. Mr Malthus notices an observation, which was first made by Hume,[1] that a rise of prices has a magic effect on industry: he states the effects of a fall to be proportionally depressing.* A rise of prices has been stated to be one of the advantages, to counter-balance the many evils attendant on a depreciation of money,

* "Grounds," &c., p. 32.

[1] [Essay XXV. *Of Money:* "Accordingly we find, that, in every kingdom, into which money begins to flow in greater abundance than formerly, everything takes a new face: labour and industry gain life, &c."]

from a real fall in the value of the precious metals, from raising the denomination of the coin, or from the over-issue of paper-money.

It is said to be beneficial, because it betters the situation of the commercial classes at the expense of those enjoying fixed incomes ;—and that it is chiefly in those classes, that the great accumulations are made, and productive industry encouraged.

A recurrence to a better monetary system, it is said, though highly desirable, tends to give a temporary discouragement to accumulation and industry, by depressing the commercial part of the community, and is the effect of a fall of prices : Mr Malthus supposes that such an effect will be produced by the fall of the price of corn. If the observation made by Hume were well founded, still it would not apply to the present instance :—for every thing that the manufacturer would have to sell, would be as dear as ever : it is only what he would buy that would be cheap, namely, corn and labour, by which his gains would be increased. I must again observe, that a rise in the value of money lowers all things ; whereas a fall in the price of corn, only lowers the wages of labour, and therefore raises profits.

If, then, the prosperity of the commercial classes will most certainly lead to accumulation of capital, and the encouragement of productive industry ; these can by no means be so surely obtained as by a fall in the price of corn.

§ 17. I cannot agree with Mr Malthus in his approbation of the opinion of Adam Smith,[1] "that no equal quantity of productive labour employed in manufactures, can *ever* occasion so great a re-production as in agriculture." I suppose that he must have overlooked the term ever in this passage, otherwise the opinion is more consistent with the doctrine of the Economist, than with those which he has maintained ; as he has stated, and I think correctly, that in the first settling of a new country, and in every stage of its improvement, there is a portion of its capital employed on the land, for the

[1] [On this see *Principles*, Chapter II., § 28, p. 53, note.]

profits of stock merely, and which yields no rent whatever. Productive labour employed on such land never does in fact afford so *great* a reproduction as the same productive labour employed in manufactures.

The difference is not indeed great, and is voluntarily relinquished, on account of the security and respectability which attends the employment of capital on land. In the infancy of society, when no rent is paid, is not the re-production of value in the coarse manufactures, and in the implements of husbandry with a given capital, at least as great as the value which the same capital would afford if employed on the land?

This opinion indeed is at variance with all the general doctrines of Mr Malthus, which he has so ably maintained in this as well as in all his other publications. In the "Inquiry," speaking of what I consider a similar opinion of Adam Smith, he observes, "I cannot, however, agree with him in thinking that all land which yields food must necessarily yield rent. The land which is successively taken into cultivation in improving countries, may only pay profits and labour. A fair profit on the stock employed, including, of course, the payment of labour, will always be a sufficient inducement to cultivate." The same motives will also induce some to manufacture goods, and the profits of both, in the same stages of society, will be nearly the same.

In the course of these observations, I have often had occasion to insist, that rent never falls without the profits of stock rising. If it suit us to-day to import corn rather than grow it, we are solely influenced by the cheaper price. If we import, the portion of capital last employed on the land, and which yielded no rent, will be withdrawn; rent will fall and profits rise, and another portion of capital employed on the land will come under the same description of only yielding the usual profits of stock.

If corn can be imported cheaper than it can be grown on this rather better land, rent will again fall and profits rise, and another and better description of land will now be cultivated, for profits only. In every step of our progress, profits of stock increase and rents fall, and more land is abandoned; besides which, the country saves all the difference between the price at which corn can be grown, and the price at which it can be imported, on the quantity we receive from abroad.

§ 18. Mr Malthus has considered, with the greatest ability, the effect of a cheap price of corn on those who contribute to the interest of our enormous debt. I must fully concur in many of his conclusions on this part of the subject. The wealth of England would, I am persuaded, be considerably augmented by a great reduction in the price of corn, but the whole money value of that wealth would be diminished. It would be diminished by the whole difference of the money value of the corn consumed, —it would be augmented by the increased exchangeable value of all those commodities which would be exported in exchange for the corn imported. The latter would, however, be very unequal to the former; therefore the money value of the commodities of England would, undoubtedly, be considerably lowered.

But, though it is true, that the money value of the mass of our commodities would be diminished, it by no means follows that our annual revenue would fall in the same degree. The advocates for importation ground their opinion of the advantages of it on the conviction that the revenue would not so fall. And, as it is from our revenue that taxes are paid, the burden might not be really augmented.

Suppose the revenue of a country to fall from 10 to 9 millions, whilst the value of money altered in the proportion of 10 to 8, such country would have a larger neat revenue, after paying a million from the smaller, than it would have after paying it from the larger sum.

That the stockholder would receive more in real value than what he contracted for, in the loans of the late years, is also true; but, as the stockholders themselves contribute very largely to the public burdens, and therefore to the payment of the interest which they receive, no inconsiderable proportion of the taxes would fall on them; and, if we estimate at its true value the additional profits made by the commercial class, they would still be great gainers, notwithstanding their really augmented contributions.

The landlord would be the only sufferer by paying really more, not only without any adequate compensation, but with lowered rents.

It may, indeed, be urged, on the part of the stockholder, and those who live on fixed incomes, that they have been by far the greatest sufferers by the war. The value of their revenue has been diminished by the rise in the price of corn, and by the depreciation in the value of paper-money, whilst, at the same time, the value of their capital has been very much diminished from the lower price of the funds. They have suffered, too, from the inroads lately made on the sinking fund, and which, it is supposed, will be still further extended,—a measure of the greatest injustice,—in direct violation of solemn contracts; for the sinking fund is as much a part of the contract as the dividend, and, as a source of revenue, utterly at variance with all sound principles. It is to the growth of that fund that we ought to look for the means of carrying on future wars, unless we are prepared to relinquish the funding system altogether. To meddle with the sinking fund is to obtain a little temporary aid at the sacrifice of a great future advantage. It is reversing the whole system of Mr Pitt, in the creation of that fund: he proceeded on the conviction that, for a small present burden, an immense future advantage would be obtained; and, after witnessing, as we have done, the benefits which have already resulted from his inflexible determination to leave that fund untouched, even when he was pressed by the greatest financial distress, when 3 per cents. were so low as 48, we cannot, I think, hesitate in pronouncing that he would not have countenanced, had he still lived, the measures which have been adopted.

To recur, however, to the subject before me, I shall only further observe, that I shall greatly regret that considerations for any particular class are allowed to check the progress of the wealth and population of the country. If the interests of the landlord be of sufficient consequence, to determine us not to avail ourselves of all the benefits which would follow from importing corn at a cheap price, they should also influence us in rejecting all improvements in agriculture, and in the implements of husbandry; for it is as certain that corn is rendered cheap, rents are lowered, and the ability of the landlord to pay taxes is, for a time at least, as much impaired by such improvements as by the importation of corn. To be consistent, then, let us by the same act arrest improvement, and prohibit importation.

ON PROTECTION

TO

AGRICULTURE

FOURTH EDITION

1822

INTRODUCTION

It cannot, I think, be denied that, within these few years, great progress has been made in diffusing correct opinions on the impolicy of imposing restrictions on the importation of foreign corn; but, unhappily, much prejudice yet exists on this subject, and it is to be feared that the generally prevailing errors in the minds of those who are suffering from the distressed state of our agriculture, may lead to measures of increased restriction, rather than to the only effectual remedy for those distresses, the gradual approach to a system of free trade. It is to the present corn-law that much of the distress is to be attributed, and I hope to make it appear, that the occupation of a farmer will be exposed to continual hazard, and will be placed under peculiar disadvantages, as compared with all other occupations, while any system of restriction on the importation of foreign corn is continued, which shall have the effect of keeping the price of corn in this country habitually and considerably above the prices of other countries.

Before I proceed, however, to this, which is the main object that I have in view, I wish to notice some of the prevailing opinions which are daily advanced on the subject of the causes of the present distress; on the doctrine of remunerating price; on taxation; on currency, &c.: after disposing of these, we shall be better able to examine the important question of what ought to be the permanent regulations of this country, respecting the trade in corn, in order to afford the greatest security to the people, for a cheap and steady price, with an abundant supply of that essential article.

ON PROTECTION TO AGRICULTURE

SECTION I.

On Remunerating Price.

§ 1. The words Remunerative Price are meant to denote the price at which corn can be raised, paying all charges, including rent, and leaving to the grower a fair profit on his capital. It follows from this definition, that in proportion as a country is driven to the cultivation of poorer lands for the support of an increasing population, the price of corn, to be remunerative, must rise: for even if no rent is paid for such poorer land—as the charges on its cultivation must, for the same quantity of produce, be greater than on any other land previously cultivated, those charges can only be returned to the grower by an increase of price. "I know districts of the country,"* says Mr Iveson, "taking the very best qualities in them, that will produce from four to five quarters by the acre. I know there are farms that have averaged in the wheat crop, four quarters to the acre, or 32 bushels." "In what part of the kingdom?—In Wiltshire." "What would you estimate the second quality of land at?—I think the middling, or second, what I should call the middling quality of lands under good cultivation, may be taken at two quarters and a half." "And the inferior lands?—From 12 to 15 bushels an acre." Mr Harvey was asked, "What is the

* Report, Agricultural Committee, 1821, page 338.

lowest rent you have ever known to be paid for the worst land on which corn is raised ?—Eighteen-pence an acre." Mr Harvey further stated, that on an average of the last ten years he had obtained 30 bushels of wheat per acre from his land. Mr Wakefield's evidence was to the same effect as Mr Iveson's; but the difference according to him between the produce of wheat per acre on the best and worst land in cultivation was as much as 32 bushels; for he said " that on the sea coast of Norfolk, Suffolk, Essex, and Kent, the crop is thought a bad one, if it be not 40 bushels per acre;" and he added, " I do not believe that the very poor lands produce above eight bushels per acre."

Suppose now, that the population of England had only been one-half its present amount, and that it had not been necessary to take any other quality of land into cultivation than that which yielded 32 bushels of wheat per acre; what would have been the remunerative price? Can any one doubt of its being so low that, if the prices on the Continent had been at the same average at which they have been for the last five or ten years, we should have been an exporting instead of an importing country? It is true, that this land now yields 32 bushels, and would have yielded no more on the supposition that I have made; but is it not true, that the value of the 32 bushels now raised is regulated by the cost of producing the 12 or 15 bushels on the inferior lands of which Mr Iveson speaks? If the cost of raising 15 bushels of wheat is as great now as the cost was of raising 30 bushels formerly, the price must be doubled to be remunerative, for the degree in which the price must rise to compensate the producer for the charges which he has to pay does not depend on the quantity produced, nor on the quantity consumed, but on the cost of its production. The difference in the value of the quantity raised on the good land, and on the inferior land, will always constitute rent; so that the profits of the occupiers of the good and bad land will be the same, but the rent of the best land will exceed the rent of the worst by the difference in the quantity of produce, which, with the same expense, it can be made to yield. It is now universally admitted, that rent is the effect of the rise in the price of corn, and not the cause; it is also admitted, that the only permanent cause of rise in the value of corn, is an increased charge on its production, caused by the necessity of cultivating poorer lands; on which, by the expenditure of the same quantity of labour, the same quantity of produce cannot be obtained.

Is it not true that the rent on the better land is regulated by the lesser quantity of 15 bushels, with which we are now obliged to be contented on our poorer lands? The rent which is now a charge on cultivating the land which yields the 32 bushels, and which is equal to the value of 17 bushels, the difference between 15 and 32 bushels, could not have existed if no land was cultivated but such as yielded 32 bushels. If, then, with the charge of rent, the cost of raising 15 bushels on the rich land—and without the payment of rent, the cost of raising the same quantity on the poor land, is now as great as the cost of raising 30 bushels was formerly on the rich land, when no rent was paid, the price must be doubled.

§ 2. It appears, then, that, in the progress of society, when no importation takes place, we are obliged constantly to have recourse to worse soils to feed an augmenting population, and with every step of our progress the price of corn must rise, and with such rise, the rent of the better land which had been previously cultivated, will necessarily be increased. A higher price becomes necessary to compensate for the smaller quantity which is obtained; but this higher price must never be considered as a good—it would not have existed if the same return had been obtained with less labour—it would not have existed if, by the application of labour to manufactures, we had indirectly obtained the corn by the exportation of those manufactures in exchange for corn. A high price, if the effect of a high cost, is an evil, and not a good; the price is high, because a great deal of labour is bestowed in obtaining the corn. If only a little labour was bestowed upon it, more of the labour of the country, which constitutes its only real source of wealth, would have been at its disposal to procure other enjoyments which are desirable.

SECTION II.

On the Influence of a Rise of Wages on the Price of Corn.

§ 3. Much of what has been said in the foregoing section, would probably be allowed by some of those who are the advocates for a restricted trade in corn; they would, however, add, that though it could be shown that no protecting duties on the importation of corn could be justifiable, merely on account of the increased expenditure of labour necessary to obtain a given quantity in this country; yet such duties were necessary to protect the farmer against the effects of high wages in this country, caused by the taxation which falls on the labouring classes, and which must be repaid to them by their employers, by means of high wages. This argument proceeds on the assumption, that high wages tend to raise the price of the commodities on which labour is bestowed. If the farmer, they say, could, before taxation, and the high wages which are the effect of it, compete with the foreign grower of corn, he can no longer do so now he is exposed to a burden from which his competitor is free.

§ 4. This whole argument is fallacious,—the farmer is placed under no comparative disadvantage in consequence of a rise of wages. If, in consequence of taxes paid by the labouring class, wages should rise, which they in all probability would do, they would equally affect all classes of producers. If it be deemed necessary that corn should rise in order to remunerate the growers, it is also necessary that cloth, hats, shoes, and every other commodity should rise, in order to remunerate the producers of those articles. Either, then, corn ought not to rise, or all other commodities should rise along with it.

If neither corn, nor any other commodity, rise, they will of course be all of the same relative value as before; and if they do all rise, the same will be true. All must require protecting duties, or none.

§ 5. To impose protecting duties on all commodities would be absurd, because nothing would be gained by it—it would in no way alter the relative value of commodities; and it is only by altering the relative value of commodities that any particular trade is protected, not merely by an alteration of price. If England gave a yard of superfine cloth to Germany for a quarter of wheat, she would neither be more nor less disposed to carry on this trade, if both cloth and corn were raised 20 per cent. in price. All foreign trade finally resolves itself into an interchange of commodities; money is but the measure by which the respective quantities are ascertained. No commodity can be imported unless another commodity is exported; and the exported commodity must be equally raised in price by the rise of wages. It is essential that a drawback should be allowed on the exported article, if the one imported be protected by a duty. But it comes to the same thing, if no drawback be allowed on the one, nor protection granted to the other, because, in either case, precisely the same quantity of the foreign commodity will be obtained for a given quantity of the home-made commodity.

If a quarter of corn be raised from 60s. to 75s., or 25 per cent. by a rise of wages, and a certain quantity of hats or cloth be raised in the same proportion by the same cause, the importer of corn into England would lose just as much by the commodity which he exports as he would gain by the corn which he imports. If trade were left free, corn would not rise from 60s. to 75s., notwithstanding the rise of wages; nor would cloth, or hats, or shoes rise from this cause. But, if I should allow that they would rise, it would make no difference to my argument; we should then export money in exchange for corn, because no commodity could be so profitably employed in paying for it; for, by the supposition, every other commodity is raised in price. The exportation of money would gradually lessen the quantity, and raise its value in this country, while the importation of it into other countries would have a contrary effect in them; it would increase the quantity, and sink its value, and thus the price of corn, of cloth, of hats, and of all other things in England, would bear the same relation to the prices of the same commodities in other countries as they bore before wages were raised. In all cases, the rise of wages, when general, diminishes profits, and does not raise the prices of commodities. If the prices of commodities rose, no producer would be benefited; for of what consequence could it be to him to sell his commodity at an advance of 25 per cent., if he, in his turn, were obliged to give 25 per cent. more for every commodity which he purchased? He would be precisely in the same condition, whether he sold his corn for 25 per cent. advance, and gave an additional 25 per cent. in the price of his hats, shoes, clothes, &c., &c., as if he sold his corn at the usual price, and bought all the commodities which he consumed at the prices which he had before given for them. No one class of producers, then, is entitled to protection on account of a rise of wages, because a rise of wages equally affects all producers; it does not raise the prices of commodities because it diminishes profits; and, if it did raise the price of commodities, it would raise them all in the same proportion, and would not, therefore, alter their exchangeable value. It is only when commodities are altered in relative value, by the interference of Government, that any tax, which shall act as a protection against the importation of a foreign commodity, can be justifiable.

§ 6. It is by many supposed, that a rise in the price of corn will raise the price of all other things; this opinion is founded on the erroneous view which they take of the effect of a general rise of wages. Corn rises because it is more difficult to produce, and its cost is raised; it would be no rise at all if all other things rose with it. It is a real rise to the hatter and clothier, if they are obliged, one to give more hats, the other more cloth, for their corn; it would be no rise at all to them, and it would be impossible to show who paid for the increased cost, if their commodities also rose, and exchanged for the same quantity of corn.

It may be laid down as a principle, that any cause which operates in a country to affect equally all commodities, does not alter their relative value, and can give no advantage to foreign competitors, but that any cause which operates partially on one does alter its value to others, if not countervailed by an adequate duty; it will give advantage to the foreign competitor, and tend to deprive us of a beneficial branch of trade.

SECTION III.

On the Effects of Taxes imposed on a particular Commodity.

§ 7. For the same reasons that protecting duties are not justifiable on account of the rise of wages generally, from whatever cause it may proceed, it is evident that they are not to be defended when taxation is general, and equally affects all classes of producers. An income tax is of this description; it affects equally all who employ capital, and it has never yet been suggested by those most favourable to protecting duties that any would be necessary on account of an income tax. But a tax affecting equally all productions is precisely of the same description as an income tax, because it leaves them, after the tax, of the same relative value to each other as before it was imposed. The rise of wages, a tax on income, or a proportional tax on all commodities, all operate in the same way; they do not alter the relative value of goods, and therefore they do not subject us to any disadvantage in our commerce with foreign countries. We suffer indeed the inconvenience of paying the tax, but from that burden we have no means of freeing ourselves.

A tax, however, which falls exclusively on the producers of a particular commodity tends to raise the price of that commodity, and if it did not so raise it the producer would be under a disadvantage as compared with all other producers; he would no longer gain the general and ordinary profits by his trade. By rising in price, the value of this commodity is altered as compared with other commodities. If no protecting duty is imposed on the importation of a similar commodity from other countries, injustice is done to the producer at home, and not only to the producer but to the country to which he belongs. It is for the interest of the public that he should not be driven from a trade which, under a system of free competition, he would have chosen, and to which he would adhere if every other commodity were taxed equally with that which he produces. A tax affecting him exclusively is, in fact, a bounty to that amount on the importation of the same commodity from abroad; and to restore competition to its just level, it would be necessary not only to subject the imported commodity to an equal tax, but to allow a drawback of equal amount, on the exportation of the home-made commodity.

The growers of corn are subject to some of these peculiar taxes, such as tithes,[1] a portion of the poor's rate, and perhaps, one or two other taxes, all of which tend to raise the price of corn, and other raw produce, equal to these peculiar burdens. In the degree, then, in which these taxes raise the price of corn, a duty should be imposed on its importation. If from this cause it be raised 10s. per quarter, a duty of 10s. should be imposed on the importation of foreign corn, and a drawback of the same amount should be allowed on the exportation of corn. By means of this duty and this drawback, the trade would be placed on the same footing as if it had never been taxed, and we should be quite sure that capital would neither be injuriously for the interests of the country, attracted towards, nor repelled from it.

The greatest benefit results to a country when its Government forbears to give encouragement, or oppose obstacles, to any disposition of capital which the proprietor may think most advantageous to him. By imposing tithes, &c. on the farmer exclusively, no obstacle would be opposed to him, if there were no foreign competition, because he would be able to raise the price of his produce, and if he could not do so he would quit a trade which no longer afforded him the usual and ordinary profits of all other trades. But if importation was allowed, an undue encouragement

[1] [In this opinion as to tithes Ricardo was at one with most of the best writers of the time. Some part of the burden was removed by commutation. In addition, tithe was redeemed in many cases, particularly when land came under enclosure.]

would be given to the importation of foreign corn, unless the foreign commodity were subject to a duty, equal to tithes or any other exclusive tax imposed on the home grower.

But the home grower would still have to complain, if he was refused a drawback on exportation, because he might then say, " Before your duty, and before the price of my produce was raised in consequence of it, I could compete with the foreign grower in foreign markets; by making the remunerating price of my corn higher, you have deprived me of that advantage, therefore give me a drawback equal to the duty, and you, in every respect, restore me to the position, as it regards both my own countrymen, as producers of other commodities, and foreign growers of raw produce, in which I was before placed." On every principle of justice, and consistently with the best interests of the country, his demand should be acceded to.

SECTION IV.

On the Effect of Abundant Crops on the Price of Corn.

§ 8. In a former section I have endeavoured to show, that the price of corn, to be remunerative, must pay all the charges of its production, including in those charges the ordinary profits of the stock employed. It is, in fact, by these conditions being fulfilled, that the supply, on an average of years, is regulated. If the price obtained be less than remunerative, profits will be depressed, or will entirely disappear. If it be more than remunerative, profits will be high. In the first case, capital will be withdrawn from the land, and the supply will gradually conform to the demand. In the second case, capital will be attracted to the land, and the supply will be increased. But, notwithstanding this tendency of the supply of corn to conform itself to the demand, at prices which shall be remunerative, it is impossible to calculate accurately on the effects of the seasons. Sometimes, for a few years successively, crops will be abundant; at other times they will, for an equal period, be scanty and insufficient. When the quantity of corn at market, from a succession of good crops, is abundant, it falls in price, not in the same proportion as the quantity exceeds the ordinary demand, but very considerably more. The demand for corn, with a given population, must necessarily be limited; and, although it may be, and undoubtedly is, true, that when it is abundant and cheap, the quantity consumed will be increased, yet it is equally certain, that its aggregate value will be diminished. Suppose 14 millions of quarters of wheat to be the ordinary demand of England, and that, from a very abundant season, 21 millions are produced. If the remunerative price were 3*l.* per quarter, and the value of the 14 millions of quarters 42,000,000*l.*, there cannot be the least doubt, that the 21 millions of quarters would be of very considerably less value than 42,000,000*l.* No principle can be better established, than that a small excess of quantity operates very powerfully on price.[1] This is true of all commodities; but of none can it be so certainly asserted as of corn, which forms the principal article of the food of the people. The principle, I believe, has never been denied by those who have turned their attention to this subject. Some, indeed, have attempted to estimate the fall of price which would take place, under the supposition of the surplus bearing different proportions to the average quantity. Such calculations, however, must be very deceptious, as no general rule can be laid down for the variations of price in proportion to quantity. It would be different in different countries; it must essentially depend on the wealth or poverty of the country, and on its means of holding over the superfluous quantity to a future season. It must depend, too, on the opinions formed of the probability of the future supply being adequate or otherwise to the future demand. This, however, is, I think, certain, that the

[1] [The enunciation and discussion of this point by Ricardo deserves notice.]

aggregate value of an abundant crop will always be considerably less than the aggregate value of an average one; and that the aggregate value of a very limited crop will be considerably greater than that of an average crop. If 100,000 loaves were sold every day in London, and the supply should all at once be reduced to 50,000 per day, can any one doubt but that the price of each loaf would be considerably more than doubled? The rich would continue to consume precisely the same number of loaves, although the price was tripled or quadrupled. If, on the other hand, 200,000 loaves, instead of 100,000, were daily exposed for sale, could they be disposed of without a fall of price, far exceeding the proportion of the excess of quantity? Why is water without value, but because of its abundance? If corn were equally plenty, it would have no greater value, whatever quantity of labour might have been bestowed on its production.

In proof of the correctness of this view, I may refer to the prices of wheat in this country in different seasons of plenty, when it will be seen that, notwithstanding we were in a degree relieved by exportation, yet, from the abundance of crops, corn has been known to fall 50 per cent. in three years. Now, to what can this be imputed but to excess of quantity? The document which follows is copied from Mr Tooke's evidence before the committee of 1821.

	s.	*d.*		Quarters.
In 1728 the price of wheat was	48	5½	with an excess of import of	70,757
1732	23	8½	with an excess of export of	202,058
1740	45	0½	. . . . . .	46,822
1743	22	1	. . . . . .	371,429
1750	28	10¾	. . . . . .	947,323
1757	53	4	excess of import	130,017
1761	26	10¾	excess of export	441,956

Page 229, *Agricultural Report.*

Because it has been said, that abundance may be prejudicial to the interests of the producers, it has been objected that the new doctrine on this subject is, that the bounty of Providence may become a curse to a country; but this is essentially changing the proposition. No one has said that abundance is injurious to a country, but that it frequently is so to the producers of the abundant commodity. If what they raised was all destined for their own consumption, abundance never could be hurtful to them; but if, in consequence of the plenty of corn, the quantity with which they go to market to furnish themselves with other things is very much reduced in value, they are deprived of the means of obtaining their usual enjoyments; they have, in fact, an abundance of a commodity of little exchangeable value. If we lived in one of Mr Owen's parallelograms, and enjoyed all our productions in common, then no one could suffer in consequence of abundance; but as long as society is constituted as it now is, abundance will often be injurious to producers, and scarcity beneficial to them.

SECTION V.

On the Effect produced on the Price of Corn by Mr Peel's Bill for restoring the Ancient Standard.

§ 9. Much difference of opinion prevails on the effect produced on the price of corn by Mr Peel's bill for restoring the ancient standard. On this subject there is a great want of candour in one of the disputing parties; and I believe it will be found, that many of those who contended, during the war, that our money was not depreciated at all, now endeavour to show that the depreciation was then enormous, and that all the distresses which we are now suffering have arisen from restoring our currency from a depreciated state to par.

It is also forgotten that, from 1797 to 1819, we had no standard whatever by which to regulate the quantity or value of our money. Its quantity and its value depended entirely on the Bank of England, the Directors of which establishment, however desirous they might have been to act with fairness and justice to the public, avowed that they were guided in their issues by principles which, it is no longer disputed, exposed the country to the greatest embarrassment. Accordingly, we find that the currency varied in value considerably during the period of twenty-two years, when there was no other rule for regulating its quantity and value but the will of the Bank.

In 1813 and 1814 the depreciation of our currency was probably at its highest point, gold being then 5*l.* 10s. and 5*l.* 8s. per ounce; but, in 1819, the value of paper was only 5 per cent. below its ancient standard, gold being then 4*l.* 2s. or 4*l.* 3s. per ounce. It was in 1819 that Mr Peel's bill passed into a law. At the time of passing that bill, Parliament had to deal with the question as it then presented itself. It was thought expedient that an end should be put to a state of things which allowed a company of merchants to regulate the value of money as they might think proper; and the only point which could then come under consideration was, whether the standard should be fixed at 4*l.* 2s., which was the price of gold, not only at the time when Parliament was legislating, but its price for nearly the whole of the four preceding years; or the ancient standard of 3*l.* 17s. 10½d. should be restored. Between these two prices Parliament was constrained to determine, and, I think, in choosing to go back to the ancient standard, it pursued a wise course. But when it is now said that money has been forcibly raised in value,—25 per cent., according to some; 50, and even 60 per cent., according to others,—they do not refer to 1819, the period at which that bill passed, but to the period of the greatest depression; and they charge the whole increase in the value of the currency to Mr Peel's bill. Now, it is to the system which allowed of such variations in the value of money that Mr Peel's bill put an end. If, indeed, in 1819, or immediately preceding 1819, gold had been at 5*l.* 10s. an ounce, no measure could have been more inexpedient than to make so violent a change in all subsisting engagements, as would have been made by restoring the ancient standard; but the price of gold, as I have already said, was then, and had been for four years, about 4*l.* 2s., never above, and frequently rather under, that price; and no measure could have been so monstrous as that which some reproach the House of Commons for not having adopted, namely, of fixing the standard at

5*l*. 10s.; that is, in other words, after the currency had regained its value within 5 per cent. of gold, under the operation of the bad system, again to have degraded it to 30 per cent. below the value of gold.

§ 10. It will be remembered, that a plan was by me submitted to the country for the restoration of a fixed standard, which would have rendered the employment of any greater quantity of gold than the Bank then possessed wholly unnecessary.[1]

That plan was to make the Bank liable to the payment of a certain large and fixed amount of their notes in gold bullion at the Mint price of 3*l*. 17s. 10½d. an ounce, instead of payment in gold coin. If that plan had been adopted, not a particle of gold would have been used in the circulation,—all our money must have consisted of paper, excepting the silver coin necessary for payments under the value of a pound. In that case it is demonstrable, that the value of money could only have been raised 5 per cent. by reverting to the fixed ancient standard, for that was the whole difference between the value of gold and paper. There was nothing in the plan which could cause a rise in the value of gold, for no additional quantity of gold would have been required, and therefore 5 per cent. would have been the full extent of the rise in the value of money.* Mr Peel's bill adopted this plan for four years, after which payments in coin were to be established. If for the time specified by the bill the Bank Directors had managed their affairs with the skill which the public interest required, they would have been satisfied with so regulating their issues, after Mr Peel's bill passed, that the exchange should continue at par, and consequently no importation of gold could have taken place; but the Bank, who always expressed

* With 4*l*. 2s. in bank notes, any one could purchase precisely the same quantity of commodities as with the gold in 3*l*. 17s. 10½d.; the object of the plan was to make 3*l*. 17s. 10½d. in bank notes, as valuable as 3*l*. 17s. 10½d. in gold. To effect this object, could it have been necessary, could it, indeed, have been possible, to lower the value of goods more than 5 per cent., if the value of gold had not been raised?

[1] [*Proposals for an Economical and Secure Currency*, §§ 11—14. This pamphlet was published 1816.]

a decided aversion to the plan of bullion payments, immediately commenced preparations for specie payments. Their issues were so regulated, that the exchange became extremely favourable to this country; gold flowed into it in a continuous stream, and all that came the Bank eagerly purchased at 3*l*. 17s. 10½d. per ounce. Such a demand for gold could not fail to elevate its value compared with the value of all commodities. Not only, then, had we to elevate the value of our currency 5 per cent., the amount of the difference between the value of paper and of gold before these operations commenced, but we had still farther to elevate it to the new value to which gold itself was raised by the injudicious purchases which the Bank made of that metal. It cannot, I think, be doubted, that if bullion payments had been fairly tried for three out of the four years between 1819 and 1823, and had been found fully to answer all the objects of a currency regulated by gold at a fixed value, the same system would have been continued, and we should have escaped the further pressure which the country has undoubtedly undergone from the effects of the great demand for gold which specie payments have entailed upon us.

The Bank Directors urge in defence of the measures which they have pursued the complaints which were made against them on account of the frequent executions for forgery, which rendered it indispensable that they should withdraw the one-pound notes from circulation for the purpose of replacing them with coin. If they could not substitute a note better calculated to prevent forgery than the one which they have hitherto used, this plea is a valid one, for the sacrifice of a small pecuniary interest could not be thought too great if it took away the temptation to the crime of forgery, for which so many unfortunate persons were annually executed; but this excuse comes with a bad grace from the Bank of England, who did not discover the importance of preventing forgery by the issue of coin till 1821, after they had made such large purchases of gold that they were under the necessity of applying to Parliament for a bill to enable them to issue coin in payment of their notes, which, by Mr Peel's bill, they were prevented from doing till 1823. How comes it that they did not make this discovery in 1819, when the committees of the Lords and Commons were sitting on bank payments? Instead of being eager at that period to commence specie payments, they remonstrated, in a manner which many thought unbecoming, against any plan of metallic payments which did not leave the uncontrolled power of increasing or diminishing the amount of the currency in their hands. It surely is not forgotten, that, on an application by the Lords' Committee to the Bank, dated the 24th March, 1819, asking if "the Bank had any and what objections to urge against the passing a law to require it should pay its notes in bullion on demand, but in sums not less in amount than 100*l.*, 200*l.*, or 300*l.*, at 3*l.* 17s. 10½d., and to buy gold bullion at 3*l.* 17s. 6d. by an issue of its notes, the said plan to commence after a period to be fixed for that purpose;" the Directors answered, "the Bank has taken into consideration the question sent by the Committee of the House of Lords, under date of the 24th March, and is not aware of any difficulty in exchanging, for a fixed amount of bank notes, gold bullion of a certain weight provided it be melted, assayed, and stamped by his Majesty's Mint.

"The attainment of bullion by the Bank at 3*l.* 17s. 6d. is, in the estimation of the Court, so uncertain, that the Directors, in duty to their proprietors, do not feel themselves competent to engage to issue bullion at the price of 3*l.* 17s. 10½d.; but the Court beg leave to suggest, as an alternative, the expediency of its furnishing bullion of a fixed weight to the extent stated at the market price as taken on the preceding foreign post-day, in exchanging for its notes, provided a reasonable time be allowed for the Bank to prepare itself to try the effect of such a measure."

If this proposal had been acceded to, the Bank would itself have determined the price at which it should have sold gold from time to time to the public, because by extending or curtailing their issues, they had the power to make the price of gold just what they pleased, 4*l.* or 10*l.* an ounce, and at that price to which they might choose to elevate it, they graciously proposed to sell it, "provided a reasonable time be allowed to prepare itself to try the effect of such a measure."

After this proposal, after the representation made to the Chancellor of the Exchequer by the Directors of the Bank of England on the 20th May 1819,* it will not be said that the question of forgery appeared so urgent to the Directors that they were eager to substitute coin for their small notes in 1819, however important the question became in their view in 1820.

It is a question exceedingly difficult to determine what the effect has been on the value of gold, and consequently on the value of money produced by the purchases of bullion made by the Bank. When two commodities vary, it is impossible to be certain whether one has risen, or the other fallen. There are no means of even approximating to the knowledge of this fact, but by a careful comparison of the value of the two commodities, during the period of their variation, with the value of many other commodities.

Even this comparison does not afford a certain test, because one-half of the commodities to which they are compared, may have varied in one direction, while the other half may have varied in another: by which half shall the variation of gold be tried? If by one it appears to have risen, if by the other to have fallen. From observations, however, on the price of silver, and of various other commodities, making due allowance for the particular causes which may have specially operated on the value of each, Mr Tooke, one of the most intelligent witnesses examined by the Agricultural Committee, came to the conclusion that the eager demand for gold made by the Bank in order to substitute coin for their small notes, had raised the value of currency about 5 per cent. In this conclusion, I quite concur with Mr Tooke. If it be well founded, the whole increased value of our currency since the passing of Mr Peel's bill in 1819, may be estimated at about 10 per cent. To that amount, taxation has been increased by the measure for restoring

* See Appendix A.

specie payment; to that amount the fall of grain, and with it of all other commodities, has taken place as far as this cause alone has operated on them; but all above that amount, all the further depression which the price of corn has sustained, must be accounted for by the supply having exceeded the demand; a depression, which would have equally occurred, if no alteration whatever had been made in the value of the currency.

§ II. It is, indeed, alleged by many of the landed interest, that to one cause alone, all the distress in agriculture is to be ascribed. They go so far as to say, that there is now no surplus produce on the land, but what is paid to the Government for taxes; that there is nothing whatever left for rent or profit; that whatever rent is paid, is derived from the capital of the farmer, and all these effects they charge on the alteration in the value of the currency.

It is evident that those who advance this most extravagant proposition, do not know how the alteration in the value of the currency affects the different interests of a country. If it injures the debtor, it in the same degree benefits the creditor; if its pressure is felt by the tenant, it must be advantageous to the landlord, and to the receivers of taxes. They, then, who maintain this doctrine, must be prepared to contend that all that fund, which formerly constituted the rent of the landlord and the profits of the farmer, are, by the alteration in the value of money, transferred to the State, and are now paid to the receivers of taxes, and, among them, the stock-holders. That the situation of the stock-holder is improved, by his dividends being paid in a currency increased in value, there can be no doubt; but what evidence is there to show that his situation is so much improved, that he has now at his disposal, in addition to his former means of enjoyment, all those which were before at the disposal of the whole of the tenantry, and of the landlords of the country? So wild an assertion cannot be for a moment entertained; we have not heard of splendid equipages and superb mansions having been built by the stock-holders since, and in consequence of, the bill of 1819. Besides, if this were true, how comes it that the profits of the merchant and manufacturer have escaped the fund-holder, this devouring monster, as he has been called? Are not their profits governed by the same principle, and by the same law, as the profits of the farmer? How have they contrived to exempt themselves from this desolating storm? The answer is plain, there is no truth in the allegation. Agriculture has been depressed by causes of which the currency forms only a little part. The peculiar hardships which the landed interest are suffering, are of a temporary character, and will continue only while the supply of produce exceeds the demand. A remunerative price is impossible while this cause of low value continues; but the situation of things which we now witness cannot have any permanence.

Is it not quite certain, that if the pressure on the farmers, from the alteration in the value of currency. and the increased taxation consequent upon it, has been so great as to take from them all the profits of their capital, it must also have taken away the profits of all other persons employing capital? for it is quite impossible that one set of capitalists should be permanently without any profit at all, whilst others are making reasonable profits.

On the part of the landlords it may be said, that they are encumbered with fixed charges on their estates, such as dowers, provision for daughters, and younger children, mortgages, &c. It cannot be denied that an alteration in the value of currency must greatly affect such engagements, and must be very burdensome to landlords; but they should remember that they or their fathers benefited by the depreciation of the value of the currency. All their fixed engagements, their taxes included, were for many years paid in the depreciated medium.[1] If they suffer injustice now, they profited by injustice at a former period; and if the account were fairly made up, it would, I believe, be found that, as far as alteration in the value of currency is concerned, they have little just cause for complaint.

[1] [That is, during the period of the Bank Restriction Act.]

§ 12. But, on the score of money engagements, which are now affected by the increased value of currency, have the commercial interest no cause for complaint? Are they not debtors in as large an amount as the landed interest? How many persons have retired from business, whose capitals are, directly or indirectly, still employed by their successors? What vast sums are employed by bankers and others in discounting bills? For the whole of this value there must be debtors, and the increased value of money could not have failed very much to aggravate the pressure of their debts.

I mention these circumstances to show that if the real efficient cause of the distress of the landed gentlemen was the increased value of money, it ought to have produced similar distress in other quarters;—it has not done so, and therefore I have a right to infer, that the cause of the distress has been mistaken.

The profits of the farmer must bear some uniform proportion to the profits of the other classes of capitalists; they are subject to temporary fluctuations, perhaps, in a greater degree than the profits of others; but the circumstances of which they complain, though severe and aggravated at the present time by other causes, yet are by no means new or uncommon.

Mr Tooke, in his evidence before the Agricultural Committee, in pages 230 and 231, has furnished us with extracts from publications in the last century, in which the ruin of the landed interest was foretold in terms not very unlike those used in the present day. Those difficulties have passed, and the present ones will, with a little good legislation, soon only be matter of history.

At a late Court of proprietors of Bank Stock, the Directors said that, so far from having reduced the amount of the circulation since 1819, they had considerably increased it, and that it was this year actually more by 3,000,000*l.* than the amount of the circulation at the same period last year or the year preceding. If the Directors were quite correct in this statement, it is no answer to the charge of their having kept the circulation too low, and thereby caused the great influx of gold. My question to them is, "Was your circulation so high as to keep the exchange at par ?" To this they must answer in the negative ; and therefore I say, that if in consequence of the importation of gold, that metal is enhanced in value, and the pressure on the country is thereby increased, it is because the Bank did not issue a sufficient quantity of notes to keep the exchange at par. This charge is of the same force whether the amount of bank notes has, in point of fact, been stationary, increasing, or diminishing.

But I dispute the fact of the circulation having been even half a million higher in amount in 1822 than in 1821 and 1820. The mode of proving the proposition adopted by the Bank is not satisfactory ; they say, in 1821 we had 23,800,000*l.* in circulation, and now the notes in circulation, with the sovereigns we have since issued, amount to 3,000,000*l.* more. But as sovereigns are circulated in Ireland, and in other districts of the United Kingdom, how can they affirm, that in the same channel in which 23,800,000*l.* bank notes circulated in 1821, 26,800,000 bank notes and sovereigns together, are now in circulation ? I believe the contrary to be the fact, for I find that the amount of notes of five pounds and above, which have been in circulation for several years past, in the month of February, is as follows :—

Years.		£
1815	..	16,394,359
1816	..	15,307,228
1817	..	17,538,656
1818	..	19,077,951
1819	..	16,148,098
1820	..	15,393,770
1821	..	15,766,270
1822	..	15,784,770

And as the notes of five pounds and upwards have not increased 400,000*l.* since 1820, I find it impossible to believe that the circulation of a smaller denomination can have increased in any much larger proportion.

§ 13. Before I conclude this section I must observe, that the complaints made against the Bank for refusing to lend money on discount at 4 per cent. are without any good foundation. The reason for such complaints is, that by lending at 4 per cent. they would lower the rate of interest generally, and the landed interest would be benefited by being able to raise money on mortgage on cheaper terms than they now pay for it. I believe, however, that no amount of loans which the Bank might make, and no degree of lowness of interest at which they might choose to lend, would alter the permanent rate of interest in the market. Interest is regulated chiefly by the profits that may be made by the use of capital; it cannot be controlled by any bank, nor by any assemblage of banks. During the last war the market rate of interest for money was, for years together, fluctuating between 7 and 10 per cent.; yet the Bank never lent at a rate above 5 per cent. In Ireland, the Bank, by its charter, is obliged to lend at a rate of interest not exceeding 5 per cent., yet all other persons lend at 6 per cent.

A Bank has fulfilled all its useful functions when it has substituted paper in the circulation for gold; when it has enabled us to carry on our commerce with a cheap currency, and to employ the valuable one which it supplants productively: provided it fulfils this object, it is of little importance at what rate of interest it lends its money.

One argument used by a very enlightened member of Parliament, during a late discussion on the rate of interest charged by the Bank, was rather a singular one: he said that the Bank of France, and other banks on the Continent, lent at a low rate, and therefore the Bank of England should do so. I can see no connexion between his premises and conclusion. The Bank of France ought to be governed by the market rate of interest and the rate of profits in France; the Bank of England by the market rate of interest and the rate of profit in England. One may be very different from the other. From the whole of his argument, I should infer that he considered a low rate of interest, in itself, beneficial to a country. The very contrary, I imagine, is the truth. A low rate of interest is a symptom of a great accumulation of capital; but it is also a symptom of a low rate of profits, and of an advancement to a stationary state; at which the wealth and resources of a country will not admit of increase. As all savings are made from profits,[1] as a country is most happy when it is in a rapidly progressive state, profits and interest cannot be too high. It would be a poor consolation, indeed, to a country for low profits and low interest, that landlords were enabled to raise money on mortgage with diminished sacrifices. Nothing contributes so much to the prosperity and happiness of a country as high profits.[2]

This complaint against the Bank, which comes, I think, with an ill grace from a member of Parliament, as representing the public interest, might be consistently urged by a Bank proprietor at a general meeting of their body, for it is difficult to account on what principle of advantage to the concern which they manage the Directors can think it right to lend their proprietors' money at 3 per cent. to Government * when they could obtain 4 per cent. from other borrowers; but with this the public have no concern, and they and their proprietors should be left to settle this matter as they please.

SECTION VI.

On the Effects of a Low Value of Corn on the Rate of Profits.

§ 14. When I use the term—a low value of corn, I wish to be clearly understood. I consider the value of corn to be low, when a large quantity is the result of

* The Bank are now in advance many millions to the Government on exchequer bills at 3 per cent., besides the fixed advance of their capital, also at 3 per cent., which latter they are, by their charter, obliged to lend at that rate of interest.

[1] [This, of course, is open to dispute. No grounds whatever are given for it. It is purely dogmatic.]

[2] [The argument is, that though a low rate points to a large accumulation of capital it indicates also the approach to a stationary condition, whereas a high rate necessarily brings about advance, leads to activity and implies the existence of opportunity for further growth. It is bound up with the very dogmatic assumption criticised in the previous note.]

a moderate quantity of labour. In proportion, as for a given quantity of labour a smaller quantity of corn is obtained, corn will rise in value. In the progress of society there are two opposite causes operating on the value of corn ; one, the increase of population, and the necessity of cultivating, at an increased charge, land of an inferior quality, which always occasions a rise in the value of corn ; the other, improvements in agriculture, or the discovery of new and abundant foreign markets, which always tend to lower the value. Sometimes one predominates, sometimes the other, and the value of corn rises or falls accordingly.

In speaking of the value of corn, I mean something rather different from its price—when its value rises, its price generally rises, and would always do so, if money, in which price is uniformly estimated, were invariable in value. But corn may not vary as compared with all other things—it may not be the result of either more or less labour, and yet it may rise or fall in price, because money may become more plentiful and cheap, or more scarce and dear. Nothing is of so little importance to the community collectively, as an alteration in the *price* of corn, caused by an alteration in the value of money merely ; nothing of greater importance, as far as its profits and its wealth are concerned, than a rise or fall in the price of corn, when money continues of a fixed and invariable value. We will suppose money to continue at a fixed and invariable value, that we may ascertain the effects of a rise or fall in the value of corn ; which, on this supposition, will be synonymous with a rise or fall in its price.

Corn being one of the chief articles on which the wages of labour are expended, its value to a great degree, regulates wages. Labour itself is subject to a fluctuation of value in the same manner as every thing which is the subject of demand and supply, but it is also particularly affected by the price of the necessaries of the labourer ; and corn, as I have already observed, is amongst the principal of those necessaries.[1] In a former

[1] [In this sentence Ricardo brings into connexion the influence on wages of the necessary standard and of the quantity of labour.]

section I have endeavoured to show, that a general rise of wages will not raise the prices of commodities on which labour is expended. If wages rose in one trade, the commodity produced in that trade must rise, to place the producer of it on a par with all other trades; but when wages affect all producers alike, a rise in the value of all their commodities must, as I have on a former occasion remarked, be a matter of great indifference to them, as whether they were all at a high price or at a low price, their relative values would be the same, and it is the alteration of their relative values only which gives to the holders of them a greater or less command of goods. Every man exchanges his goods, finally, for other goods, or for labour, and he cares little whether he sells his own goods at a high price, if he is obliged to give a high price for the goods he purchases, or sells them at a low price, if, at the same time, he can also procure the goods he wants at a low price. In either case his enjoyments are the same.

With a permanently high price of corn, caused by increased labour on the land, wages would be high; and, as commodities would not rise on account of the rise of wages, profits would necessarily fall. If goods worth 1000*l.* require at one time labour which cost 800*l.*, and at another the price of the same quantity of labour is raised to 900*l.*, profits will fall from 200*l.* to 100*l.* Profits would not fall in one trade only, but in all. High wages, when general, equally affect the profits of the farmer, the manufacturer, and the merchant. There is no other way of keeping profits up but by keeping wages down. In this view of the law of profits, it will at once be seen how important it is that so essential a necessary as corn, which so powerfully affects wages, should be at a low price; and how injurious it must be to the community generally, that, by prohibitions against importation, we should be driven to the cultivation of our poorer lands to feed our augmenting population.

§ 15. Besides the impolicy of devoting a greater portion of our labour to the production of food than would otherwise be necessary, thereby diminishing the sum of our enjoyments and the power of saving, by lowering profits, we offer an irresistible temptation to capitalists to quit this country, that they may take their capitals to places where wages are low and profits high. If landlords could be sure of the prices of corn remaining steadily high, which happily they cannot be, they would have an interest opposed to every other class in the community; for a high price, proceeding from difficulty of production, is the main cause of the rise of rent: not that the rise of rent, the advantage gained by the landlord, is an equivalent for the disadvantage imposed on the other classes of the community, in being prevented from importing cheap corn we have not that consolation: for to give a moderate advantage to one class, a most oppressive burden must be laid on all the other classes.

§ 16. This advantage to the landlords themselves would be more apparent than real; for, to complete the advantage, they should be able to calculate on steady as well as high prices. Nothing is so injurious to tenants as constantly fluctuating prices, and under a system of protection to the landlord, and prohibition against the importation of foreign corn, tenants must be exposed to the most injurious fluctuations of profits, as I shall attempt to show in the next section. When the profits of a farmer are high, he is induced to live more profusely, and to make his arrangements as if his good fortune were always to continue; but a reverse is sure to come: he has then to suffer from his former improvidence, and he finds himself entangled in expenses which render him utterly unable to fulfil his engagements with his landlord.

The landlord's rent is, indeed, nominally high, but he is frequently in the situation of not being able to realize it; and little doubt can exist, that a more moderate and steady price of corn, with regular profits to the tenant, would afford to the landlord the best security for his happiness and comfort, if not for the receipt of the largest amount of rent.

It appears, then, that a high but steady price of corn is most advantageous to the landlord; but, as steadiness in a country situated as ours, is nearly incompatible with a price high in this country, as compared with other countries, a more moderate price is really for his interest. Nothing can be more clearly established, than that low prices of corn are for the interest of the farmer, and of every other class of society; high prices are incompatible with low wages, and high wages cannot exist with high profits.[1]

I must here notice an error, which has been supported by one of those, whose talents give them great authority in the place where the opinion was delivered; it is, that though the manufacturer has it in his power to raise the price of his commodity when it is taxed, and even, on some occasions, to profit by its being taxed, yet the farmer cannot so indemnify himself, and that, consequently, at the end of his lease, if not before, the whole weight of the tax must fall on his landlord. This is an error of long standing, for it is supported by no less an authority than Adam Smith. The subject of rent, and the laws by which its fall and rise are regulated, have been explained since the time of Adam Smith; and all those men who are acquainted with this explanation, are incapable of falling into the error. I am not now going into the question of rent; that subject has been well elucidated by several able writers. But I would ask those who still adhere to Adam Smith's doctrine, on whom the tax on land could fall when it was equal to 3s. per acre, if the land cultivated were of the description mentioned by Mr Harvey in his evidence, and to which I have already referred, land for which 1s. 6d. only is paid as rent? The farmer must either get lower profits

[1] [This statement must not be taken by itself. With reference to it see Ricardo's *Principles*, Introductory Essay, § 15, p. xxxvi, &c.

In the *Influence of a Low Price of Corn on the Profits of Stock*, § 14, it is urged that "greater profits would lead to further accumulation; and thus would a stimulus be given to population by really high wages, which could not fail for a long time to ameliorate the condition of the labouring classes." It is assumed that ultimately this *might* be partly absorbed by an increase of population.

The sentences at the end of § 7 in the same essay should be remembered by those who attribute a sinister meaning to the reference to "low wages."]

than other farmers who pay higher rents, or he must be able to transfer this charge to the consumer. But why should he remain in an occupation in which his profits are below the profits of all other capitalists in the community? He might require time to remove himself from an unprofitable employment; but he would not perseveringly continue in it, more than any other person similarly circumstanced in other occupations.

I have taken the instance mentioned by Mr Harvey, because, as he is a practical man, weight will be given to his information; but I am myself fully persuaded that a large quantity of corn is raised in every country, for the privilege of raising which, no rent whatever is paid. Every farmer is at liberty to employ an additional portion of capital on his land after all that which is necessary for affording his rent, has already been employed. The corn raised with this capital, can only afford the usual profits if no rent is paid out of it. Impose a tax on producing it, without admitting a compensation by a rise of price, and that moment you offer an inducement to the withdrawing of that portion of capital from the land, thereby diminishing the supply. No point is more satisfactorily established in my opinion, than that every tax imposed on the production of raw produce falls ultimately on the consumer, in the same way as taxes on the production of manufactured commodities fall on the consumers of those articles.

SECTION VII.

Under a System of Protecting Duties established with a view to give the Monopoly of the Home Market to the Home Grower of Corn, Prices cannot be otherwise than fluctuating.

§ 17. Protecting duties on the importation of corn must always be imposed on the supposition that corn is cheaper in foreign countries, by the amount of such duties; and that if they were not imposed, foreign corn would be imported. If foreign corn were not cheaper, no protecting duty would be necessary, for, under a system of free trade, it would not be imported. To the amount, then, of the protecting duty, the ordinary and average price of corn must be supposed to be higher in the country imposing it than in others, and when abundant harvests occur, before any corn can be exported from a country so circumstanced, corn must fall from its usual and average price, not only by the amount of the duty, but also by the further amount of the expenses of exporting the corn. Under a system of free trade, the price of corn in two countries could not materially differ more than the expenses attending the exportation of it from one country to the other; and therefore, if an abundant harvest occurred in either, and was not common to both, after an inconsiderable fall of price, a vent for the superfluous produce would be immediately found in exportation. But under a system of protecting duties, or of prohibitory laws, the fall in the price of corn from an abundant crop, or from a succession of abundant crops, must be ruinous to the grower, before he can relieve himself by exportation. If we could listen to Mr Webb Hall's recommendation of a fixed duty of 40s. on the importation of foreign corn; and if he be right in supposing that 40s. is the difference of the natural price of corn in England and in the corn countries, on every occasion of abundant harvests, corn must actually fall 40s., before it can be the interest of any party to export it to the Continent; a fall so great that, if the farmers were subjected to it, they would be totally unable to pay their rents in abundant seasons, without a great sacrifice of capital.

§ 18. The same observation is applicable to the present corn law,[1] which prohibits importation till the price

[1] [In this paragraph the peculiar defects of sliding scales are well brought out. The argument may be briefly summarised. It is true that a high price of corn is advantageous to the landowner and to those interested in land. But it is equally to their advantage that prices should be steady. Where high prices are sought by means of protection, a cause of fluctuation is introduced; and this is more particularly the case where protection is given under such a scale as that described.]

rises to 80s. The effect of this law is to make the price of corn in this country habitually and considerably above the price in other countries; and, therefore, on occasion of abundant crops, it must fall below the price of those other countries, before any relief can be afforded to the grower by exportation. Its effect, indeed, in this view, is precisely the same as that of the high fixed duty which we have been already considering.

But the present law has another capital defect, from which the system of fixed duties is free. When the average price of wheat reaches 80s. per quarter, the ports are now open for three months, for an unlimited importation of foreign wheat, duty free. With prices somewhat about 40s. per quarter on the Continent, in average years, the temptation to import into this country, during the three months that the ports are open, must operate to the introduction of an enormous quantity.

During these three months, and for a very considerable time afterwards, for the effect cannot cease with the shutting of the ports, the home grower and the foreign grower are placed in a state of free competition, to the ruin of the former. By prohibitory duties he is encouraged to employ his capital on the poorer lands of this country, which require a great expense for a small produce; and when he has an unusually short crop, and most stands in need of a high price, he is all at once exposed to the free competition of the grower of corn on the Continent, to whom a price of 40s. would be amply sufficient to compensate him for the whole cost of production. A system of fixed duties protects the farmer against this particular danger, but it leaves him exposed, in the same degree as on the present system, to all the evils which arise from abundant crops, and which can never fail to accompany every plan of a corn law, which shall elevate the price of corn in the country in which they prevail, considerably above the level of the prices of other countries.

§ 19. It must not be supposed, however, that to obviate this difficulty, the importation of corn should be at all times allowed without the payment of any duty whatever; that is not, under our circumstances, the course which I should recommend. I have already shown in Section III., that with a view to the real interest of the consumer, in which the interests of the whole community are, and ever must be, included, whenever any peculiar tax falls on the produce of any one commodity, from the effects of which all other producers are exempted, a countervailing duty to that amount, but no more, should on every just principle be imposed on the importation of such commodity; and, further, that a drawback should be allowed, to the same amount also on the exportation of the like commodity. If, before any taxation, the remunerating price of wheat was 60s. per quarter, both in England and on the Continent, and in consequence of the imposition of a tax, such as tithes, falling exclusively on the farmer, and not on any other producer, wheat was raised in England to 70s., a duty of 10s. should be also imposed on the importation of foreign corn. This tax on foreign corn, and on home corn also, should be drawn back on exportation. However large the aggregate amount might be of the drawback given to the exporter, it would only be returning to him a tax which he had before paid, and which he must have to place him in a fair state of competition in the foreign markets, not only with the foreign producer, but with his own countrymen who are producing other commodities. It is essentially different from a bounty on exportation, in the sense that the word bounty is usually understood; for by a bounty is generally meant a tax levied on the people for the purpose of rendering corn unnaturally cheap to the foreign consumer, whereas, what I propose, is to sell our corn at the price at which we can really afford to produce it, and not to add to its price a tax which shall induce the foreigner rather to purchase it from some other country, and deprive us of a trade, which, under a system of free competition, we might have selected.

The duty which I have here proposed is the only legitimate countervailing duty,[1] which neither offers inducements to capital to quit a trade, in which for us

[1] [Cf. § 27.]

it is the most beneficially employed, nor holds out any temptations to employ an undue proportion of capital in a trade to which it would not otherwise have been destined. The course of trade would be left precisely on the same footing as if we were wholly an untaxed country, and every person was at liberty to employ his capital and skill in the way he should think most beneficial to himself. We cannot now help living under a system of heavy taxation, but to make our industry as productive to us as possible, we should offer no temptations to capitalists, to employ their funds and their skill in any other way than they would have employed them if we had had the good fortune to be untaxed, and had been permitted to give the greatest development to our talents and industry.

§ 20. The Report of the Committee on Agricultural Distress in 1821, contains some excellent statements and reasonings on this subject.

To that important document I can with confidence refer, in support of the principles which I am endeavouring to lay down on the impolicy of protecting corn laws. The arguments in it in favour of freedom of trade appear to me unanswerable; but it must be confessed, that in that same Report, recommendations are made utterly inconsistent with those principles.

After condemning restrictions on trade, it recommends measures of permanent restriction; after showing the evils resulting from prematurely taking poor lands into cultivation, it countenances a system which, at all sacrifices, is to keep them in tillage. In principle, nothing so odious as monopoly and restriction; in practice, nothing so salutary and desirable.

The Committee on Agriculture this year avoid taking any notice of the sound doctrines entertained by the last Committee, but have founded their whole Report on the erroneous ones; and conclude their recommendations to the House in the following words:—" If the circumstances of this country should hereafter allow the trade in corn to be permanently settled upon a footing constantly open to all the world, *but subject to such a fixed and uniform duty as might compensate to the British grower the difference of expense at which his corn can be raised and brought to market, together with the fair rate of profit upon the capital employed, compared with the expense of production, and other charges attending corn grown and imported from abroad, such a* system would, in many respects, be preferable to any modification of regulations depending upon average prices, with an ascending and descending scale of duties; because it would prevent the effects of combination and speculation, in endeavouring to raise or depress those averages, and render immaterial those inaccuracies which, from management or negligence, have occasionally produced, and may again produce such mischievous effects upon our market; but your Committee rather look forward to such a system as fit to be kept in view for the ultimate tendency of our law, than as practicable within any short or definite period."

The system which we are to keep in view for the ultimate tendency of our law, we are told, is one of a fixed duty; but on what principle is the fixed duty to be calculated? not on that which I have endeavoured to show is the only sound one, namely, that the duty should accurately countervail the peculiar burdens to which the grower of corn is subject, but a fixed duty which should compensate to the British grower the difference of expense at which his corn can be raised and brought to market, compared with the expense of production, and other charges attending corn grown and imported from abroad. Instead of holding out any hope to the consumer that we shall at any future time legislate on a principle which shall enable him to purchase corn at as cheap a price as British industry shall be enabled to obtain it for him,—instead of giving any security to the British capitalist that wages shall not be unnaturally raised in this country, by obliging the labourer to purchase corn at a dear, and not at a cheap rate—a security so essential to the keeping up the rate of profits,—instead of bidding the farmer look forward to a time when he will be spared from the fluctuations in the price of the commodity which he raises, and which are so destructive to his interests, we are told that the present mode in which the price of corn is kept in this country habitually and considerably above its price in other countries, is not, perhaps, the best mode of effecting that object, as it may be more conveniently done by means of a fixed duty instead of a varying duty; but, at any rate, corn is to be rendered habitually and considerably dearer in this country than in others. A duty calculated upon the principle of the Committee cannot fail to perpetuate a difference of price between this and other countries, equal to the difference of expense of growing corn in this country beyond the expense of growing it in others. If we had not already pushed the endeavour of providing food for ourselves too far,—if we had not, by our own acts, made the expense of growing corn in this country greater than in others, such a law would be nugatory, because no difference of expense would exist. Is it not, then, in the highest degree absurd first to pass a law, under the operation of which the necessity is created of cultivating poor lands, and then, having so cultivated them at a great expense, make that additional expense the ground for refusing ever to purchase corn from those who can afford to produce it at a cheaper price? I can produce a quantity of cloth which affords me a remunerating price at 60*l.*, which I can sell to a foreign country, if I will lay out the proceeds in the purchase of thirty quarters of wheat at 2*l.* per quarter; but I am refused permission to do so, and am obliged, by the operation of a law, to employ the capital which yielded me 60*l.* in cloth, in raising fifteen quarters of wheat at 4*l.* per quarter.

The exchange of the cloth for wheat,—the production of the cloth is wholly prevented by the countervailing duty of 2*l.* per quarter on the importation of wheat, which obliges me to raise the corn, and prevents me from employing my capital in the making of cloth for the purpose of exchanging it for wheat.

It is true, indeed, that in both cases I raise a commodity worth 60*l.*, and to those who look only at money, and not money's worth, either of these employments of my capital appears equally productive; but a moment's reflection will convince us that there is the greatest difference imaginable between obtaining (with the same quantity of labour, mind) thirty quarters of wheat, and fifteen quarters, although either should, under the circumstances supposed, be worth 60*l*.

If the principle recommended by the Committee were consistently followed, there is no commodity whatever which we can raise at home which we should ever import from abroad; we should cultivate beet-root, and make our own sugar, and impose a duty on the importation of sugar equal to the difference of expense of growing sugar here, and growing it in the East or West Indies. We should erect hot-houses, and raise our own grapes for the purpose of making wine, and protect the maker of wine by the same course of policy. Either the doctrine is untenable in the case of corn, or it is to be justified in all other cases. Does the purchaser of a commodity ever inquire concerning the terms on which the producer can afford to raise or make it? His only consideration is the price at which he can purchase it. When he knows that, he knows the cheapest mode of obtaining it; if he can himself produce it cheaper than he can purchase it, he will devote himself to its production rather than to the production of the commodity with which he, in fact, must otherwise purchase it.

But there are persons, and of the number of those, too, who are considered of authority on these matters, who say this reasoning would be correct if we were about to employ capital on the land with a view to obtain more corn; that then it would undoubtedly be wise to consider whether we could purchase it from abroad cheaper than we could grow it at home, and govern our proceedings accordingly; but that, when capital has been expended on the land, it is quite another question, since much of that capital would be lost, if we then resolved rather to import cheap corn from abroad than grow it at a dear price at home. That some capital would be lost cannot be disputed, but is the possession or preservation of capital the end, or the means? The means, undoubtedly. What we want is an abundance of commodities, and if it could be proved that, by the sacrifice of a part of our capital, we should augment the annual produce of those objects which contribute to our enjoyment and happiness, we ought not, I should think, to repine at the loss of a part of our capital.

Mr Leslie has invented an ingenious apparatus, by the use of which we might fill our ice-houses with ice. Suppose a capital of half a million were expended on these machines, would it not nevertheless, be wise in us to get our ice, without any expense, from the frozen ponds in our neighbourhoods, rather than employ the labour, and waste the acid or other ingredients in the manufacture of ice, although, by so doing, we should for ever sacrifice the 500,000*l.* which we had expended on air-pumps?

In this recommendation, which must have the effect of perpetuating the difference between the price of corn here and its price in other countries, we should naturally conclude that the Committee did not admit the evils which from time to time must thence inevitably arise in this country. Quite the contrary; they admit them to the fullest extent, and they refer to the statements made on that subject in a former report, for the purpose of expressing their approbation of the reasoning which is founded on them. They say, "The excessive inconvenience and impolicy of our present system have been so fully treated and so satisfactorily exposed in the report already alluded to (pp. 10 and 12,) that it is unnecessary to do more than to refer to it, adding only, that every thing which has happened subsequent to the presentation of that report, as well as all our experience since 1815, has more and more tended to demonstrate how little reliance can be placed upon a regulation which contains an absolute prohibition up to a certain price, and an unlimited competition beyond that price; which, so far from affording steadiness to our market, *may at one time reduce prices, already too low, still lower than they might have been even under a free trade;* and at another, unnecessarily enhance the prices already too high, which tends to aggravate the evils of scarcity, *and render more severe the depression of profits from abundance.*"

Here the two evils of our corn law are very fairly stated; and against one of them, that of unlimited competition beyond the price of 80s., a remedy, though by no means the best which might have been temporarily established, is recommended; but, instead of suggesting any means of alleviating or remedying the other evil, proceeding from abundance, which is so fully acknowledged, measures are recommended for immediate and temporary adoption; and others are suggested as desirable to be at a future time permanently adopted, which cannot fail to perpetuate this evil, because they cannot fail to make the price of corn constantly and considerably higher in this than in any other neighbouring country.

§ 21. One of the grounds advanced for high duties on the importation of corn is, that the manufacturer is protected by high duties against the competition of the foreign manufacturer, and that the cultivator of the soil should have a similar protection against the foreign grower of corn. To this it is impossible to give an answer in language more satisfactory than has been done by Lord Grenville.

"If the measures which had formerly been adopted for the protection of trade and manufactures were right, let them be continued; if wrong, let them be abrogated; not suddenly, but with that caution with which all policy, however erroneous, so engrafted into our usage by time, should be changed; but let it be consecrated as a principle of legislation, that in no case should the grounds for advising the Legislature to afford any particular protection, rest on the protection which might have been afforded in any other quarter. In fact, he could not well conceive how the noble earl could argue, that measures which he admitted to have been wrong with respect to manufactures, would nevertheless be right with respect to agriculture.

"It would be an extraordinary mode of doing justice, thus to declare that, because a large, the largest, part of the community were already oppressed by favours shown to one particular class, they should be still farther oppressed by favours shown to another particular class."—*Speech,* March 15, 1815.

If any thing more is required against this pretension of

protection for the land, it is furnished in the following passage of the Report of the Agricultural Committee of last year :—

"They (the Committee) observe, that one of the witnesses, in order to illustrate his ideas and the wishes of the petitioners, has furnished a table of the duties payable on foreign manufactured articles, of which several are subject to duties of excise in this country; and upon which the importation duty, as, for instance, upon the article of glass, is imposed in a great measure to countervail the duty upon that article manufactured in this kingdom.

"But the main ground upon which your Committee are disposed to think that the House will look with some mistrust to the soundness of this principle, is—first, that it may be well doubted whether (with the exception of silk) any of our considerable manufactures derive benefit from this assumed protection in the markets of this country: for how could the foreign manufactures of cotton, of woollens, of hardware, compete with our own in this country, when it is notorious that we can afford to undersell them in the products of those great branches of our manufacturing industry, even in their own markets, notwithstanding that cotton and wool are subject to a direct duty on importation, not drawn back upon their export in a manufactured state, as well as to all the indirect taxation which affects capital in these branches, in common with that capital which is employed in raising the productions of the soil?"

This is followed by other passages which are excellent, and all tend to show, that the protection which manufactures are said to possess, is not really afforded them; though, if it were, Lord Grenville's argument is conclusive against that being a ground for extending protection to agriculture.

It is to be hoped that we shall, even in the present session of Parliament, get rid of many of these injurious laws; a better spirit of legislation appears likely to prevail in the present day; and that absurd jealousy which influenced our forefathers, will give way to the pleasing conviction, that we can never, by freedom of commerce, promote the welfare of other countries without also promoting our own.

The passage from the Report is useful in another respect: it shows us that the writer of it understood well what a countervailing duty is, and should be; for he states that the duty on the importation of glass "is imposed in a great measure to countervail the duty upon that article manufactured in this kingdom." How is this passage to be reconciled with the recommendation in both Reports, that, in imposing a duty on the importation of corn, "it should be calculated fairly to countervail the difference of expense, including the ordinary rate of profit, at which corn, in the present state of this country, *can be grown and brought to market* within the United Kingdom, compared with the expense, including also the ordinary rate of profit, of producing it in any of those countries from whence our principal supplies of foreign corn have usually been drawn, joined to the ordinary charge of conveying it from thence to our markets"?

SECTION VIII.

On the Project of advancing Money on Loan, to Speculators in Corn, at a low Interest.

§ 22. It is allowed by the Report, that "the universal rule of allowing all articles, as much as possible, to find their own natural level, by leaving the supply to adjust itself to the demand," discouraged the Committee from recommending that Government should employ money, in making purchases of corn, with a view to sell it when the price rose; but the Committee do not appear to have seen that the same universal rule, of which they speak with approbation, ought to have discouraged them also from recommending that Government should advance money, at a low rate of interest, to persons who should purchase wheat, to deposit it in the King's warehouses, while it was under 60s. per quarter.

Will not such an advance of money at a low rate of

interest, and for twelve months certain, if the parties desire it, prevent the article from "finding its own level," and "will the supply be left to adjust itself to the demand?"

If the cause of the low price of corn be owing to an abundant quantity in the country, and not to an abundant quantity hurried prematurely to market by the distress of the farmers, the proposed remedy will be really mischievous, as in that case we must go through the ordeal of low prices, and increased consumption, which is always in a degree consequent on low price, before the supply will adjust itself to the demand, and prices become again remunerative. By the encouragement thus given to storing corn for a twelvemonth, the period of glut may be retarded, but it must come at last. On the other supposition, that from alarm or distress more than a due portion of corn is prematurely sent to market, and that before the next harvest the whole supply will, in consequence, prove deficient, and the price will rise; I must observe, that sharp-sighted individuals, prompted by a regard to their interest, can discover this, if it be so, with more certainty than Government. Money is not wanted to purchase the wheat thus unduly brought to market; nothing is required but a conviction of the probability of a diminished supply, or an increased demand, and a probable rise of price, to awaken the spirit of speculation. If there were any well-founded opinion of such a rise, we should soon witness a more than usual activity among the corn-dealers. When there was a prospect of continued wet weather, just before the harvest of last year, did we not see an immediate spring in the price of corn? On what was such rise founded, but on an anticipation of probable scarcity, and an increased price? If, then, there be any good foundation for a probable deficiency before the wheat of the next harvest comes into use, individuals will be found to speculate without any encouragement from Government; the difference between a rate of interest of 3 per cent. and of 5 per cent. must be of little importance in such a transaction, and as far as the public is concerned may be wholly neglected, when we are considering the advantages of such a measure.

It has been said that similar advances have been made to the commercial interest on more than one occasion, why then should the agricultural interest be excluded from a similar benefit? In the first place, I doubt whether the measure be justifiable in any case whatever; but it cannot be disputed that the commercial class made their application for this indulgence under very different circumstances from the agricultural class. The commercial class are liable to stagnation of business; a market for which they have prepared their goods may, during war (and it is only during war that such advances have been made) be shut against them. On the probability of selling their goods, they have given bills which are becoming due, and their character and fortune depend on fulfilling their engagements. All they want is time; by forbearing to produce more of the commodity for which there is a diminished demand, they are sure, though probably with great loss, to dispose of their articles. Is the situation of the farmer any thing like this? Has he any bills becoming due? Do all his future transactions depend on his momentarily sustaining his credit? Are markets ever wholly shut against him? Is it a mere supply of money to meet his bills that he requires? The cases are most widely different, and the analogy which is attempted to be set up between them fails in every particular.

SECTION IX.

Can the present State of Agricultural Distress be attributed to Taxation?

§ 23. The present distress is caused by an insufficient price for the produce of the land, which it appears impossible, with any degree of fairness, to ascribe to taxation. Taxation is of two kinds, it either falls on the producer of a commodity in his character of producer, or it falls on him as a consumer. When a farmer has to pay an agricultural horse-tax, tithes, land-tax, he is taxed as a producer, and he seeks to repay himself, as all other producers do, by imposing an additional price, equivalent to the tax, on the commodity which he produces. It is the consumer, then, that finally pays the tax, and not the producer, as nothing can prevent the latter from transferring the tax to the consumer, but the production of too great a quantity of the commodity for the demand. Whenever the price of a commodity does not repay to the producer all the charges of every description which he is obliged to incur, it fails to give him a remunerating price ; it places him under a disadvantage, as compared with the producers of other commodities ; he no longer gets the usual and ordinary profits of capital, and there are only two remedies by which he can be relieved : one, the diminution of the quantity of the commodity, which will not fail to raise its price, if the demand do not at the same time diminish ; the other, the relieving him from the taxes which he pays as a producer. The first remedy is certain and efficacious ; the second is of a more doubtful description, because, if the price of the commodity did once remunerate the producer, after the tax was imposed, it could only fall afterwards from increased supply, or diminished demand.

The repeal of the tax will not diminish quantity ; and if it does not further lower the price, it will not increase demand. If the price falls still lower, then the repeal of the tax will not afford relief to the producer. It is only in the case of the commodity falling no lower, although the producer is relieved from one of the charges of production, that he can be said to be benefited by the repeal of a tax on production ; and a very reasonable doubt may be entertained, whether the competition of the sellers may not further diminish the price of the commodity in consequence of the repeal of the tax. That taxes on production may be the cause of an excess of the supply above the demand, is true, when the tax is a new one and when the consumers are unwilling to re-pay, in the additional price, the additional charge imposed on the producer. But this is not the case in this country at the present moment; the taxes are not new ones; the prices of raw produce were sufficiently high, notwithstanding the taxes, to afford a remunerating price to the producer; and no doubt can exist, that if there had been no such taxes, raw produce would have been considerably lower than it now is. The same cause which made wheat fall from 80s. to 60s., or 25 per cent., would have made it fall from 60s. to 45s., if, in consequence of fewer taxes on the land, 60s. and not 80s. had been the ordinary average price. Some of the charges of production have actually been diminished, while there is every reason to conclude, that the quantity consumed by the people has been increasing.

The alteration in the value of money has been generally supposed to be favourable to the working classes, as their money wages are said not to have fallen in proportion to the increased value of money, and the fall in the price of necessaries. Their condition is then bettered, and their power of consuming increased; but prices can never stand against a great augmentation of quantity, and therefore there is no other rational solution of the cause of the fall of agricultural produce but abundance.

Taxes on consumers affect consumers generally, and will in no way account for the distress of a particular class, or for an insufficient price of the commodity which they grow or manufacture. The taxes on candles, soap, salt, &c., &c., are not only paid by farmers, but by all persons who consume those commodities. The repeal of those taxes would afford relief to all, and not to the agricultural class particularly.

Those who maintain, that on no reasonable grounds can it be shown, that taxation is the cause of agricultural distress and of the low price of corn, are sometimes represented as maintaining that a repeal of taxes will afford no relief; such a conclusion shows a want of candour or of intelligence, for it is perfectly consistent to maintain, that taxation is not the cause of some particular distress, and at the same time insist that a repeal of taxes would afford relief. When Lord John Russell's horse falls because he trips over a stone, and is enabled to get up again when relieved from the burden of his harness, it would surely be incorrect to say that the horse fell because he was burdened with harness; though it would be right to assert that the tripping over the stone threw him down, while the relief from the confinement of the harness enabled him to get up again.

For my own part, then, being of opinion that almost all taxes on production fall finally on the consumer, I think that no repeal of taxes could take place which would have any other effect than to relieve consumers generally of a part of the burdens which they now bear. Although I am at all times a friend to the most rigid economy in the public expenditure, yet I am also convinced, that there are causes of distress, to the producers of a particular commodity, arising from abundant quantity, from which no practicable repeal of taxes could materially relieve, particularly if the commodity be agricultural produce, and if its ordinary price be kept above the level of the prices of other countries by restrictions on importation.

Against such distress no country, and more particularly no country having a bad system of corn laws, is exempted. If we were absolutely without any taxes whatever; if the public expenditure was the most economical possible, and was supported by a revenue drawn from lands appropriated for that purpose; if we had no national debt, no sinking fund, we yet should be exposed to a destructive fall of price from occasional abundance. It is impossible to read Mr Tooke's able evidence before the Agricultural Committee of 1821, without being struck with the surprising effects which an excess of supply produces on price, and for which there is, in fact, no effectual remedy but a reduction of quantity. If there be any other remedy, why do not those who complain of the distress, and who have been in situations so favourable to make themselves heard, state it? With the exception of a reduction of taxation, new and additional protection against the competition of foreigners for every description of agricultural produce, direct purchases to be made by Government, or encouragements to others to make them, I have heard no remedies suggested; and as to the efficacy of these remedies, I must leave that to the reader's judgment; my own opinion of them having been already most decidedly expressed.

§ 24. On the causes which have produced the degree of abundance to which I attribute all that part of the fall of raw produce since 1819, which cannot fairly be ascribed to the alteration in the value of the currency,* it will not be necessary for me to say much; we are, I think, justified in ascribing it to a succession of good crops, to an increasing importation from Ireland, and to the increase of tillage which the high prices and the obstacles opposed to importation during the war occasioned. Many of the gentlemen who gave evidence before the Committee concurred in describing the harvests of 1819 and 1820 as unusually abundant. Mr Wakefield said on the 5th April 1821, "I think there is a wonderful quantity of corn in the country; I now think that there is as much corn left in the country, as generally, in common years, there is after harvest." "I think, that if you were to have for the next two or three years, fair average crops, it would leave you with a great stock in hand."

Mr Iveson.—"I think the last crop was abundant; the crop of 1820 was considerably beyond an average." —P. 338.

Mr J. Brodie.—"The crop in Scotland was very abundant last year."

"The crop of the year before was above an average crop too."—P. 327.

Besides this abundant crop at home, the importations from Ireland were unusually great, as will be seen by the following account of the importation of oats, wheat, and wheat-flour, the production of Ireland, imported into Great Britain, which was laid before the Agricultural Committee of 1821.

* To that cause it will have been seen I ascribe a fall of 10 per cent.

Years ending 5th Jan.	Oats—Qrs.	Wheat—Qrs.	Wheat flour—Cwt.
5th Jan. 1818	594,337	50,842	16,238
... 1819	1,001,247	95,677	33,258
... 1820	759,608	127,308	92,893
... 1821	892,605	351,871	180,375
For three months.			
From 5th Jan. 1821 to 5th April 1821	437,245	218,764	99,062

It will be seen by the above account how greatly the importation from Ireland has increased, which, coming in addition to the abundant quantity yielded by the harvests of 1819 and 1820, will, I think, sufficiently account for the depression of price.

To trace this abundance to its source is not, however, necessary in this case; it is sufficient to show that the low price cannot have arisen from any other cause but an increased supply, or a diminished demand, to be convinced that the evil admits of no other effectual remedy but a reduction of quantity, or an increased demand.

That an abundant quantity has been exposed to sale will be shown by the accounts of the sales in Mark Lane.* It will be found, too, that an unusually large quantity has arrived in the port of London from ports in Great Britain and Ireland.

It must, indeed, not be forgotten that the fall of price is attributed to the abundant quantity actually in the market, and the reasoning founded on the doctrine of abundance being the cause of low price would in no degree be invalidated if, before the next harvest, our supply should be found to be below the demand, and there should be a great increase of price. We can have no unequivocal proof of abundance but by its effects. I believe in the existence of an abundant quantity, but I should not think my argument in the least weakened if corn should, before next harvest, rise to 80s. per quarter.

* See Appendix B.

CONCLUSION.

§ 25. Having disposed of most of the subjects which are intimately connected with the question of the policy which it would be wise for this country to adopt, respecting the trade in corn, I shall briefly recapitulate the opinions which will be found more at large in various parts of this inquiry.

The cause of the present low price of agricultural produce is partly the alteration in the value of the currency, and mainly, an excess of supply above the demand. To Mr Peel's bill, even in conjunction with the operation of the Bank, no greater effect on the price of corn can, with any fairness, be attributed than 10 per cent., and to that amount the far greatest part of the taxation of the country has been increased; but this increased taxation does not fall on the landed interest only; it falls equally on the funded interest, and every other interest in the country. Suppose the land to pay one half of the whole taxation of the country, after deducting that part of the expenditure which depends on the value of money, and which would therefore be augmented in proportion as money fell in value, the whole increase of taxation which, since 1819, has fallen upon the landed interest, taking tenants and landlords together, cannot have exceeded 2 millions; but, suppose it 4 millions per annum,* is 4 millions per annum the amount of the whole loss sustained by landlords and tenants together by the fall in the price of agricultural produce? Impossible; because, by the allegations of the landed interest, all rent is now paid from capital, leaving nothing for profit; and, therefore, if the only cause of distress be the alteration in the value of the currency, 4 millions must have constituted all the net income both of landlords and tenants before such

* The whole amount of taxes paid to the public creditor and sinking fund, is 36 millions; suppose the other fixed charges to be 4 millions, then the whole taxation on which the altered value of money has operated, is 40 millions. I estimate the increase 10 per cent., or 4 millions, which falls on all classes—landlords, merchants, manufacturers, labourers, and, though last not least, stockholders.

alteration—a proposition which no man would venture to sustain. To what other cause, then, is the distress to be attributed? To what other cause are we to ascribe the extreme depression of all agricultural produce? The answer is, I think, plain, intelligible, and satisfactory;—to the general prevalence of abundance, arising from good crops, and large importations from Ireland.

§ 26. This fall has been increased by the operation of the present corn laws, which have had the effect of driving capital to the cultivation of poor lands, and of making the price of corn in average years in this country greatly to exceed the price in other countries. The price, under such circumstances, must be high, but in proportion as it is raised, so is it liable to a greater fall; for, in abundant seasons, the whole increased quantity gluts our own market, and if it be above the quantity which we can consume, rapidly depresses the price, without our having any vent from exportation, till the fall of price is ruinous to the interests of farmers, who are never so secure as when the resource of exportation can be easily had recourse to.

§ 27. To obviate, as far as is practicable, this enormous evil, all undue protection to agriculture should be gradually withdrawn. The policy which we ought at this moment of distress to adopt, is to give the monopoly of the home market to the British grower till corn reaches 70s. per quarter. When it has reached 70s., all fixed price and system of averages should be got rid of, and a duty of 20s. per quarter on the importation of wheat, and other grain in proportion, might be imposed.

This change would do but little in protecting us from the effects of abundant crops, but it would be greatly beneficial in preventing an unlimited importation of corn when the ports were opened. Under the payment of a fixed duty, corn would be imported only in such quantities as it might be required, and as no one would fear the shutting of the ports, no one would hurry corn to this country till we really wanted it. Against the effects of glut, caused by an unlimited supply from abroad, we should be then amply protected.

This measure, however, although a great improvement on the present corn law, would be very deficient if we proceeded no farther. To establish measures which should at once drive capital from the land would, under the present circumstances of the country, be rash and hazardous, and, therefore, I should propose that the duty of 20s. should every year be reduced 1s. until it reached 10s. We should also allow a drawback of 7s. per quarter on the exportation of wheat; and these should be considered as permanent measures.

A duty of 10s. per quarter on importation, to which I wish to approach, is, I am sure, rather too high as a countervailing duty for the peculiar taxes which are imposed on the corn grower, over and above those which are imposed on the other classes of producers in the country; but I would rather err on the side of a liberal allowance than of a scanty one, and it is for this reason that I do not propose to allow a drawback quite equal to the duty. As far as the producer of corn was concerned, when the duty had fallen to 10s. the trade would to him have all the advantages of a free trade, within the trifling amount of 3s. per quarter. Whenever his crops were abundant, he could be relieved by exportation, after a very moderate fall of price, unless, indeed, the abundance and fall were general in all countries; but, at any rate, the price of his corn would be nearer the general rate of prices of the rest of the world by 20s. or 25s. than it is under the existing regulations, and this alteration would be invaluable to him.

Before I conclude, it will be proper to notice an objection which is frequently made against freedom of trade in corn, viz. the dependence in which it would place us for an essential article of subsistence on foreign countries. This objection is founded on the supposition that we should be importers of a considerable portion of the quantity which we annually consume.

In the first place, I differ with those who think that the quantity which we should import would be immense; and, in the second, if it were as large as the objection requires, I can see no danger as likely to arise from it.

From all the evidence given to the Agricultural

Committee, it appears that no very great quantity could be obtained from abroad, without causing a considerable increase in the remunerating price of corn in foreign countries. In proportions as the quantity required came from the interior of Poland and Germany, the cost would be greatly increased by the expenses of land carriage. To raise a larger supply, too, those countries would be obliged to have recourse to an inferior quality of land, and, as it is the cost of raising corn on the worst soils in cultivation, requiring the heaviest charges, which regulates the price of all the corn of a country, there could not be a great additional quantity produced without a rise in the price necessary to remunerate the foreign grower. In proportion as the price rose abroad, it would become advantageous to cultivate poorer lands at home ; and therefore, here is every probability that, under the freest state of demand, we should not be importers of any very large quantity.

But suppose the case to be otherwise, what danger should we incur from our dependence, as it is called, on foreign countries for a considerable portion of our food ? If our demand was constant and uniform, which, under such a system, it would undoubtedly be, a considerable quantity of corn must be grown abroad expressly for our market. It would be more the interest, if possible, of the countries so growing corn for our use, to oppose no obstacles to its reaching us, than it would be ours to receive it.

Let us look attentively at what is passing in this country before our eyes. Do we not see the effects of a small excess of quantity on the price of corn ? What would be the glut if England habitually raised a considerable additional quantity for foreign consumption ? Should we be willing to expose our farmers and landlords to the ruin which would overwhelm them if we voluntarily deprived them of the foreign market, even in case of war ? I am sure we should not. Whatever allowance we may make for the feelings of enmity, and for the desire which we might have to inflict suffering on our foe by depriving him of part of his usual supply of food, I am sure that at such a price as it must be inflicted, in the case which I am supposing, we should forbear to exercise such a power. If such would be our policy, so would it also be that of other countries in the same circumstances; and I am fully persuaded that we should never suffer from being deprived of the quantity of food for which we uniformly depended on importation.

All our reasoning on this subject leads to the same conclusion, that we should, with as little delay as possible, consistently with a due regard to temporary interests, establish what may be called a substantially free trade in corn. The interests of the farmer, consumer, and capitalist, would all be promoted by such a measure; and, as far as steady prices and the regular receipt of rents is more advantageous to the landlord than fluctuating prices and irregular receipt of rents, I am sure his interest well understood would lead to the same conclusion; although I am willing to admit, that the average money rents, to which he would be entitled if his tenants could fulfil their contracts, would be higher under a system of restricted trade.

APPENDIX.

A.

REPRESENTATION, AGREED UPON THE 20TH DAY OF MAY 1819, BY THE DIRECTORS OF THE BANK OF ENGLAND, AND LAID BEFORE THE CHANCELLOR OF THE EXCHEQUER.

Ordered by the House of Commons to be Printed, 21st May, 1819.

At a Court of Directors at the Bank, on Thursday, 20th May 1819

THE Directors of the Bank of *England*, having taken into their most serious consideration the Reports of the Secret Committees of the two Houses of Parliament, appointed to inquire into the state of the Bank of England with reference to the expediency of the resumption of cash payments at the period now fixed, have thought it their duty to lay before His Majesty's Ministers, as early as possible, their sentiments with regard to the measures suggested by these Committees, for the approbation of Parliament.

In the *first* place, it appears that, in the view of the Committees, the measures of the Bank recommencing cash payments on the 5th of July next, the time prescribed by the existing law, " is utterly impracticable, and would be entirely inefficient, if not ruinous."

Secondly, it appears that the two Committees have come to their conclusion at a period when the outstanding notes of the Bank of England do not much exceed 25,000,000*l.*; when the price of gold is about 4*l.* 1s. per ounce; and when there is great distress from the stagnation of commerce, and the fall of prices of imported articles.

It must be obvious to His Majesty's Ministers, that as long as such a state of things shall last, or one in any degree similar, without either considerable improvement on one side, or growing worse on the other, the Bank, acting as it does at present, and keeping its issues nearly at the present level, could not venture to return to cash payments with any probability of benefit to the public, or safety to the establishment.

The two Committees of Parliament, apparently actuated by

this consideration, have advised that the Bank shall not open payments in coin for a period of four years, but shall be obliged, from the 1st of May 1821, to discharge their notes in standard gold bullion, at Mint price, when demanded in sums not amounting to less than thirty ounces. And, as it appears to the Committees expedient that this return to payments at Mint price should be made gradually, they propose that, on the first day of February next, the Bank should pay their notes in bullion, if demanded in sums not less than sixty ounces, at the rate of 4*l.* 1s. an ounce, and from the 1st of October 1820 to the 1st of May following, at 3*l.* 19s. 6d. an ounce.

If the Directors of the Bank have a true comprehension of the views of the Committees in submitting this scheme to Parliament, they are obliged to infer, that the object of the Committees is, to secure, at every hazard, and under every possible variation of circumstances, the return of payments in gold, at Mint price, for bank notes, at the expiration of two years; and that this measure is so to be managed, that the Mint price denominations shall ever afterwards be preserved, leaving the market or exchange price of gold to be controlled by the Bank, solely by the amount of their issue of notes.

It further appears to the Directors, with regard to the final execution of this plan, and the payment of bank notes in gold at Mint price, that discretionary power is to be taken away from the Bank; and that it is merely to regulate its issues, and make purchases of gold, so as to be enabled to answer all possible demands, whenever its treasury shall be again open for the payment of its notes.

Under these impressions, the Directors of the Bank think it right to observe to His Majesty's Ministers, that being engaged to pay on demand their notes in statutable coin, at the Mint price of 3*l.* 17s. 10½d. an ounce, they ought to be the last persons who should object to any measure calculated to effect that end; but as it is incumbent on them to consider the effect of any measure to be adopted, as operating upon the general issue of their notes, by which all the private banks are regulated, and of which the whole currency, exclusive of the notes of private bankers, is composed, they feel themselves obliged, by the new situation in which they have been placed by the restriction act of 1797, to bear in mind not less their duties to the community at large, whose interests, in a pecuniary and commercial relation, have in a great degree been confided to their discretion.

The Directors being thus obliged to extend their views, and embrace the interests of the whole community in their consideration of this measure, cannot but feel a repugnance, however involuntary, to pledge themselves in approbation of a system which, in their opinion, in all its great tendencies and operations, concerns the country in general more than the immediate interests of the Bank alone.

It is not certainly a part of the regular duty of the Bank, under its original institution, to enter into the general views of policy by which this great empire is to be governed in all its commercial and pecuniary transactions, which exclusively belong to the administration, to Parliament, and to the community at large; nor is it the province of the Bank to expound the principles by which these views ought to be regulated. Its peculiar and appropriate duty is the management of the concerns of the banking establishment, as connected with the payment of the interest of the national debt, the lodgments consigned to its care, and the ordinary advances it has been accustomed to make to Government.

But when the Directors are now to be called upon, in the new situation in which they are placed by the restriction act, to procure a fund for supporting the whole national currency, either in bullion or in coin, and when it is proposed that they should effect this measure within a given period, by regulating the market price of gold by a limitation of the amount of the issue of bank notes, with whatever distress such limitation may be attended to individuals or the community at large, they feel it their bounden and imperious duty to state their sentiments thus explicitly, in the first instance to his Majesty's Ministers, on this subject, that a tacit consent and concurrence at this juncture may not, at some future period, be construed into a previous implied sanction on their part, of a system which they cannot but consider fraught with very great uncertainty and risk.

It is impossible for them to decide beforehand what shall be the course of events for the next two, much less for the next four, years; they have no right to hazard a flattering conjecture, for which they have not real grounds, in which they may be disappointed, and for which they may be considered responsible. They cannot venture to advise an unrelenting continuance of pecuniary pressures upon the commercial world, of which it is impossible for them either to foresee or estimate the consequences.

The Directors have already submitted to the House of Lords the expediency of the Bank paying its notes in bullion at the market price of the day, with a view of seeing how far favourable commercial balances may operate in restoring the former order of things, of which they might take advantage: and, with a similar view, they have proposed that Government should repay the Bank a considerable part of the sums that have been advanced upon exchequer bills.

These two measures would allow time for a correct judgment to be formed upon the state of the bullion market, and upon the real result of those changes which the late war may have produced in all its consequences, of increased public debt, increased taxes, increased prices, and altered relations as to interest, capital, and commercial dealings with the Continent; and how far the alterations thus produced are temporary or permanent; and to what extent, and in what degree, they operate.

It was the design of the Directors, in pursuance of the before mentioned two measures, to take advantage of every circumstance which could enable the Bank to extend its purchases of bullion, as far as a legitimate consideration of the ordinary wants of the nation for a sufficient currency could possibly warrant. Beyond this point, they do not consider themselves justified in going, upon any opinion, conjecture, or speculation, merely their own; and when a system is recommended which seems to take away from the Bank anything like a discretionary consideration of the necessities and distresses of the commercial world, if the Directors withhold their previous consent, it is not from a want of deference to his Majesty's Government, or to the opinion of the Committees of the two Houses of Parliament, but solely from a serious feeling that they have no right whatever to invest themselves, of their own accord, with the responsibility of countenancing a measure in which the whole community is so deeply involved, and possibly to compromise the universal interests of the empire, in all the relations of agriculture, manufacture, commerce, and revenue, by a seeming acquiescence or declared approbation on the part of the Directors of the Bank of England.

The consideration of these great questions, and of the degree in which all these leading and commanding interests may be affected by the measure proposed, rests with the legislature; and it is for them, after solemn deliberation, and not for the Bank, to determine and decide upon the course to be adopted.

Whatever reflections may have from time to time been cast upon the Bank, whatever invidious representations of its conduct may have been made, the cautious conduct it adopted, in so measuring the amount of currency as to make it adequate to the wants both of the nation and of the Government, at the same time keeping it within reasonable bounds when compared with what existed before the war, as is shown in the Lords' reports, pages 10, 11, 12, and 13; the recent effort to return to a system of cash payments, which commenced with the fairest prospects (but which was afterwards frustrated by events that could not be foreseen nor controlled by the Bank), are of themselves a sufficient refutation of all the obloquy which has been so undeservedly heaped upon the establishment.

The Directors of the Bank of England, in submitting these considerations to his Majesty's Ministers, request that they may be allowed to assure them, that it is always their anxious desire, as far as depends upon them, to aid, by every consistent means, the measures of the legislature for furthering the prosperity of the empire.

ROBERT BEST, *Sec.*

B.

CORN ARRIVED IN THE PORT OF LONDON FROM PORTS IN GREAT BRITAIN AND IRELAND.

	1817. No. of Quarters.	Average Price.	1818. No. of Quarters.	Average Price.	1819. No. of Quarters.	Average Price.	1820. No. of Quarters.	Average Price.	1821. No. of Quarters.	Average Price.	1822. No. of Quarters.	Average Price.
WHEAT.												
1st Quarter,	93,624	101s.	78,671	86s.	49,047	78s.	103,589	65s.	77,227	54s.	133,913	48s.
2d Do.	69,842	104s.	45,541	88s.	44,201	72s.	103,938	71s.	78,260	54s.		
3d Do.	77,293	91s.	51,869	83s.	91,741	74s.	71,461	72s.	107,024	55s.		
4th Do.	96,505	80s.	60,086	81s.	100,552	66s.	87,680	60s.	165,804	58s.		
	337,264		236,167		285,541		366,668		428,315			
BARLEY.												
1st Quarter,	99,853	50s.	87,538	46s.	84,020	60s.	121,063	34s.	97,707	25s.	99,062	19s. 6d.
2d Do.	64,054	51s.	39,901	51s.	15,454	45s.	55,632	35s.	46,943	24s.		
3d Do.	17,559	48s.	14,731	54s.	8,461	39s.	10,678	36s.	14,416	26s.		
4th Do.	93,941	43s.	120,373	61s.	87,196	37s.	59,420	29s.	71,868	29s.		
	275,407		262,543		195,131		246,793		230,934			
OATS.												
1st Quarter,	142,721	30s.	147,959	28s.	110,373	33s.	197,476	23s.	127,351	19s.	199,057	
2d Do.	80,872	34s.	102,204	31s.	94,669	28s.	188,723	26s.	138,781	18s.		
3d Do.	89,137	36s.	194,603	34s.	98,841	27s.	82,131	28s.	149,106	20s.		
4th Do.	155,564	27s.	88,977	35s.	136,352	25s.	91,100	22s.	152,934	21s.		
	468,294		533,743		440,235		559,430		568,170			

AN ACCOUNT of the Number of Quarters of Wheat, Barley, and Oats, sold in Mark Lane, as appears from the Inspector's Returns, at the following Periods.

	WHEAT. Quarters.	BARLEY. Quarters.	OATS. Quarters.
From 1st November 1818 to 1st March 1819, ...	65,804	107,764	137,272
From 1st November 1819 to 1st March 1820, ...	100,582	117,144	164,017
From 1st November 1820 to 1st March 1821, ...	106,465	96,703	134,586
From 1st November 1821 to 1st March 1822, ...	170,621	96,127	216,870